THE BEGINNINGS OF WELSH POETRY

da filius ebba · tenuit regiones in sinistrali parte
brittanniae · id est umbri maris · & regnauit annis
duodecim · & iunxit dinguayrdi guurthberne
ich ·

unc dutigirn · in illo tempore fortiter dimica
bat contra gentem anglorum · Tunc talhaern
tat aguen in poemate claruit · & neirin · & ta
liessin · & bluchbard · & cian qui uocatur gue
nith guaut · simul uno tempore in poema
te brittannico claruerunt ·

ailcunus magnus rex apud brittones regna
bat · id est in regione guenedote · quia at
tauus illius id est cunedag · cum filiis suis · quorum
numerus octo erat · uenerat prius de parte si
nistrali id est de regione que uocatur manau
guotodin centum quadraginta sex annis
antequam mailcun regnaret · & scottos
cum ingentissima clade expulerunt ab istis re
gionibus · & nusquam reuersi sunt iterum ad ha
bitandum ·

dda filius ida regnauit annis octo ·
aedlric filius adda regnauit quattuor
annis · Deoric filius ida regnauit septem
annis · Friodolguald regnauit sex
annis · In cuius tempore regnum cantorum
mittente gregorio baptismum suscepit ·
Hussa regnauit annis septem · Contra il
los quattuor reges urbgen · & riderch
hen · & guallauc · & morcant dimicauerunt ·
Deodric contra illum urbgen cum filiis dimi
cabant fortiter · In illo autem tempore ali
quando hostes nunc ciues uincebantur · & ip
se conclusit eos tribus diebus & tribus noctibus
in insula metcaud · & dum erat in expedi
tione iugulatus est · morcanto destinante pro in
uidia · quia in ipso prae omnibus regibus uirtus ma
xima erat in instauratione belli · Eadfered
flesaurs regnauit duodecim annis ·

Harleian MS. 3859 *fol.* 188b.
(By courtesy of the British Museum)

# THE BEGINNINGS OF WELSH POETRY

STUDIES BY SIR IFOR WILLIAMS,
D. LITT., LL.D., F.B.A.

Edited by Rachel Bromwich

Second Edition

CARDIFF
UNIVERSITY OF WALES PRESS
1980

First edition 1972
Second edition 1980

**British Library Cataloguing in Publication Data**

Williams, *Sir* Ifor

The beginnings of Welsh poetry. – 2nd ed.
1. Welsh poetry – To 1550 – History and criticism
I. Title II. Bromwich, Rachel.
891.6′6′1109 PB2227

ISBN 0-7083-0744-2



*Published on behalf of the Language and Literature Committee of the Board of Celtic Studies of the University of Wales*

Printed in Great Britain at the
University Press, Cambridge

# CONTENTS

# PLATES

# INTRODUCTION

At a meeting held at Easter 1967, in Sir Ifor's former study at Hafod Lwyd, I was one of a small group of former pupils and colleagues who were invited by Gwynn ab Ifor and Gwenno Caffell to discuss plans for re-issuing certain of their father's works. Amongst other projects, it was agreed that it would be desirable to bring together a number of important articles which had been long out of print, and which had been published over a period of many years, and in a variety of periodicals. Since many of these articles had been written in English, it was felt that a collection of the most important of Sir Ifor's writings in English would have the additional advantage of making available some part of the fruits of his scholarship to a wider audience than before. I was invited to make a selection of these articles and to prepare them for publication.

The title which I have chosen for this selection, *The Beginnings of Welsh Poetry*, could equally well serve as a comprehensive title for the prime concern of Sir Ifor's whole career, the interest which dominated all others among his multiple scholarly activities. A major part of his published work was based, either directly or indirectly, upon his researches into problems which were related to the origins of the Welsh poetic tradition. He demonstrated repeatedly in his writings how philology, history, and archaeology have each their separate contributions to make towards the elucidation of these problems. It is therefore appropriate that a selection which brings together under this title his two articles in English on 'The Poems of Llywarch Hen' (Sir Ifor's address to the British Academy in 1932; chapter VIII), and on 'The Gododdin Poems' (chapter V)—both of them preliminary surveys which anticipated by several years his magistral Welsh editions of the poems concerned—should commence with three of Sir Ifor's important discussions of the language of the early Welsh inscriptions (chapters I–III). To Sir Ifor, indeed, the question of the date of the development of Welsh out of its parent-language Brittonic or British, and the nature of the linguistic changes which were involved in this development, was 'the chief and most urgent problem confronting the student of Early Welsh Literature' (chapter I, p. 1). In an article on 'Welsh' in the *Encyclopaedia Britannica*,[1] Sir Ifor has vividly summarised

[1] *Encyclopaedia Britannica*, V (London, etc., 1964), 'Celtic Languages: Welsh', p. 151.

the linguistic situation in Britain as it was towards the end of the period of the Roman occupation:

> Latin by then had long been the language of the army, administration, law, commerce, and town life generally. British lived on in the wilder country districts, where romanization was not so complete. On the departure of the Romans, the men of the hills were called on to take the lead in repelling the raids of Picts, Scots, and Saxons. These new leaders and their followers spoke a different language: a rough, uncouth, clipped form of the old British. By A.D. 550 this had been developed into a language fit to be employed by bards to sing the praises of the new heroes. Aneirin sang to the Gododdin, Taliesin to Urien, the opponent of Ida (547–559), and to Cynan, the father of Selyf who fell at the battle of Chester in *circa* 615. That is the Welsh tradition, and it fits the known facts.

In a literary context, therefore, this problem could for him have but one meaning: had the Welsh language, with its structural features essentially as they are today, come into being in time for the famous Cynfeirdd or 'Early Bards' to have composed their verse in it? To put the question in another way: can any part of the poetry which is attributed in medieval manuscripts to bards whom Nennius synchronises with historical figures of the sixth century, be really as old as is claimed for it by the concerted literary tradition of the country? The importance of the linguistic evidence provided by the earliest inscriptions for its bearing on this problem was always to the forefront in Sir Ifor's mind: for instance, he compared the complexities of the task which confronted him in interpreting the sparse onomastic remains of Primitive Celtic in Britain and in Gaul with those which would confront English scholars if they had nothing but the inscriptions on Elizabethan tombstones and other contemporarary artefacts as evidence from which to deduce the language of Shakespeare (chapter I, p.3). After interpreting the Towyn inscription, he discerned in its concluding words *tricet nitanam* ('grief and loss remain') evidence for the existence of 'a true poet' in the hall of the chieftain who was commemorated in this earliest monumental epitaph in the Welsh language (chapter III, p. 37). In yet another place[2] he alluded to 'the wild background of these early grave-stones' and recalled in reference to them the opening line of the *Stanzas of the Graves*: they are *Y Beddeu ae gwlych y glaw* ('the graves which the rain wets'), and he went on to speak of 'the thrill I get from a massive pillar of rough granite with streaks of Ogam

[2] *Trans. Hon. Soc. Cymmrodorion* (1943–4), p. 152 (from a review of R. A. S. Macalister's *Corpus Inscriptionum Insularum Celticarum*, I).

on its ribs, standing boldly all alone on a headland or a mountain side'.

To these pioneer studies on the poets and on the emergence of the language which was their medium, I have added certain essays, lectures, and broadcast talks which were published at various later dates, together with editions (accompanied in each case by full linguistic and historical discussion) of certain poems or poetic fragments which Sir Ifor showed could be ascribed with confidence to the Old Welsh period (before *circa* 1100). The only complete articles which I have translated from the original in Welsh are Sir Ifor's discussions of the two sets of early *englynion* preserved in the Cambridge Juvencus manuscript (chapter VII). I believe the inclusion of these poems to be essential for the preservation of a thematic unity in this volume, and it seemed also that their re-issue was long overdue. Their interpretation formed an important step in Sir Ifor's researches into the literary affiliations and metrical antecedents of the *englynion* associated with the name of Llywarch Hen (chapter VIII). The only other piece which I have translated from the Welsh is Sir Ifor's introduction to the poem *Etmic Dinbych* or 'The Praise of Tenby' (chapter IX); the translation and notes to it were written by Sir Ifor in English. With the addition of these few pieces in translation, I believe that this volume contains all but one of Sir Ifor's major publications in English which are relevant to the subject under discussion. The single exception to this is the slim volume containing his three *Lectures on Early Welsh Poetry*, delivered in Dublin during the war, and published by the Dublin Institute for Advanced Studies in 1944 (reprinted in 1954, 1970). The *Lectures* form an essential complement to the articles which are collected here, and I have made frequent references to them in the accompanying notes.

I had originally intended to include in the volume translations or abstracts in summary form of some of the more important of Sir Ifor's essays and introductions, containing material which was only available in Welsh: in particular, the substance of his introductions to *Canu Aneirin* (1938), *Armes Prydein* (1955), and *Canu Taliesin* (1960), with some account of *Marwnad Cynddylan* and *Moliant Cadwallon*—two poems which are only preserved in a corrupt form in late manuscripts, but which Sir Ifor showed to be of a probable antiquity comparable to that of the Gododdin. But the three years which have intervened since 1967 have seen such unprecedented advances in the publication of responsible translations into English from early Welsh poetry, and of books and articles in English concerning it, that such an essay in synthesis has been rendered largely unnecessary by the labours of others. Two works in particular require special mention here: Professor K. H. Jackson's translation and discussion of the Gododdin[3] has made available for English readers the substance of Sir Ifor's introduction to *Canu Aneirin*, together with a useful working translation of the poem; and Professor J. E. Caerwyn Williams has provided a no less welcome rendering into English of the introduction and notes to *Canu Taliesin* in *The Poems of Taliesin*, published by the Dublin Institute for Advanced Studies in 1968. My own translation of *Armes Prydein* ('The Prophecy of Britain') is in the press, and will follow *The Poems of Taliesin* in the Dublin Institute's *Medieval and Modern Welsh Series*. Important recent articles by Professors I. Ll. Foster, Thomas Jones and A. O. H. Jarman have dealt with different aspects of the early poetry, and have made valuable additions to the number of authoritative translations available.[4]

In bringing together these studies within the covers of a single volume, it has seemed to me to be preferable to preserve a consecutive chronology in the subjects dealt with, rather than to observe the somewhat arbitrary chronology of the original dates of their publication—for these dates would have little bearing upon the periods when the respective subjects were uppermost in their author's mind. Each and all of them had been under consideration for long periods before they eventually received written form. Where repetitions occur, I have made a few minor deletions. But it has not been possible wholly to avoid overlap in the subject-matter dealt with. A rather special instance of this is the repetition several times over of the passage from the *Historia Brittonum* in which Nennius commemorated the names of Aneirin and Taliesin together with those of others of the Cynfeirdd. It is almost inevitable that this passage should constitute the point of departure for

[3] *The Oldest Scottish Poem: The Gododdin* (Edinburgh, 1969).

[4] See I. Ll. Foster, 'The Emergence of Wales' in I. Ll. Foster and G. E. Daniel (eds.), *Prehistoric and Early Wales* (1965) (this includes an account of *Marwnad Cynddylan* and *Moliant Cadwallon*); ibid. 'Wales and North Britain', the Presidential Address to the Cambrian Archaeological Association, *Archaeologia Cambrensis* (1969), pp. 1–16: Thomas Jones, 'The Black Book of Carmarthen "Stanzas of the Graves"', *Proceedings of the British Academy* (1967), pp. 97–137; A. O. H. Jarman, 'The Heroic Ideal in Early Welsh Poetry' in W. Meid (ed.) *Beiträge zur Indogermanistik und Keltologie* (Pokorny festschrift) (*Innsbrucker Beiträge zur Kulturwissenschaft* XIII; Innsbruck, 1967). (This article originally appeared as 'Y Delfryd Arwrol yn yr Hen Ganu', *Llên Cymru*, VIII, 125–49.) Generous selections from the early poetry in translation have also been given recently by A. Conran in *The Penguin Book of Welsh Verse* (1967) and by J. P. Clancy in *The Earliest Welsh Poetry* (1970).

any discussion of the early poetry, and it is quoted in translation by Sir Ifor no less than four times in the following chapters (with some unimportant variants between them in the wording of his translation). Throughout his career, Sir Ifor gave continuous attention to the many and varied questions bearing on the sources and composition of the *Historia Brittonum*, (cf. pp. 72-3)[5] but it is obvious that the central core of his interest lay in the passage which concerns the poets. In 'Wales and the North' (chapter VI) he decribes this as 'the most important Nennian comment of all, at any rate for the student of early Welsh literature' (p. 76). Each one of the four citations of this passage is vital to his argument in a way which will not admit of excision. A facsimile reproduction of this passage from fol. 188*b* of Harleian MS 3859 is perhaps as appropriate a frontispiece as any which could be devised for this volume.

Many younger generations of students have now grown up for whom Sir Ifor's major editions of early Welsh poetry have been a formative influence extending over many years, and who have not known a time when his works were not at hand to provide the essential data of their subject. To them it may well prove difficult to re-create imaginatively a period when the interpretations which we have for so long taken for granted were new and original. I believe, however, that these articles still convey something of the excitement of the era in which they first appeared, and of the exhilaration brought about by the first impact of this poetry when it was elucidated by Sir Ifor. To those of us who are old enough to have been among his pupils, Sir Ifor's writings will always forcibly invoke his whole personality, his manner of lecturing, and of his teaching in class. More than one of his old pupils has indeed recalled his gift of imparting in class to his students a sense of being participants with him in his most immediate and up-to-the-moment discoveries. Of no man has it been more true that teacher, lecturer, and writer were all one; and that it was impossible to separate the scholar from the man, for his human qualities and his individual personality shone out in all his scholarship. The disarming grace of his style of writing, whether in Welsh or in English, has crystallised the essence of Sir Ifor's mode of address, whether in class or on the public platform: relaxed and conversational, it treats subjects of complex learning with a deceptive simplicity which endeared him to audiences of all

[5] 'Hen Chwedlau', *Trans. Hon. Soc. Cymmrodorion* (1946–7), pp. 34 ff.; 'Notes of Nennius', *Bulletin of the Board of Celtic Studies*, VII, 380–9; 'The Nennian Preface: A Possible Emendation', ibid. IX, 342–4; etc.

kinds by its rare combination of wisdom, shrewdness, broad humanity, humility, and wit.[6] Like the final 'author' of the *Four Branches of the Mabinogi* (who manifests a remarkably similar combination of qualities, when all allowance is made for the social and intellectual changes which have taken place over eight centuries) his style is one which remains so close to the spoken word in which it originated, that to read what he has written is almost as if it were to hear him speak.

In spite of the diffidence which Sir Ifor frequently expressed about writing in English, these characteristic qualities come out clearly in his written style in both languages, and the articles collected here go far to exemplify the truth of Professor Foster's observation that Sir Ifor was 'as lucid and attractive a writer in English as in Welsh'.[7] It has been frequently regretted, and by many people, that Sir Ifor did not choose to disclose more fully in English the results of researches which have so obvious a value for students in all the disciplines concerned, and not only for students of Welsh literature and history. The English reading public has certainly been the loser from his reticence in this respect. Perhaps it will be sufficient to observe here that Sir Ifor had only a limited interest in communicating his discoveries, unless it were on a direct personal basis. To him it was the discovery itself which meant everything; and though it came naturally to him to wish to share his ideas with an intimate circle of friends and pupils (and as an extension of this circle, with the many local audiences whom he was always ready to address) he had considerably less interest in any wider audience, unseen and unknown, which might lie outside his own country. When he undertook the task of writing, he did so primarily for the benefit of this limited and defined circle, and particularly for the benefit of his own students. This sense of intimate personal communication permeates his style, and is conveyed to some degree in everything which he wrote. It is in itself a sufficient explanation of his strong preference for writing in his mother-tongue, in which he felt himself to be most at ease. Professor J. E. Caerwyn Williams has recalled his having said that 'You cannot give your allegiance to more than one language'.[8]

Sir Ifor would have been the first to recognise the extent to which certain aspects of his earlier work have been superseded. Indeed, at the

[6] With respect to the latter, some characteristic (but by no means isolated) examples of 'Iforisms' will be found below on pp. 1, 57, 89, 152.

[7] I. Ll. Foster, 'Sir Ifor Williams, 1881–1965', *Proceedings of the British Academy*, LIII, 375.

[8] *Y Dyfodol* (Bangor students' periodical), Rhagfyr 10 (1965).

time of his retirement he expressed the wish that he could re-edit each one of his books 'since new light breaks in upon us constantly as we struggle forwards'.[9] In a later work he referred to the 'immense progress' which Old Welsh studies had achieved during the preceding forty years;[10] and he believed that in the light of this progress (which we may justly attribute to his own work beyond that of all others) scholars of the future would be able to correct some of his mistakes. In spite of his generous recognition that there are 'few one-man haystacks',[11] and of the emphasis which he continually placed upon our common indebtedness to all those who have preceded us in our researches, it can nevertheless have been given to few to have erected in their lifetime so colossal a one-man haystack as did Sir Ifor—or to have come so very close as he did (except, regrettably, for the remainder of the *Book of Taliesin*)—to achieving all that they can have planned and intended to accomplish.

In editing, it has seemed to me that it would be helpful to the present-day reader to supplement Sir Ifor's generally very brief notes and references by adding some more ample footnotes dealing with sources, and referring in particular to such relevant works as have appeared since the original date of publication of these articles. This has involved re-numbering all Sir Ifor's footnotes, and interspersing them with my own. To distinguish between his and mine, I have placed between square brackets any words which I have added to Sir Ifor's original note; and, in those instances in which the whole note is my own contribution, I have placed square brackets round the number which introduces it, thus [10].

Chapter I, 'When Did British Become Welsh?', is based upon a lecture delivered at Bangor before the Cambrian Archaeological Association on 1 September 1937, and published in the *Transactions of the Anglesey Antiquarian Society and Field Club* (1939), pp. 27–39.

Chapter II, 'The Personal Names in the Early Anglesey Inscriptions', appeared first as 'The Personal Names in the Early Inscriptions' in *An Inventory of the Ancient Monuments of Wales and Monmouthshire*, VIII, *Anglesey* (London, Stationery Office, 1937), Appendix VI, pp. cxiv–cxvii.

Chapter III, 'The Towyn Inscribed Stone', was the presidential address delivered to the Cambrian Archaeological Association at

[9] *Y Cymro*, Hydref 17 (1947).
[10] *Canu Taliesin* (1960), p. xxiii.
[11] *Y Cymro*, *loc. cit.*

Harlech on 30 August 1949, and published in *Archaeologia Cambrensis*, C (1949), 160–72.

Chapter IV, 'The Earliest Poetry', is reprinted from *The Welsh Review*, VI (1947), 238–43. It was published in an abbreviated form in *The Listener* (12 June 1947), p. 919, under the title 'How Old is Welsh Poetry?'.

Chapter V, 'The Gododdin Poems', is reprinted from *Trans. Anglesey Antiq. Soc.* (1935), pp. 25–39. This article is in the main an English *résumé* of the results of researches which had been made known much earlier in Welsh in a series of articles in vols. I and II of *Y Beirniad* (1911 and 1912).

Chapter VI, 'Wales and the North', is based upon a lecture delivered at the annual general meeting of the Cumberland and Westmorland Antiquarian and Archaeological Society, held at Carlisle on 30 August 1950, and published in their *Transactions*, LI (1952), 73–88.

Chapter VII, 'The Juvencus Poems', is here translated from the *Bulletin of the Board of Celtic Studies*, VI (1933), where the two sections were originally published as two articles under the titles of 'Tri Englyn y Juvencus', pp. 101–10, and 'Naw Englyn y Juvencus', pp. 205–24.

Chapter VIII, 'The Poems of Llywarch Hen', was the Sir John Rhŷs Memorial Lecture, delivered before the British Academy on 1 February 1933. It may be noted here that (in contrast to the substance of chapter V) this lecture was Sir Ifor's earliest public exposition of a subject which we know from his own testimony to have been for him the most exciting of all his discoveries; as indeed it is in some ways the most far-reaching of them all in its ultimate literary implications. This re-issue includes also three passages taken from a broadcast talk given by Sir Ifor on the Third Programme on 22 November 1952 (re-broadcast on 13 January 1953) under the title 'The Llywarch Hen Poems'. I have introduced these passages into their present contexts in the belief that they amplify the matters under discussion in the earlier lecture, and that each deserves preservation in its own right. (I have indicated the interpolation of these three passages by brackets.)

Chapter IX, 'Two Poems from the *Book of Taliesin*', gives the text, translation, and discussion of *Etmic Dinbych* 'The Praise of Tenby' as published in the *Transactions of the Honourable Society of Cymmrodorion* (1940), pp. 66–83, under the title 'Moliant Dinbych Penfro'; and of the poem beginning *Echrys ynys* (BT 68) published in the *Trans. Angelsey Antiq. Soc.* (1941), pp. 23–30, as 'An Early Anglesey Poem' (with a postscript containing some minor revisions in TAAS 1942, 19–24.) Sir Ifor showed that these two poems have a common interest as exemplifying bardic verse from a period which is sparsely represented in our records, the period of the late Cynfeirdd (late ninth to eleventh centuries).

Chapter x, 'An Old Welsh Verse', is reprinted from the *Journal of the National Library of Wales*, II (1941), 69–75. This is a stray englyn, of considerable historical interest, which Sir Ifor also attributes to the late Old Welsh period (thus corroborating Bradshaw's independent dating on palaeographical grounds).

I wish to thank the editors of all the journals listed above, together with the Controller of H.M. Stationery Office, for giving their permission to reprint these works.

I owe an especial debt of gratitude to Alun Eirug Davies for generous bibliographical assistance, given to me in advance of the publication of his invaluable bibliography of the works of Sir Ifor Williams.[12] My thanks are also due to Gwynn ab Ifor for his encouragement towards an undertaking which I should not have otherwise embarked upon; and for making available to me the script of the broadcast talk from which I have quoted extracts in chapter VIII. I am indebted, as always, to Professor Idris Foster for giving me unstinted help and advice on many points and in a variety of ways. I wish also to express my thanks to Dr D. Ellis Evans for his guidance on some details concerning the Gaulish material which is discussed in chapter I. My final thanks are due, as a *sine qua non*, to the Board of Celtic Studies and to the University of Wales Press for undertaking the publication of this book, to Dr R. Brinley Jones for his care and helpfulness in guiding it through the press, and to the printers and staff of the Cambridge University Press for the high quality of their craftsmanship.

RACHEL BROMWICH

*January 1972*

[12] *Ifor Williams: A Bibliography* (University of Wales Press, 1969: reprinted from *Studia Celtica* IV, 1–55).

# ABBREVIATIONS

AC The *Annales Cambriae*, ed. E. Phillimore, *Cy.* IX, 141 ff.

ACL Wh. Stokes and K. Meyer, *Archiv für celtische Lexicographie* (Halle, 1900–7).

ACS A. Holder, *Alt-Celtischer Sprachschatz* (Leipzig, 1896–1913).

AL I, II Aneurin Owen, *Ancient Laws and Institutes of Wales* (London, Public Record Commissioners, 1841).

ALMA R. S. Loomis (ed.), *Arthurian Literature in the Middle Ages* (Oxford, 1959).

AMCA *An Inventory of the Ancient Monuments of Wales and Monmouthshire,* VIII, *Anglesey* (London, H. M. Stationery Office, 1937).

*Ann. Tig.* *The Annals of Tigernach*, ed. and trans. Wh. Stokes, RC, XVI–XVIII (1895–7).

AP Ifor Williams, *Armes Prydein o Lyfr Taliesin* (Caerdydd, 1955).

$AP^2$ ibid. Translated (with addional notes) by Rachel Bromwich (Dublin Institute for Advanced Studies, 1972).

*Arch. Cam.* *Archaeologia Cambrensis.*

B *The Bulletin of the Board of Celtic Studies.*

BBC *The Black Book of Carmarthen*, ed. J. G. Evans (Pwllheli, 1907).

BD Henry Lewis, *Brut Dingestow* (Caerdydd, 1942).

BT *The Book of Taliesin*, ed. J. G. Evans (Llanbedrog, 1910).

CA Ifor Williams, *Canu Aneirin* (Caerdydd, 1938).

*Cart. Red.* *The Cartulary of Redon* ed. A. de Courson (Paris, 1863).

*Chr. Br.* J. Loth, *Chrestomathie bretonne* (Paris, 1890).

CIIC R. A. S. Macalister, *Corpus Inscriptionum Insularum Celticarum* I, II (Dublin, 1945, 1949).

CIL K. Meyer, *Contributions to Irish Lexicography* (Halle, 1906).

CLlH Ifor Williams, *Canu Llywarch Hen* (Caerdydd, 1935).

CLl. aLl. Ifor Williams, *Cyfranc Lludd a Llevelys* (Bangor, 1910).

*Contribb.* *Contributions to a Dictionary of the Irish Language.* Published by the Royal Irish Academy (Dublin, 1942– ). In progress.

CS N. K. Chadwick (ed.), *Celt and Saxon* (Cambridge, 1963).

CT Ifor Williams, *Canu Taliesin* (Caerdydd, 1960).

*Cy.* *Y Cymmrodor.*

*Cymm. Trans.* *Transactions of the Honourable Society of Cymmrodorion.*

D J. Davies, *Dictionarium Duplex Latino–Britannicum* (London, 1632).

DGVB L. Fleuriot, *Dictionnaire des gloses en vieux Breton* (Paris, 1964).

EC *Études Celtiques.*

ECMW V. E. Nash-Williams, *The Early Christian Monuments of Wales* (Cardiff, 1950).

ECNE C. Fox and B. Dickins (eds.), *The Early Cultures of North-West Europe* (Cambridge, 1950).
ECNP K. Jackson, *Early Celtic Nature Poetry* (Cambridge, 1935).
EHR *The English Historical Review.*
EL H. Lewis, *Yr Elfen Ladin yn yr Iaith Gymraeg* (Caerdydd, 1943).
ES H. M. Chadwick, *Early Scotland* (Cambridge, 1949).
EWGP K. Jackson, *Early Welsh Gnomic Poems* (Cardiff, 1935).
EWGT P. C. Bartrum, *Early Welsh Genealogical Tracts* (Cardiff, 1966).
EWP J. P. Clancy, *The Earliest Welsh Poetry* (London, 1970).
EWS W. M. Lindsay, *Early Welsh Script* (Oxford, 1912).
FAB W. F. Skene, *The Four Ancient Books of Wales* (Edinburgh, 1868).
G J. Lloyd-Jones, *Geirfa Barddoniaeth Gynnar Gymraeg* (Caerdydd, 1931–63).
GC² Caspar Zeuss, *Grammatica Celtica* (2nd edn, Berlin, 1871).
GML Timothy Lewis, *A Glossary of Mediaeval Welsh Law* (Manchester, 1913).
GMW S. Evans, *A Grammar of Middle Welsh* (Dublin, 1964).
GOI R. Thurneysen, *A Grammar of Old Irish.* Translated from the German by D. A. Binchy and Osborn Bergin (Dublin, 1946).
GPC *Geiriadur Prifysgol Cymru: A Dictionary of the Welsh Language.* Published by the Board of Celtic Studies of the University of Wales (Cardiff, 1950– ). In progress.
GPN D. Ellis-Evans, *Gaulish Personal Names* (Oxford, 1967).
H J. Morris-Jones a T. H. Parry-Williams, *Llawysgrif Hendregadredd* (Caerdydd, 1933).
*Harl.* Harleian MS.
HB The *Historia Brittonum* of Nennius: (i) Ed. Th. Mommsen, *Chronica Minora Saeculi IV, V, VI, VII* (Berlin, 1898); (ii) ed. F. Lot (Paris, 1934).
HE Bede's *Historia Ecclesiastica Gentis Anglorum*, ed. C. Plummer (Oxford, 1896).
*HGCr* Henry Lewis, *Hen Gerddi Crefyddol* (Caerdydd, 1931).
HI A. O. H. Jarman, 'The Heroic Ideal in Early Welsh Poetry' in *Beiträge zur Indogermanistik und Keltologie zum 80. Geburtstag J. Pokorny*, ed. W. Meid (Innsbruck, 1967).
Hübner, Emil Huebner, *Inscriptiones Britanniae Christianae* (Berlin, 1876).
HW J. E. Lloyd, *A History of Wales from the Earliest Times to the Edwardian Conquest* (London, 1911).
ITS The Irish Texts Society.
IW Ifor Williams.
*Lap. W.* J. O. Westwood, *Lapidarium Walliae* (Oxford, 1876–9).
*Llan.* Llanstephan MS.
LBS S. Baring-Gould and J. Fisher, *Lives of the British Saints,* 4 vols. (London, 1907–13).
LEWP Ifor Williams, *Lectures on Early Welsh Poetry* (Dublin, 1944, 1954, 1970).

LHEB K. Jackson, *Language and History in Early Britain* (Edinburgh, 1953).

Ll.A. J. Morris-Jones and J. Rhŷs, *Llyvyr Agkyr Llandewivrevi* (Oxford, 1894).

LL J. Rhŷs and J. G. Evans, *The Text of the Book of Llan Dâv* (Oxford, 1893).

LP H. Lewis and H. Pedersen, *A Concise Comparative Celtic Grammar* (Göttingen, 1937).

MA Owen Jones, Edward Williams and William Owen Pughe, *The Myvyrian Archaiology of Wales,* 2nd edn (Denbigh, 1870).

MC Glosses on Martianus Capella, ed. W. Stokes, *Arch. Cam.* (1873), pp. 1–21.

Ml. Br. Medieval Breton.

M.W. Modern Welsh.

NLW The National Library of Wales.

O.B. Old Breton.

O.I. Old Irish.

O.W. Old Welsh.

Ox.I. Glosses from *Codex Oxoniensis Prior* (*Bodleian Auctor F.4.32*) ed. IW in B v, 226 ff. (See LHEB 47.)

OSPG K. Jackson, *The Gododdin: The Oldest Scottish Poem* (Edinburgh, 1969).

PBA Proceedings of the British Academy.

*Pen.* Peniarth MS.

PEW I. Ll. Foster and Glyn Daniel, *Prehistoric and Early Wales* (London, 1965).

PH R. Atkinson, *Passions and Homilies from the Leabhar Breac* (Dublin, 1887).

PKM Ifor Williams, *Pedeir Keinc y Mabinogi* (Caerdydd, 1930).

PT Ifor Williams, *The Poems of Taliesin*: English version by J. E. Caerwyn Williams (Dublin, 1968).

RBB J. Rhŷs and J. G. Evans, *The Text of the Bruts from the Red Book of Hergest* (Oxford, 1890).

RBH *The Red Book of Hergest.*

RBP J. G. Evans, *The Poetry from the Red Book of Hergest* (Llanbedrog, 1911).

RC *Revue Celtique.*

*Rep.* J. G. Evans, *Report on MSS. in the Welsh Language* (London, H. M. Stationery Office, 1898–1902).

RM J. Rhŷs and J. G. Evans, *The Text of the Mabinogion from the Red Book of Hergest* (Oxford, 1887).

SE D. Silvan Evans, *Dictionary of the Welsh Language* (Carmarthen, 1888–1906).

SEBC N. K. Chadwick (ed.), *Studies in the Early British Church* (Cambridge, 1958).

SEBH N. K. Chadwick (ed.), *Studies in Early British History* (Cambridge, 1954; 2nd edn. 1959).

SG *Y Seint Greal*; vol. 1 in *Selections from the Hengwrt MSS.* ed. R. Williams (London, 1876).

## ABBREVIATIONS

TAAS *Transactions of the Anglesey Antiquarian Society and Field Club.*
*Tal.* J. Morris-Jones, 'Taliesin', *Cy.* XXVIII (1918).
T.W. Thomas Wiliems, *Dictionarium Duplex* (1632); second part.
TYP R. Bromwich, *Trioedd Ynys Prydein* (Cardiff, 1961).
*Voc. Corn.* *Vocabularium Cornicum*, ed. E. Norris, *Ancient Cornish Drama* (Oxford, 1895), II, 311 ff.; see LHEB pp. 60–1.
VKG H. Pedersen, *Vergleichende Grammatik der keltischen Sprachen* (Göttingen, 1909–13).
VVB J. Loth, *Vocabulaire Vieux Breton* (Paris, 1884).
WG J. Morris-Jones, *A Welsh Grammar* (Oxford, 1913).
WM J. G. Evans, *The White Book Mabinogion* (Pwllheli, 1907).
*Wör.* E. Windisch, *Irische Texte mit Wörterbuch* (Leipzig, 1880).
YCM *Ystorya de Carolo Magno*, ed. S. J. Williams (Caerdydd, 1930).
ZfcPh. *Zeitschrift für celtische Philologie.*

## *Chapter I*

# WHEN DID BRITISH BECOME WELSH?

DR MACALISTER, in the introduction to his lecture at Aberafan on the inscriptions of Wales, remarks that they can be studied from several different viewpoints. 'We may take them', he says, 'as memorials of *language*—the philological viewpoint. We may consider them as illustrations of steps in the *history of writing*—the epigraphic viewpoint. We can regard them as *historical* and *biographical* monuments. And, as they are frequently accompanied by ornamental detail, we may add that they can be also treated as approximately datable monuments of the *history of art*.'[1] In this lecture I intend to confine myself to the strictly philological investigation, though that method of approach may not be very interesting to all of you. It is curious how sane and well-balanced people as a rule keep clear of philology. The inmates, however, enjoy themselves hugely, and carry on a chronic uncivil war amongst themselves.

Tonight I will try to answer one question, and one only, namely, are there indications of date in the language of our inscriptions? Or I might put it this way: do our inscriptions help in any way to date the development of Welsh from British or Brittonic? This is the chief and most urgent problem confronting the student of early Welsh literature, and any fresh light on it must be welcome.

Celtic, that great branch of the Aryan or Indo-European language, at some time or other in the dim past forked into (at least) two. One may be called Goidelic (for it developed into Irish, Manx, Gaelic), and the other Brittonic or British (for it produced Welsh, Cornish, Breton). The old Celtic languages of Spain, Gaul, northern Italy, south Germany, Austria, Galatia, probably had affinities with both. Here and now we are only concerned with British. When Caesar attacked Britain in the first century B.C., the Gauls of northern France and Belgium were closely connected in race and language with the inhabitants of the opposite coast. The same tribal and personal names occur on both sides of the English Channel. So also names of rivers, mountains, forts and towns. The language seems to have been at the same

1 R. A. S. Macalister, 'The Ancient Inscriptions of Wales', *Arch. Cam.* (1928), p. 285.

stage of development in Britain and on the Continent, though there were probably minor differences, or what may be called dialectal variations in form and vocabulary. On the whole, this old Celtic tongue resembled Latin more closely than any other Indo-European language.[2] It was a fully inflected language, with several declensions of nouns and conjugations of verbs.

The resemblance of Celtic to Latin had two results. On the one hand Gauls and Britons probably found it easier, for this reason, to adopt the language of their conquerors, and to forget their own. On the other hand, as the two languages were so closely akin, Celtic words and idioms were admitted rather freely into the Latin of Gaul and Britain. The Celtic accent brought about many modifications in the quantity and quality of Latin vowels.[3] And so with the consonants. That is why French is so different from Italian, though both are derived from Latin. Probably British died out rather quickly in the thoroughly Romanised parts of Britain, the eastern and southern districts,[4] which were afterwards the first to be overrun by the Angles and Saxons. These later invaders learnt more Latin than British from their captives and slaves, if one may safely judge from the scarcity of British elements in English as compared with the number of early Latin borrowings.

A good deal of what I have just said is controversial and hypothetical. My next point, however, is certain. Of primitive Celtic we have only scraps left. There are, of course, hundreds of proper names and place names preserved in Greek and Latin authors; also a few

[2] For more recent discussions of the relation between Italic and Celtic see Myles Dillon, 'Italic and Celtic', *American Journal of Philology* LXV (1944), 124–34; ibid. 'Celtic and the other Indo-European Languages', *Trans. Philological Society* (1947), pp. 15–34; Calvert Watkins, 'Italo-Celtic Re-visited' in J. Puhvel (ed.), *Ancient Indo-European Dialects* (Berkeley, 1966). The problem is briefly summarised by Ceri Lewis, 'The Welsh Language' in *The Cardiff Region: A Survey prepared for the Meeting of the British Association in Cardiff 1960* (Cardiff, 1960), pp. 148–9.

[3] 'There must have been a strong stress accent in British on the penult, so that the syllables before and after it were pronounced lightly. In the course of time this led to the universal dropping of final syllables, and in many cases other unaccented syllables were either lost or their vowels were shortened. The first change, when completed, marks the passing of British into Welsh.' IW's article on 'Welsh' in *Encyclopaedia Britannica* (1964), V, 151.

[4] The nature of the interaction between the two languages has been fully discussed by K. Jackson, 'On the Vulgar Latin of Roman Britain', *Medieval Studies in Honour of J. D. M. Ford*, ed. U. T. Holmes and J. Denomy (Harvard, 1948), pp. 83–100; esp. p. 95 ff. Jackson concludes that 'the situation (was) very similar to that of English and Irish in eighteenth-century Ireland, or English and the Indian languages in twentieth-century India'. See further LHEB, ch. 3.

score inscriptions in various parts of the Continent,[5] dedications to Celtic deities, altars, memorial tablets, inscriptions on coins, graffiti on bits of pottery, etc. But not a single manuscript written in Celtic has survived: no poem, no chronicle, no treatise. Luckily some of the inscriptions are long enough to provide examples of complete sentences, so that we know how a simple sentence was put together in Celtic.[6] And that is about all. We have a certain amount of material, but it is woefully inadequate. Imagine what would be the plight of English scholars if they had to guess what Shakespeare's language was like from fragments of tombstones found in the churchyard at Stratford-on-Avon, and inscriptions on mugs and flagons discovered in the ruins of the local inn.

Speaking generally, Celtic scholars have to be content with individual words, mostly proper names, and an analysis of their component parts. A few years ago the publication of the graffiti of La Graufesenque potters gave us the ordinal numbers up to ten, a very welcome and important addition to our stock.[7] They were discovered on the site of the old *Condatomagos* 'the plain of the confluence', i.e. the confluence of the rivers Tarn and Dourbie, close to Millau, dép. Aveyron, in the basin of the Garonne, 300 miles south of Paris, and just over a hundred from the Pyrenees. This was one of the most important potteries in Gaul, if not in the Roman Empire, during the first century A.D. and the beginning of the second, and its signed vases have been found as far north as Carlisle and Corbridge on the Roman Wall, York, Chester, Wroxeter, and other Roman sites in England. In the British Museum alone, according to the 1908 catalogue, there were 889 vases made and stamped by La Graufesenque potters. Many of these men had good Celtic names, like *Damonus*, *Cassidanus*, *Bilicatus*; amongst them was a *Maponus*, the Welsh *Mabon*.[8] The Welshman, however, is

[5] A major accession to the knowledge and interpretation of early Celtic personal names attested on the Continent has been provided by D. Ellis Evans, *Gaulish Personal Names: a Study of some Continental Celtic Formations* (Oxford, 1967) (henceforth GPN).

[6] H. Lewis, 'The Sentence in Welsh', PBA (1942).

7 First discovery 1882; full account by Frédéric Hermet (Paris, 1934). [See further GPN, pp. 31–4, and references there cited.]

[8] Hermet, *op. cit.* pp. 202, 204 (nos. 18, 47, 92). *Cassidanus* is now thought to be a title rather than a personal name of a potter, GPN pp. 168, 189. For the other three names see A. Oxé, 'La Graufesenque', *Bonner Jährbucher* CXL–CXLI (1936), 381 ff. (nos. 28, 78, 137). The stamps give the potters' names in the genitive, so that in this last instance OF MAPONI (= *oficina Maponi*) has been listed by Oxé as *Maponius*; so also Whatmough, *Dialects of Ancient Gaul* (Harvard, 1969), p. 132. (I am indebted to Dr Ellis Evans for these references.) For *Maponos*/*Mabon* in mythology and early Welsh literature, see Anne

not a relation of the potter; his pedigree is much more elevated, for in Durham, Cumberland, and Northumberland altars have been found, dedicated to *Apollo Maponos*. Evidently the Britons worshipped a youthful god (as the name *Mabon* implies), whom the Romans and Greeks equated with Apollo. He is the *Mabon fab Madron* of early Welsh legend.

On broken pottery these potters scratched lists or accounts, which show that they manufactured 183,150 of one type of vessel, and 137,600 of another, numbers which show the scale of their operations. First of all they wrote *Tvthos* or *Tuththos*, a word meaning list or series; then came *cintu*, *al(l)os*, *tritos*, *petuarios*, *pinpetos*, *svexos*, *sextametos*, *oxtumetos*, *navmetos* (= ? *namet* [*os*]), *decametos*. Scholars were delighted to see in these forms the prototypes of the Welsh ordinals, *cynt-af*, *ail* or *all*, *trydydd*, *pedwerydd*, *pumed*, *chwech-ed*, *seithfed*, *wythfed*, *nawfed*, *degfed*. The importance of the discovery is obvious. We know the dates of these potters, A.D. 40 to 120 or so. We know where they lived in the south of France. It is of immense interest to us to know that the Celtic spoken so far south as the Garonne basin, within a hundred miles of the Pyrenees, resembled closely the parent language of Welsh and Breton, our British. Indo-European *qu*, as attested by Latin *quattuor*, *quatruus*, *quinque*, *quintus*, gave *c* in Irish (cf. *cethir*, 4; *cóic*, 5), and *p* in Welsh (*pedwar*, *pump*). These Gauls wrote *petvar-* and *pinp-*; so their brand of Celtic was more like British than Goidelic. And further, the change of *qu* to *p* had been completed by A.D. 40, at latest. (So when we find at Margam a cross called the Cross of *Ilquici*[9] from the name carved on it in ninth-century minuscules, it is useless to try and explain the name as if it contained a primitive *qu*, for that sound had developed into *p* at any rate nine hundred years earlier at Condatomagos.) A local tribe was called *Petrucorii* (a name preserved in the modern *Périgueux*), a compound of *petru* (cf. Welsh *pedry-fan*) and *cori* (Welsh *cordd* 'family, tribe').[10] A coin of the Remi, whose name is preserved in Rheims, is stamped *Pennovindos*, our *pen-wyn* 'white-head'. The *Parisi* had a settlement in Yorkshire, called *Petuaria*.[11] So the change of *qu* to *p* was not accidental or local at La Graufesenque.

Ross, *Pagan Celtic Britain* (London, 1967), pp. 359, 363–4, 368–70; TYP pp. 433–6; and references there cited.

[9] ECMW no. 236. The cross at Margam which bears this name has been assigned by Nash-Williams to the eleventh century.

[10] For *Petrucorii* > *Périgueux* see GPN p. 373. On *petr-* in compounds 'four-square, perfect, complete' see TYP p. 279.

[11] The name is recorded by Ptolemy; LHEB p. 473.

Taking *decametos* to be the first century British form of the ordinal 'tenth', what happened to it later? The main accent must have been on the penult, *-met-*, for both the termination *-os*, and the *-a-* preceding the accented syllable disappeared. By easy stages *decametos* became *dec'-met-'*, *degfed*, as the unaccented vowels dropped and the consonants softened. These changes are typical. British became Welsh when the unaccented medial syllables and the unaccented terminations were dropped; the medial consonants during this process underwent regular changes or mutations, so that *-c-* became *g*, *-m-* became *-v-* (*f*), and *-t-* became *d* in the word we are studying. Both the dropping of the unaccented vowels and the various mutations of consonants were gradual processes, and several centuries passed away before the orthography was adapted to the changed pronunciation. When, however, these changes had taken place in the living speech, British may be said to have become Welsh.

Here I must ask your indulgence while I make a digression. Third-declension nouns in Latin are regularly longer by a syllable or two in the oblique cases than in the nominative singular. Or to put it more neatly, the nominative singular is shorter by a syllable than the genitive.[12] So *rex*, *regis*; *index*, *indicis*; *trinitas*, *trinitatis*. A thousand Latin words borrowed by the Britons survive in Welsh, and as they developed on the lips of British speakers exactly like words of Celtic origin, the phonetic development of the one class helps us to understand that of the other. The exact form of the Latin word at the period of borrowing, say eighteen or nineteen centuries ago, is proved by the classics, so that the philologist has a more or less simple problem to solve, namely, how did this particular form become modified to the form found a thousand years later in a Welsh manuscript? What phonetic laws, or regular sound changes, must be assumed to have been in operation? And we can assume further that these phonetic laws were in full operation in the case of the Celtic elements in our vocabulary, though here, unfortunately, the early forms can only be inferred, or guessed, unless they happen to occur in a Gaulish inscription, or are quoted by Roman or Greek authors.[13]

12 It is, of course, shorter also than the dative and ablative singular, and all plural cases.

[13] The phonetic changes which marked the development of Brittonic (or British) into Welsh before the latter half of the sixth century have been fully treated by K. Jackson in LHEB. A parallel development took place in the treatment of Latin loanwords. For a convenient summary of these changes see Ceri Lewis, *op. cit.* pp. 151–2.

An interesting fact is that we have quite frequently in Welsh both a short and a long form of the borrowed third-declension Latin word, the first from the nominative singular, and the other from an oblique case, e.g. *trinet* 'Trinity' in Old Welsh, from *trinitas*; and *trindawd*, later *trindod*, from *trinitatem*, *trinitatis*, *trinitati*, *trinitate*. The long form may derive also from the plural in *-ates*, but for the purpose of this paper I need not consider forms of that type. We will take the genitive singular as our representative of the long group. So *trined* and *trindod* both mean 'Trinity'; one comes from the Latin nominative and the other from the genitive. As the long form may actually derive from any one of four cases, it stands a better chance of surviving than the short, which can only represent the nominative. Words were not borrowed from dictionaries but from sentences, and the inflected forms occur much more frequently than the simple nominative in the usual type of sentence. That is why so many of our Welsh borrowings can only be explained by reference to the Latin genitive stem.

There must have been in British also a declension like the Latin third declension, and the story of the Latin borrowings must be kept in mind when we try to trace its modern equivalents. For instance, the old name of Ireland was *Iueriô*, with *Iuerionos* as its genitive. The first gave Welsh *Iwerydd*, as in *Môr Iwerydd* 'Irish Sea', and the latter *Iwerddon* 'Ireland'. Take any pedigree. The first name is in the nominative; every other name is in the genitive, whether you talk in Latin, Celtic, Old Irish or Old Welsh. In the course of centuries these genitives would tend to become fixed. People forgot that they were genitives. Just as *Iwerddon* became the current name of Ireland, and ousted the old nominative *Iwerydd*, so did the genitive of many a personal name become the usual form. The old nominatives became obsolete, or survived here and there as doublets. If then we can find in our inscriptions a name in its genitive form used as a nominative, we shall have a clear indication of a late period. On the other hand a true nominative may be early or late, for occasionally such nominatives managed to survive, and their presence in a document or on a stone does not help us to fix the date.

I shall now take one or two typical forms. The first is *rix* 'king', a common element in personal names, Latin *rex*, Irish *rí*, Welsh *rhi*. The Celtic genitive was *rigos*, Old Irish *rigas*, Latin *regis*. In composition with *teuto-* 'tribe, people', it gave *Teutorix* 'lord of the tribe', its genitive being *Teutorigos*. Both survived in Welsh; the first became

*Tudyr*, later *Tudur*, and the latter *Tudri*. How? *Teutorix* developed in this way. The final long *i* modified or affected the *o* of the second syllable to *y*, before it dropped. But the dropping of the final syllable did not take place all at once. The tail was not amputated, but gradually shed, little by little. The first change was probably that of *-x* to *-ss* or *-s*. British *s* was very unstable. Initially and medially it gave *h* in Welsh; so *-ris* gave *-rih*; and then the *h* was dropped. The *-i* was shortened after the accent, and at last disappeared altogether. The *Teut* of the first element became *tud*. So *Tudyr*. Later the *y* was assimilated to the preceding *u*, giving *Tudur*.

The genitive *Teutorigos* passed through the following stages. The second element was changed to *-rigis* (perhaps by vowel assimilation, helped by the analogy of the Latin *regis*), then *-rigi-*; finally *-rig*, *-ri*, for *-g-* between vowels disappeared. The accent in the British period was on the penult *-rig-*, and the unaccented *-o-* preceding it disappeared. So *Teutorigos*, *Teutorigis*, *Teutorigi*, *Tut' rig'*, *Tudri*.

Are there any traces of these intermediate forms in our inscriptions? On the Rhuddgaer lead coffin, kindly loaned to the College Museum by Mr Lloyd Hughes, we have *Camuloris*.[14] *Camulus* was the Celtic god of war.[15] Dedications in the form *Deo Marti Camulo* are quoted by Holder. A town called after him *Camulodunum* is now Colchester. A king dedicated to his service might well be styled *Camulorix*. The *-ris* of this inscription shows the first and earliest stage on the way to Welsh.

The next stage, when the final *-s* has gone, is seen in the Llangefni *Culidori*,[16] and the Penmachno *Cantiori*.[17] On the Brynkir bilingual stone we have in Latin letters *Icori filius Potentini*, and in Old Irish Ogam, the genitive *Icorigas*.[18] Rhŷs[19] in his report hesitates between *Icoris* of the *-i* declension and a form of *Icorix*. The Ogam *Icorigas* must turn the scale in favour of the latter, for *-rigas* is the Old Irish genitive of *rix*; and I class this form with the other two. The Welsh equivalent

[14] CIIC no. 322; ECMW no. 28 (where *Camuloris* is interpreted as genitive); early fifth century, LHEB p. 627.

[15] Anne Ross, *op. cit.* p. 68, and *passim*.

[16] CIIC no. 320; ECMW no. 26. Fifth to early sixth century. See below p. 22 and cf. n. [43] to this chapter.

[17] CIIC no. 394; ECMW no. 103. Fifth to early sixth century. Cf. p. 13 below, and LHEB p. 188 n.

[18] CIIC no. 380; ECMW no. 84; sixth century. The evidence for dating provided by this and by the other bilingual Ogam inscriptions in British has been discussed by K. Jackson, 'Notes on the Ogam Inscriptions of Southern Britain', ECNE pp. 205 ff.

19 *Arch. Cam.* (1910), p. 110.

of *Icorix* would be *Igyr*; with a doublet *Igri* from the genitive *Icorigos*, cf. the *Egri* of Anglesey records.[20] To this stage also belongs *Carantorius*,[21] if I am right in reading it as *Carantori* with the Latin *-us* tacked on 'for good form', and not as *carant-* with the Latin termination *-orius*. My reason for differing from Rhŷs on this point is that the Latin *-orius* would give *-ur* in Welsh, but *Carantorix* (a compound of *carantis-* 'kin, family', and *rix* 'lord') is the exact form required to explain the *Cerenhir* of the *Book of Llan Dâv*.[22]

The Trawsfynydd *Porius*[23] does not belong here, for the name occurs in Suetonius in that form. But the Gildas vocative *Vortipori* (read *Votepori*)[24] should be classed with this group. The epithet of Coel *Godebawg* proves a Celtic *votepo-*, Welsh *godeb*;[25] and the discovery of the Llanfallteg stone (now in the Carmarthen museum) with its *Memoria Voteporigis protictoris*[26] settles the question, if, as is extremely

[20] *Plant Egri o Dalebolion* are listed in a number of genealogical collections preserved in manuscript. These have been edited by P. C. Bartrum, EWGT p. 86; *NLW Journal* XIII (1963), 93 ff. as 'Pedigrees of the Welsh Tribal Patriarchs'. § 58 in this latter collection gives the genealogy of *Iarddur ap Egri ap Morien Mynac ap March ap Meirchion arglwydd ar dalm o Wynedd oedd hwnnw* from *Peniarth MS.* 134, pp. 131–2.

21 Hubner no. 69. [At Kenfig, Glam. (with accompanying Ogam), sixth century; ECMW no. 198; LHEB p. 627, CIIC no. 409.]

22 LL p. 239.

[23] ECMW no. 289. Late fifth to early sixth century.

[24] Ed. Hugh Williams (*Cymmrodorion Record Series* no. 3; London, 1899), p. 72. Cf. the form *Guortepir* in *Harl. Gen.* no. 2 (EWGT 10).

[25] *Godeb* 'refuge'. O.W. *Guotepauc* 'shelterer, protector, defender' is attested both as a personal name and as an epithet, which is attached to Coel (Hen). For the first cf. *Harl. Gen.* no. 10, *Coyl Hen map Guotepauc* (EWGT p. 10); *Life of St Cadoc* § 46, *Guotepauc genuit Coilhen* (EWGT p. 25); *Jesus Gen.* 5, *Coyl hen m. Godebawc* (EWGT p. 44), CA line 131, *meibyon Godebawc*. As against this, *Godebawc* appears as Coel's epithet in the *Life of Gruffudd ap Cynan*, in the *Mostyn Pedigrees*, and in certain later sources (see index to EWGT). The early genealogies in fact show considerable uncertainty as to whether *Godebawc* was originally Coel's epithet or his patronymic. Cf. below on *Protector*.

[26] ECMW no. 138 and fig. 108; ECNE pp. 208–9; LHEB pp. 169–70, 175 and n. 1; mid-sixth century. Idris Foster relates **Voteporix* to the semantically equivalent epithets (or names—see above) *Protector*/*Guotepauc* (PEW pp. 219–20). On the close semantic correspondence between Brittonic **uo(r)-tep-*, Welsh *godeb*, and Latin *protec(t)* see further P. mac Cana, B XIX (1959), 116–17. The occurrence of the name *Protector* among those of the ancestors of *Guortepir* in *Harl. Gen.* no. 2 is evidence for a long tradition of the use of this epithet as a personal name, and may be cited in favour of the identity of Gildas's king *Vortipori(x)* with the potentate whose name appears in the genitive on the stone as *Voteporigis Protictoris*. R. Thurneysen (GOI p. 571) rejected this identification, presumably on account of the discrepancy between the prefixes *Vor-* and *Vo-*, but Jackson argues (LHEB p. 625 n.) that such a confusion of prefixes is not in itself a sufficiently strong argument against identifying the characters concerned; and this identity is in fact assumed throughout LHEB. The accompanying Ogam inscription on the stone reads *Votecorigas*.

probable, it commemorates the very prince 'so severely treated by Gildas', as Dr Macalister has already said.[27] A British *Voteporix* has become *Votepori*, through the intermediate form *Voteporis*, by the first half of the sixth century, or even earlier. Gildas is a satisfactory witness on that point. If he wrote *Votepori* about A.D. 540, the Rhuddgaer *Camuloris* must be put back to 450 or even 400. You must allow time for *-rix* to become *-ris*, and for *-ris* to become definitely *-ri* before Gildas went to school!

Now for the genitive cases of this group of names. Of *-rigos* we have no example; only Ogam *-rigas*, already quoted. The next stage *-rigis* is seen in the *Voteporigis* of the Llanfallteg stone. Then comes *Camelorigi* (or rather *Camulorigi*)[28] the genitive of the Rhuddgaer name; *Clutorigi* or *Clotorigi.*[29] *Caturugi*, an obvious carver's mistake for *Caturigi*;[30] and *Caelexti Monedorigi*[31] on the Barmouth stone. The Latin name in the latter, *Caelestis,* ended in *-is* in both the nominative and genitive cases. The scribe wrote *-x-* medially for *-s-*, a broad hint that in his day *x* had come to be pronounced *s*. The final *-s* has gone whether you take the form to be nominative or genitive. We can thus assume that *Monedorigi* also has lost its final *-s* like all the other *-rigi* genitives. Whether we can proceed to infer that they are all later than 550 because of the Llanfallteg *-rigis*, is not so certain. Some of the writers of these inscriptions were more archaic in their orthography than others. And besides, the analogy with *rex*, *regis*, was so obvious to anyone with even an elementary knowledge of Latin, that it would not be surprising if the author of *Memoria Voteporigis Protictoris* (a rather ambitious and rare

Jackson concludes that this king was Irish, and that Irish remained a living language in south-west Wales throughout the sixth century. On this see further Melville Richards, 'The Irish Settlements in South-West Wales', *Journal of the Royal Society of Antiquaries of Ireland*, LXXXIX (1959), 133–60.

[27] All these forms in *-oris*, *-ori* on the inscriptions, together with the *Vortipori* of Gildas, have been discussed in detail by Jackson, LHEB pp. 624–8. He concludes that the endings in *-ori* were not necessarily evolved regularly from the old British nominative in *-orix* (though he accepts this in the case of *Camuloris*), but that they may represent the genitive or vocative 'of a new latinizing (ending in), *-ŏrīus* or *-ŏri̯us*, actually seen (as nominative) in *Carantorius*'. On the false latinisations in the inscriptions see also H. Lewis, *op. cit.* pp. 8–9.

[28] CIIC no. 455; ECMW no. 403 (*sic. leg.*). Fifth to early sixth century.

[29] CIIC no. 435; ECMW no. 315 (reading *Clutorigi*). Fifth to sixth century.

30 *Lap. W.* p.97; [CIIC no. 379; ECMW no. 170 (reading *Caturug*); LHEB p. 626; late fifth to sixth century].

[31] CIIC no. 413; ECMW no. 272; LHEB p. 626; fifth to early sixth century. Jackson prefers to regard these forms in *-origi* as latinised genitives, rather than as developments from genuine British formations.

formula) regularised the genitive of his patron's name. He had *pro-tictoris* before him at the time as an additional inducement. Epigraphic spelling is usually on the archaic side, with a fondness for traditional rather than contemporary forms. Gildas proves that the *-s* of the nominative had disappeared, even earlier than this, when *Voteporix*, *Voteporis* was still alive.

Another common element in personal names was *cu* 'dog', Irish *cu*, Welsh *ci*, used for 'warrior, hero', by the Irish and the Welsh. The genitive was *cunos*. In compounds the stem was lengthened to *cuno-* (on the analogy of second declension formations), when it formed the first element, as in *Cunorix*, *Cunovalos*, *Cunotegirnos*. If we combine it with *maglos* 'prince', Welsh *mael*, Irish *mál*, two forms are possible, *Cuno-maglos* and *Maglocu*, the genitive of the latter being *Maglocunos*. *Cuno-maglos* gave our *Cynfael*. *Maglocu* regularly gave *Meilyg* (written *Meilic* in the *Book of Llan Dâv*),[32] for the final *ū-*, like *i*, would affect the *-o-* of the penult to *i*, *y* (cf. *Maglorix*, *Meilyr*). But the genitive *Maglocunos* quite as regularly became *Maelgwn*, so that *Meilyg* and *Maelgwn* are as much of a pair as *Tudur* and *Tudri*, or *trined* and *trindawd*. The most famous bearer of the name in our history is Maelgwn Gwynedd in the first half of the sixth century. Tradition consistently calls him *Maelgwn*, never *Meilyg*. So the chronicles, pedigrees, the early poetry. The significance of this fact has not been fully realised. It proves that the old British declension system had gone to pieces in Wales long before 540, or whatever date we ascribe to Gildas. British grammar must have been in a very bad way when a king's name was only known in the genitive case! The old school of philologists shut their eyes to the possibility, and explained *Maglo-cunos* as a compound of *maglos* and a *cunos* 'high', which they deduced from Pughe's invented *cwn* 'head, top, summit', and his wrong explanations of *cwnu*, *cynu*.[33]

The *Historia Brittonum* of Nennius was written just before A.D. 800 and contains many names in their Welsh form, and common nouns as well. He refers to Maelgwn Gwynedd at the beginning of a paragraph as *Mailcunus*, but the *-us* need not be taken seriously: it is the Latin ending tacked on to a Welsh name to give it dignity. At the end of the sentence he has become *Mailcun*.[34] The Celtic *maglo* has become *mail*;

[32] LL pp. 161, 162.

[33] W. O. Pughe's *Dictionary of the Welsh Language* (2nd edn Denbigh, 1866) gives *cwn* subst. (*cy-wn*) 'a head; a top, a summit', and *cwnu* bb. 'to arise, to support'.

[34] HB, ch. 62; cf. AC ann. 547; *Harl. Gen.* 1 (EWGT p. 9); and see LHEB p. 464. On the form *Maglocune* used by Gildas, see *Tal.* pp. 28–9.

the stem vowel -*o*, and the -*os* of the British case-ending, have been dropped. Welsh has arrived pretty definitely by 800. Corroboration is provided by the Welsh extracts and glosses in an Oxford manuscript in the Bodleian (Ox. I)[35] written in A.D. 820; as well as by the Welsh form of all the royal names on the Pillar of Elisedd, near Llangollen, set up probably about 810–20.[36] For instance the *Cunocenni* of the Trallwng inscription[37] is here written *Concenn*. British *Broccomaglos* has become *Brohcmail*. If neither Nennius, the disciple of the great Bishop Elfoddw, nor the royal scribe of Powys felt any qualms about writing these Welsh names about the year 800, it is safe to assume that the language by this time was well established, and we may say that the British inflexions had been shed a century earlier, to say the least.

There is evidence for a still earlier date. In the inscription at Llangadwaladr, Anglesey, Cadfan, the father of the Cadwallon who fell in 634 after ruling as conqueror for a full year over Northumbria, is called *Catamanus*.[38] So the monument can be dated *circa* 625. But even here the royal name is not pure Celtic or British: that would have been **Catumanduos*. The first element *catu*- is a fourth-declension noun (Welsh *cad* 'battle'), with -*u*- as its stem vowel. The *Cata*- of the stone is thus proved late. Further -*nd*- should have given -*nn*-: here we have one *n*. They were shockingly careless about doubling their consonants in the old days! What about the -*us*? Is it a real living tail, or one fixed on for show? The latter, I think. This famous inscription is carved in swaggering minuscules that fit in with the mood of the men who thought they could wrest the north of Britain once more from the hands of the invaders. A similar type is seen on the Llangaffo stone,[39] also in Anglesey, and experts tell us that it belongs to the same period. Here I have no doubt at all: the three personal names *Cini, Cuuris, -virnin*, are in their old Welsh form, i.e., the terminations have been dropped, and Llangaffo has the honour of preserving on stone the earliest testimony to the change-over from British to Welsh.

Reverting to Llangadwaladr, with its *Cataman*-, may I call your

[35] B V, 1–8, 226–48; VI, 112–15. See LHEB pp. 47, 53 f.

[36] CIIC no. 1000; ECMW no. 123; EWGT pp. 1–3 (with additions to bibliography).

[37] CIIC no. 342; ECMW no. 70. Fifth to early sixth century.

[38] CIIC no. 970; ECMW no. 13; see ch. II below, pp. 18–19; and cf. GPN pp. 67, 222–3.

[39] CIIC no. 971; ECMW no. 35; see ch. II below, pp. 17–18. Nash-Williams reads the inscription as ]VS/[ ]NIN/ FILIU[S] CUURI[S?] CINI ERE|XIT HUNC LAPI|DEM and dates it as seventh to ninth century. Cf. LHEB p. 188; seventh century.

attention to the stem vowel, the second *a* in it? A Welshman in 625 heard something between the *t* and the *m*. The original *-u-* had become an indistinct vowel, which took its colour from the vowels flanking it. The important thing is that there was some sort of vowel there, and we cannot cling any longer to the old theory that both medial and final unaccented vowels were lost at one and the same time. In 625 the medial remains, but the final is gone, at any rate in this particular name, *Catamann*. The main accent was still on the last syllable; we must assume that to account for the loss of the old British ending, and the blurring of the vowel before the accented syllable. Later on the accent moved backwards one syllable. But when this accent-shifting took place in Anglesey, the stem vowel had disappeared completely, and the name was pronounced *Cadfan*, not *Cadafan*. In some districts, however, when this change occurred, and the accent moved back to the penult, the stem vowel in a modified form was still there to receive it. That is why we have doublets like *Dyfnwal*, *Dyfnawal*; *Tudwal*, *Tudawal*; *Dingad*, *Dinagad*; *Urien*, *Urföen*.[40] The longer forms are rarer than the short, and may be dialectal. They prove that the shifting of the accent did not take place at the same time in all the districts where Welsh was spoken.

Going still further back, from 625 to 540, I can understand, with the help of Llangadwaladr and Llangaffo, why Gildas wrote *Maglocune* and *Cuneglase*. The stem vowel was still there, though blurred in the second name. Cynlas was given a Latinised vocative, second declension, *Cuneglase*: and the *-e* of *Maglocune* can be explained in the same way. The name of the second prince, as has been suggested already, is an old genitive. What I cannot find out for certain is this: had this genitive already lost its ending? Would a Welshman of Gwynedd in 520 have called his lord *Maglocunos, Maglocuno,* or *Maglocun*? If *Voteporix* could be addressed as *Votipore*, I think it safe to guess that *Maglocunos* never heard the final *s* in his name. Even the *-o* may have dropped before his time. It was a short *o*, and would be likely to disappear much

[40] On the two forms of this name, with and without composition vowel (*Urien* < *Urbgen*; *Urföen* < *Urb-o-gen*) < **Orbogenos*, see IW in B vii, 388; PT pp. xxxvii, 42. In LHEB pp. 643–56 Jackson discusses the gradual weakening and final syncope of the composition vowel, and concludes that this had been lost in nearly all instances by the latter part of the sixth century. He points out that it is only in the orthography of a few personal names that these medial vowels are found preserved in O.W. written sources, and he concludes from this that such sporadic instances of their preservation can best be accounted for as archaisms due to the conservative tendencies inherent in the forms of personal names.

earlier than the final long *i* of *Voteporix*, which furthermore was originally followed by a double consonant (*ss*, from *gs*, *x*). If the colloquial form was *Maglocun* in 520–40, Gildas could easily Latinise it into a second-declension *Maglocunus*, and get all the cases he required.

The Penmachno stone is a good example of an inscription composed in the period of muddle and confusion when British was dying and Welsh struggling to the birth; *Cantiori Hic Iacit, Venedotis Cive Fuit Consobrino -magli Magistrati.*[41] Here we have *Cantiori* as a nominative, with final *s* (from *x*) dropped: *Venedotis*, a genitive for the nominative *Venedos* 'one of the Gwynedd tribe': *Cive* for *civis*, and the *s* gone: *Consobrino* for *consobrinus* 'cousin'; *Magistrati*, a fourth-declension noun with the genitive ending of the second. With *Consobrino* one can compare the *Elmetiaco* of Llanaelhaearn,[42] another nominative.

Working on Westwood's plates in his *Lapidarium Walliae,* I picked out 50 inscriptions in uncials or capitals, and classified them thus:

A. 13, with correct nominative forms as subject to *Hic Iacit.*
B. 21, with genitives as subject to *Hic Iacit.*
C. 16, genitives only, without *Iacit* or *Hic Iacit.*

The construction in A and C is quite correct; in C a word meaning *stone* or *memorial* is to be understood. B, however, shows a confusion between the formulas found in A and C, which may be taken as evidence that the difference between genitive and nominative did not worry their authors unduly.

Traces of vowel changes are not very numerous. I shall deal with one only. Sir Cyril Fox has suggested A.D. 550 for the Mynydd Margam inscription, beginning *Bodvoci Hic Iacit.*[43] The important word here is *Bodvoci*, a genitive used as a nominative. The Britons were fond of hypocoristic names, pet-names, formed from compounds beginning with *maglos*, *tigernos*, etc., by adding *-acos* to the stem; thus *Maglacos*, *Tigernacos*, our *Maelog*, *Teyrnog*. Starting from *Bodua* 'a crow, raven, goddess of war', Old Irish *bodb,* we get not only Welsh names like *Elfoddw*, *Gwrfoddw,* but also (in a Continental inscription) *Boduacos.*[44] Why then

[41] See above p. 7 and n. 17. Jackson interprets *Venedotis* in this inscription as an adjectival formation, and not as a genitive used as nominative; LHEB p. 188 n.; CS p. 30. On *cive*—exemplifying loss of *-s* and with *e* for *i*—see LHEB p. 193.

[42] CIIC no. 381; ECMW no. 87.

[43] CIIC no. 408; ECMW no. 229. The genitive form of the name is here interpreted by Nash-Williams as depending on 'the stone of'—understood, but not expressed. This is the assumption commonly made in the case of the numerous Ogam inscriptions which consist merely of a single name in the genitive.

[44] GPN p. 151.

the Mynydd Margam *Bodvoc-i*? A study of Latin borrowings has shown that long *a* under the accent gave in Welsh first of all a back *ō*; this later on became *-aw-*, and at last, when the accent moved back from it, a short *o*. In the glosses of A.D. 820 in Ox. I the form is *-au*, pronounced *-aw*. Bede, who died in 735, in his account of the Battle of Chester, 615, states that the Welsh abbot of Bangor (on Dee) at that time was *Dinoot*.[45] This is the Latin name *Donatus* on its way to become *Dunawd* in Welsh, passing through the first stage mentioned above, a back *o*. Bede must have got this early form from a seventh-century Welsh chronicle or record. If *Bodvoci* belongs to A.D. 550, then *Catacus* (Hübner's no. 35), *Dervaci* (his no. 50) must be earlier.

Here is the place to refer to the Old Irish *trindóit* 'Trinity', a form often quoted to prove that the first missionaries to bring the gospel and the doctrine of the Trinity to Ireland were Welshmen, for this Old Irish form preserves the 'Welsh accent' of these early saints.[46] They talked much of the *trinitas*, *trinitatis*, and pronounced the long *a* of the latter as a back *o*, so that their Irish converts became believers in the *trindoit*. The *d* also is a Welsh symptom, and still more definitely so the *o*, for as a rule Latin *a* in Irish was kept unchanged. As we have been blamed so consistently and long for the unwillingness of the early Welsh to attempt the conversion of the Anglo-Saxons, I am glad of a chance to remind you that men of our race played a worthy part in the conversion of Ireland, and in addition provided her with a patron saint in the Briton Patrick.

And St Patrick can help us now. There is considerable evidence that St Patrick swore in Welsh, and Bishop Cormac (killed in A.D. 908) has preserved the words he used, *modebroth*.[47] In his glossary he says that the Irish have corrupted the Welsh, and that it should really be *muin duiu braut*, i.e., he says, *muin* 'my', *duiu* 'God', and *braut* 'judge'. Perhaps Cormac's predecessors were more accurate than he thought. I think he was wrong in explaining *braut* as 'judge'; it is the Welsh word for 'judgment'. *Dwyw brawt* is good Old Welsh for the God of judgment. Now Patrick lived in the fifth century, and if he pronounced *braut* as *brot*, then we have good evidence that the final syllable of the genitive case had either been dropped in Welsh a century before Gildas, or else there was so little of it left that nobody heard it, when the saint swore. Cormac explains *mo* as *muin* 'my'. Again I must take leave to

[45] HE II, ch. 2; LHEB pp. 41, 295. [46] Cf. GOI pp. 565–6.

[47] *Cormac's Glossary*, ed. J. O'Donovan (Calcutta, 1868), p. 106; ed. W. Stokes, *Three Irish Glossaries* (London, 1862), p. 28.

doubt. Welsh oaths usually begin with *myn* 'by'; and *Myn Duw brawd* 'by the God of Judgment' is an oath worthy of a saint. The Welsh word for 'my' is *fy* (Old Welsh *mi*), and is followed by the nasal mutation (cf. *fy Nuw*). Instead of arguing that St Patrick's oath dates from a period when the nasal mutation had not yet taken place, though that is possible, I should prefer to make another suggestion. In medieval Welsh, side by side with the *myn* formula in oaths, we find a variant *ym* or *m*, followed by the noun in its unmutated form, e.g. *ym Duw, M' Beuno*, etc. Perhaps the *mo* of Patrick's oath may be an early example, and may have meant after all 'my', as Cormac thought. At any rate, there is something to learn when holy men swear. For fear that I have tempted you beyond endurance, I will sum up very briefly.

Welsh is well established by A.D. 800: proved by Nennius, the Elisedd Pillar, and glosses in Ox. I, A.D. 820.

Bede, who died in 735, quotes a few names in their Welsh form, e.g. *Car Legion*, for Caer-lleon, Chester: *Ban-cor, Brocmail*.[48]

The *Catamanus* stone is evidence for 625; in conjunction with the *Cuuris* and *Cini* of Llangaffo it helps to show that British terminations had been dropped, but that the stem vowel of the first element in a compound, though unaccented and somewhat blurred, occasionally survived.

Bede's *Dinoot* suits A.D. 615.[49] The ending is gone, and the vowels are changing.

Gildas, 540, and the Llanfallteg stone, 550, may be archaic in their orthography. The stem vowel is preserved (partly modified, in *Cuneglase*). Nominatives and genitives have fallen together. Final consonants have gone; perhaps also short vowels in the final syllable before a single consonant. Traces remain of long vowels in this position.

The Rhuddgaer coffin is said to belong to the fifth century. Final *x* has become *s*. Unaccented syllables remain. If St Patrick has been correctly reported, he swore in Welsh, not in British, in the fifth century. He may be taken as witness to the colloquial speech, and the coffin to the more formal language of the period. Perhaps, however, the coffin may be a century earlier.

48 HE II, 2. See *Tal.* 30, 60, where Morris-Jones stresses the resemblance between O.W. and O.B. as a proof that the 'reconstruction' of a modern language out of the ruins of Brittonic had taken place before the separation of Breton and Welsh, i.e. before 450–500. [For a full discussion of the linguistic evidence provided by the Breton settlements, see now LHEB chapter I.]

[49] See LHEB pp. 41, 295 for the argument that Bede derived this name from an older written account of the Battle of Chester, rather than from an oral source of his own day.

*Chapter II*

# THE PERSONAL NAMES IN THE EARLY ANGLESEY INSCRIPTIONS

THESE inscriptions having been dated approximately,[1] it is possible to use the personal names contained in them as test-material for the study of the development of Welsh from Brittonic or British, the language of the ancient Britons. 'The great change which transformed British and converted it into Welsh and its sister dialects was the loss of the endings of stems and words, by which, for example, the four syllables of the British *Maglo-cunos* were reduced to the two of the Welsh *Maelgwn*.'[2] It was a change as complete and as definite as the growth of French or Italian from Latin, but owing to the almost complete lack of datable evidence in contemporary manuscripts, charters, etc., no one knows when it took place. Some scholars believe that it must have been accomplished by the fifth century, others hold that the seventh is early enough. Some of the Anglesey inscriptions are assigned to the fifth, and some to the seventh century. Do they provide us with evidence in support of either view? No full discussion of this difficult problem is possible here, for that would require the study of the inscriptions of the whole of Wales, and also an examination of such materials as can be gleaned from the Lives of the Saints, Nennius, the *Book of St Chad*, the *Book of Llan Dâv*, as well as Bede and Gildas. Yet the Anglesey inscriptions have a very valuable contribution to make to the general store; amongst them we have one of the rare memorials that can be dated with some certainty, the Llangadwaladr stone.[3] Here we are on solid ground; Cadfan's date is known, and his epitaph can be dated with confidence to *circa* A.D. 625. Similarities in lettering date the Llangaffo inscription[4] in the same period, so that these

[1] The previous section of AMCA, pp. civ–cxiv, gives the readings of the early medieval inscriptions as deciphered by Ralegh Radford; pp. cix–cxiii that of the Trescawen stone (ECMW no. 33, now in the Bangor Museum) as deciphered by IW. These interpretations have since been incorporated in ECMW.

2 WG p. 6.

[3] See p. 11 above, and n. [38] to chapter 1.

[4] P. 11 above, and n. [39] to chapter 1.

two definitely belong to the early seventh century. What do they tell us?

LLANGAFFO: here are three names in their Welsh forms, i.e. without the British or Latin terminations.

CINI is attested elsewhere, e.g. in an eleventh-century document in the *Book of Llan Dâv*, p. 275. The name of a farm near Clynnog, Caernarvonshire, *Prysgyni*, may well be from *Prys* 'grove, brushwood' and *Cyni*; cf. also CLlH I, 48 and p. 98—two stanzas of the Llywarch Hen saga, probably composed in the ninth century, are in honour of one of Llywarch's sons, *Keny*, with a variant *Kyni*; The *Book of Llan Dâv* has also *Cinhi* (p. 275) and *Cynhi* (p. 277); this, however, may be a different name, cf. *Gwri* and *Gwrhy*. Holder gives us a Celtic *Cinius* (with *Cinia* as a feminine); *Cintius* (and a feminine *Cintia*).[5] The name with *-h-* may derive from the second, and *Cini* from the first. Whatever the derivation may be, *Cini* is definitely Welsh, not British or Latin.

CUURIS: cf. Holder, ACS I, 1202, *Curisius*, a Celtic proper name, from which was derived *Curisiacus*, surviving in the place names *Curzac* and *Coursac*. The double U can be compared with the VV of the Llangefni stone, ORVVITE;[6] also the Ogam on the Llanwinio stone, AVVI BODDIBEVV—;[7] and the Trallwng (Brecon) Ogam, ILVVETO.[8] Still more apposite is the Glan Usk, PVVERI.[9] Some of the instances support Rhŷs's view, that VV is an attempt to express a consonantal *w*, later *gw*; but this theory does not explain CUURIS or PVVERI. I suggest that the doubling in Welsh names might have been intended to differentiate the *w* sound (Latin *u*) from the sound expressed by *u* in Welsh, which could be described as a rounded *i* down to *circa* 1600, cf. French *u*. Latin short *u* when not affected by a following vowel gave Welsh *w*; Latin long *u* and long *o* gave Welsh *u*. Assuming that CUURIS was pronounced *Cwris circa* 625, the next step would be for *w* in the penult to weaken into the obscure sound of Welsh *y*. For this Old Welsh script used *i*; Latin *culcita* had given *cilchet* in Welsh by 820, as the glosses in Ox. I prove.[10] Similarly *Cwris* would have

5 ACS col. 1020–1; [GPN pp. 176, 179–80].

[6] CIIC no. 320; ECMW no. 26.

7 J. Rhŷs, *Lectures on Welsh Philology*, p. 389; *Lap. W.* p. 91. [Cf. CIIC no. 378; LHEB pp. 180–1.]

8 J. Rhŷs, *op. cit.* p. 384. [CIIC no. 342, ECMW no. 70. Cf. LHEB p. 185 and n.; W in *Cymm. Trans.* (1943–4), p. 155.]

9 *Lap. W.* p. 73, plate 41. [CIIC no. 327; LHEB p. 171.]

[10] VVB p. 71, *cilchetou* gloss on *vela*. Cf. DGVB p. 113 (s.v. *colcet*); CLlH p. 223.

become *Ciris*, to give later *Cyris* or *Cyrys*; cf. *Cyrys* the Old (*Hen Gyrys*) in the *Red Book of Hergest* (*circa* 1400).[11] This Cyrys is said to have made a collection of Welsh proverbs; he came from Yale (*o Iâl*). As *e* and *y* occasionally interchange in the initial syllable, a variant *Cerys* or *Ceris* is possible (cf. *Merddin* side by side with *Myrddin*), and it is tempting to guess that the Llangaffo *Cuuris* might have given his name to the whirlpool, Pwll *Ceris,* in the Menai Straits. The local pronunciation is Ceris; cf. Brit. Mus. MS. 46, 54*b*, *Pwll Kerys dwll echrys dwfn,* where the internal rhyme proves that the final syllable was *-ys*; and B.M. 55, 186*b*, where it is written *Ceris.*[12] In the Nennian *Mirabilia*, the variants are *in voragine Cereuus*, or *Cerenus*, *polkerist* and *polleerist.*[13]

The first name on the stone begins with VI and ends with IH (i.e. IN). If the initial of line 2 be read R and the final letter N, the full name is *VIRNIN. I can only suggest that this may be a variant of GVERNIN,[14] a diminutive of *Gwern*, a name with Anglesey associations; in the Mabinogi Branwen's son is called *Gwern*. Though this first name on the stone is mutilated, it agrees with the other two in being without the British termination. Thus all three bear witness to the loss of final syllables which changed British to Welsh; and further they prove that the change was full and complete, and not recent. If the dropping of the final syllable had been looked upon in 625 as the slovenly habit of illiterates, the writer of the inscription would not have insulted himself and his relative or patron by using the curtailed forms of their names. *Cini* and *Cuuris* were 'respectable' forms, and had been respectable for more than two generations.

LLANGADWALADR. What has just been said on the Llangaffo names shows that CATAMANVS, with its *-us* termination, cannot have been the living form in 625. Names of kings and dignitaries of the church have had Latin forms throughout the centuries. As for *Cataman*, two things must be noted. The first element in the compound is obviously the Welsh *cad,* Old Welsh *cat*, 'battle'; but this in Celtic,

11 J. Gwenogvryn Evans, *Report on Welsh MSS.* II, 7, 9; RBH cols. 964, 1057.

12 *Report on Welsh MSS.* II, 1106, 1159.

13 HB ed. Mommsen, p. 218; [ed. F. Lot, p. 217].

14 [CIIC no. 971]; Skinner 'Ten Days' Tour Through the Island of Anglesey' (*Arch. Cam.* 1908), p. 31, in his drawing shows a horizontal stroke, which *may* be the top of a G, at the beginning of line 1. He saw the stone in December 1802, before it was moved from Fron Deg. He begins line 2 with a sprawling S or G, but it is difficult to believe that the cut still visible on the stone could ever have been part of the long curling tail of his S.

as Gaulish proves, was a *-u* stem, *catu-* (nominative *catus*, cf. Latin fourth-declension nouns). In Celtic names the first element in a compound ends in the stem vowel, and Holder gives scores of instances (vol. I, cols. 847–63) in *Catu-*, amongst them *Catumandus* (col. 858), the prototype of our Cadfan. So *Cata-* must be regarded as a late and poor tradition, which arose when the unaccented vowels in a word were becoming or had become slurred and obscure. The second element *-man* should have been written *-mann* in Old Welsh, as it derives from *-mandus* in Celtic, cf. Holder, ACS II, cols. 404–6. The meaning is uncertain, but a good case has been made for taking it as a cognate of the root seen in Greek μανθάνω (**men-dh-*) 'learn, understand',[15] if so, *Cadfan* means 'wise in battle', cf. *Tegfan*, from *Tecomandus* 'handsome and wise'. In the Gododdin poems one of the heroes is called *Cadfannan*,[16] a diminutive of Cadfan; here the *-nn-* from Celtic *-nd-* has been preserved in the orthography.

Four names are found in sixth-century inscriptions. In order of dating they stand as follows: SATURNINUS,[17] CUNOGUSI,[18] ETTORIGI,[19] MACCUDECCETI.[20]

LLANSADWRN. The name SATVRNINVS would give Sadyrnin in Welsh, not Sadwrn. As the slab probably commemorates the founder of the *llan*, it is safe, I think, to explain SATVRNINVS as a diminutive (of affection or honour), formed from *Saturnus* on the analogy of Celtic names like *Cynin* (*Cunignos*), from *Cunos*.

LLANFAELOG (BODFEDDAN). The latest reading of the name on this stone is CVNOGVS-. The name corresponds to a Celtic *Cunogussos* or *Cunogustos*. The first element, *Cuno-*, occurs in several well-known names, e.g. *Cuno-maglos*, Cynfael; *Maglo-cunos*, Maelgwn, etc. The usual meaning ascribed to it, 'high, noble', is based on three ghost words only found in late dictionaries, *cwn* 'top, summit', *cynnu* 'to rise up', and *erchynu*.[21] I take it to be the stem of the Celtic word seen in Irish *cú*, genitive *con*, and Welsh *ci* 'dog', plural *cwn*, cognate with the English *hound*; cf. names like *Gwrgi*, *Aergi*, and other

15 Boisacq, *Dict. Etym. de la Langue Grecque*, p. 607.
[16] CA lines 38, 457, 715.
[17] CIIC no. 323; ECMW no. 32; *circa* 525, LHEB p. 670.
[18] CIIC no. 319; ECMW no. 9; LHEB pp. 172, 531, etc.
[19] CIIC no. 318; ECMW no. 6; LHEB pp. 188, 456 n. 1.
[20] CIIC no. 326; ECMW no. 39; LHEB pp. 140, 172 and n., 181–2, 648.
[21] Cf. p. 10 above, and n. [33] to chapter I.

'animal' names like *Erthgi* (from *arth* 'bear', and *ci*), *Bleddyn* from *blaidd* 'wolf', and *gynt* 'tribe'. The second element has been connected with the Latin *gustus*, the *-t-* being attested by Old Welsh names, e.g. *Cingust* (Irish *Congus*), *Gurgust*, modern *Grwst* in Llan-*rwst* (Irish *Fergus*), *Ungust* (Irish *Oingus*, Scotch *Angus*). Rhŷs compares the Cilgerran inscription, *Trenegussi*, Ogam *Trenagusu*.[22] For Irish inscriptions containing *Cunagusos*, *Cunagussos*, see Macalister, *Studies in Irish Epigraphy*, part III, pp. 57, 131. If British forms contained *-st-*, and Irish *-s(s)-*, then our Bodfeddan *Cunogus* looks like an Irishman.[23] His name survives in the name of the neighbouring village, *Pencaernisiog*, a late semi-learned corruption, influenced by *caer*, of *Conysiog*, later *Conisiog*, with the regular *y* from *w* in the second syllable assimilated to the following *i*. The old name occurs in the *Record of Caernarvon*, p. 51, written *Comissok*, probably for *Conussok*.[24] Parallel formations showing *-iog* added to a man's name to denote his property or sphere of influence, are *Tudweiliog* in Lleyn, from *Tudwal*; *Peuliniog* in Dyfed 'the land of *Peulin* or Paulinus',[25] *Rhufoniog*, *Cetheiniog*, etc. So *Conysiog* 'the land of Conws'. If he had borne the Welsh name *Cynwst*, one would have expected *Cynystiog*. In Anglesey pedigrees there are a few occurrences of the name *Cwnws*[26] or *Conws*; with the latter, compare the *Con-* names in the *Book of Llan Dâv*, pp. 393–4. This *Cwnws* may be a borrowing of the Irish *Congus*, or a Welsh modification of *Cynwst*, *Conwst*, to *Cwnwst* by the assimilation of *y* or *o* to a following *w*, as in *bygwth*, *bwgwth*; *corwg*, *cwrwg*, and the loss of the final *t* on the analogy of names like *Dicws, Einws*. Whether *Cwnws* be Welsh or not, the absence of *-t* in the inscription still remains a problem.

LLANBABO. ETTORIGI bears witness to the confusion of forms and cases when Welsh was gradually being evolved out of British. Names in pedigrees, with the exception of the first, were in the genitive case, *A*, son of *B*, son of *C*, etc., and these genitives were quite as likely to survive as the nominative. British personal names in which the

[22] CIIC no. 428, ECMW no. 305; LHEB pp. 181, 190; ECNE pp. 206, 210. Cf. GOI p. 197.

23 But the rule that final *-st* should give *st* in Welsh is not universal, see VKG I, 79–80; II, 20; cf. also LL p. 393, *Conblus* and *Conblust*.

24 Ed. H. Ellis (Historical MSS. Commission, London, 1838). Also Anglesey Court Rolls, 1346; Peredur Jones, TAAS (1932), p. 49.

25 HW p. 265.

26 J. E. Griffith, *Pedigrees of Anglesey and Caernarvonshire Families*, pp. 83, 100. [For references to *Kwnws* see EWGT pp. 111, 112, 113]; *History of Gruffydd ap Cynan* (ed. A. Jones) p. 126, a chendelu m(ab) *conus o von*.

second element belonged to the third declension were longer by a syllable in the genitive than in the nominative, and as Welsh names derive from both cases, we have pairs like *Tudyr* (later *Tudur*) from *Teutorīx*, *Tudri* from *Teutorigos* the genitive; *Meilig*, *Meilyg* from *Maglo-cū*, and *Maelgwn* from *Maglocunos*. Latin borrowings developed in the same way, *trined* from *trinitas*, and *trindawd* from *trinitatis*, etc. Rhŷs has already pointed out that *Ethri* would be the Welsh name corresponding to *Ettorigi*: I think the nominative *Ettorix* survives in the *Eithir*[27] of the *Black Book of Carmarthen*, 107, l. 9. The genitive in Celtic, however, was not *Ettorigi* but *Ettorigos*, for *rix* 'king' had a genitive *rigos*.[28] This shows that the inscriptional form in *-i* is due to a confusion in spoken British between the second and third declension, or else to sheer ignorance on the part of the epigraphist as to the correct form in 'stone' Latin of the Welsh name, *Ethri*. In early script *-tt-* must have stood for our *-th-*; he added *-o-* to get the regular stem vowel, thus *Etto*. Even in Nennius (*circa* 800) *rhi* 'king', is written *rig*; so *Ettorig*. And to this 'restored' form he added the termination of the second declension genitive, though the construction required a nominative. In this he was probably influenced by earlier inscriptions, where the genitive stood by itself, with 'Stone of' understood, e.g. the Llannor VENDESETLI,[29] and the Llanaber, CAELEXTI MONEDORIGI[30] (with the same debased genitive), and others where *Hic iacit* was used with the nominative. For similar inscriptions containing a genitive form accompanied by *Hic iacit* compare Hübner's nos. 11, 17, 20, 34, 48, 50, 64, 71, 88, 108, and in particular the Penrhos–Lligwy stone above, comparing the Tavistock FILI MACCODECHETI,[31] where the name is in the genitive. So this mixture of formulas must have been fairly popular. The carver of Hübner's no. 35, CATACVS HIC FILIVS TEGERNACVS, went to the other extreme! Both types of mistakes would be impossible to men whose everyday speech was a fully inflected language like British.

PENRHOS–LLIGWY. On the difficult MACCVDECCETI see Rhŷs, *Lectures on Welsh Philology*, pp. 361, 407–12. It must be studied in connexion with the Tavistock SABINI FILI MACCODECHETI,[32]

27 The *ei-* of the first syllable is a possible misreading of O.W. *e*, which stood for our *e* and *ei*.

28 GOI p. 200; [LP p. 174, § 304].

[29] CIIC no. 390; ECMW no. 96.

[30] See p. 9 above, and n. [31] to chapter 1.

[31] CIIC no. 326; ECMW no. 39; LHEB p. 172.

[32] CIIC no. 492; LHEB p. 171, etc.

the Llywel MACCVTRENI with the corresponding form in Ogam, MAQVTRENI and the Cilgerran TRENEGVSSI FILI MACVTRENI (Ogam, TRENAGVSV MAQVI MAQITRENI).[33] Pedersen explains MACCV as an Irish word meaning great-grandson,[34] a joining of *macc* 'son' and *ua* 'grandson'. Dr Macalister's note on the inscription runs, 'Maccu, which is not a common word in the epigraphy of Wales, denotes descent from a remote ancestor, who is, in fact, the founder of the family'.[35] Rhŷs compares DECCETI to Caesar's *Decetia*, without accounting for the *-cc-* in our form. Until the Welsh *mach* 'surety' and the *mach* 'great' found in Old Bret. *Machtiern*, and Welsh *mechteyrn*[36] have been more satisfactorily explained, I prefer to suspend judgement on MACCV.

The fifth-century names are simpler.

LLANGEINWEN and LLANGEFNI. The Rhuddgaer CAMV-LORIS seems to show the first step in the deterioration of the British *Camvlorix*,[37] the final *x* weakening to *s*. The CVLIDORI[38] of the Llangefni stone may be an instance of the second stage, when the final *s* disappeared, i.e. if one can assume *Cvlidorix* to be the British form. Such a form in the nominative could have given the *Kyledyr* of the *Red Book Mabinogion*.[39] SECVNDI is a straightforward borrowing of the Latin *Secundus* in the genitive. ORVVITE, a feminine nominative in *-e*, the Welsh *Erwyd* according to Rhŷs, must be taken with similar names of women, all nominatives, occurring in our early inscriptions, *Tuncetace R*stece*, *Caune*, and perhaps *Cuniovende*.[40] With these, as evidence of a lasting Welsh tradition that *e* was the regular ending for a woman's name in its Latin form, I should compare the names entered in the

[33] ECMW no. 305. See n. 22 above.

34 VKG pp. 11, 16.

35 *Arch. Cam.* (1930), p. 471. [On *maccu*, *moccu* see also J. MacNeill in *Ériu* III (1907), 42–9; CIIC pp. xi–xiii.]

[36] For a full discussion of *mechteyrn* 'high-king, overlord' and its cognates in Cornish and Breton, see B x, 39–40; TYP pp. 71–2; and cf. AP lines 18, 100. The first element *mach-* (affected to *mech-* in Welsh, to *mych-* in Cornish) may either represent the substantive meaning 'surety, pledge' as was argued by Loth (*Chr. Br.* p. 148) in discussing the cognate Breton *machtiern*, or—as IW prefers—it may be an adj. meaning 'great, magnificent' (cf. Ir. *mass*). See further Fleuriot, *Annales de Bretagne* lxxviii (1971), 622 ff.

37 ACS I, col. 727. [See p. 7 above, and n. 27 to chapter I.]

[38] See p. 7 above, and nn. 16, 27 to chapter I. The Llangefni inscription (CIIC no. 320; ECMW no. 26) reads CVLIDOR(I?)/ IACIT/ ET ORVVIT(a)E/ MVLIERI(s) SECVNDI/ FILIUS(?).

[39] RM pp. 134, 141.

40 Rhŷs, *op. cit.* pp. 168, 212.

*Book of St Chad*, such as *Sulcene*, *Hancarate* (= Angharad), *Huilmede*, *Ourceine* (Eurgain), *Gloiumede*, *Dimnmede*.[41] These belong to the period when the manuscript was in south Wales, before it was carried off to Lichfield some time before Wynsi's episcopate (974–92).

The weakening of the terminations and the confusion of cases shown in several of the Anglesey fifth- and sixth-century names are in favour of the theory that British at this period was not the spoken language of the men who wrote these inscriptions.[42] On the other hand, the persistence of the stem vowel, though blurred in some cases, through the whole series till we reach the Llangaffo stone, shows that medial unaccented vowels were more stable than the case terminations. All unaccented syllables, medial and final, did not disappear at one and the same period. This accounts for doublets like *Dyfnwal* and *Dyfnawal, Tudwal* and *Tudawal, Urien* and *Urföen, Dingad* and *Dinogad*.[43] The British accent was on the penult. When the termination was dropped, it shifted more or less gradually to the new penult, and in some cases the old stem vowel of the first element in a compound was still there to receive it, a very significant fact for the study of the stress accent in British, as compared with Irish.

## LOST STONES

Three lost stones are on record bearing recognisable names. Drawings of two of them enable a date to be assigned to them from the form of the lettering employed. The earliest, bearing the letters MAILIS, which was formerly at Llanfaelog, by this method of dating must be assigned to the fifth century, but such an early date presents philological difficulties. *Mail* in personal names of the eighth–tenth century is fairly common; in modern Welsh it gives *Mael,* as in Maelgwn, but in the fifth–sixth centuries *Maglo* would be expected. If the early date is certain, then *Mailis* must have another origin Stokes. (*Urkeltischer Sprachschatz*, p. 204) has a root form *mailo-s* 'bald', cf. Irish *mael,* Old Welsh *mail* (gloss on *mutilum*), Welsh *moel.* The Old Welsh *mail* is a gloss in the Cambridge Martianus Capella MS. (date eighth-century according to Stokes). The Irish were fond of names like *Mail Isu* 'the slave (bald one) of Jesus', *Mail Brigit*, cf. the Welsh *Gwas*dewi, *Gwas*mihangel. In his text Skinner gives the word as MALIS, and this alternative form in the fifth century is equally obscure to me.

41 LL p. xlvii. 42 *Tal.* pp. 28–37. [43] See chapter I, pp. 12–13 above, and n. [40.]

The second stone, formerly at Capel Heilin, Llangefni, should be of sixth-century date and reads ...IACIT[44] / ...SORIS or SORII.[45] The better-attested reading, SORIS, may be the latter part of UXSORIS, a form which occurs at St Nicholas, Pembrokeshire,[46] or the original form may have been OSORII, for OSTORII, genitive of *Ostorius*.

The third stone[47] was formerly at Chwaen Wen House, in the parish of Llantrisant. Two readings are known, the more probable one being O BARRVS CONBVRRI. With *Conburr-i* cf. *Liber Landavensis*, *Convur*, variants *Convor Cinuur Cinmur*. There is an old word *burr*, 'fat', cf. Dunawd *fwr* or *vwrr* (see note in B VII, 35–6), Irish *borr* 'big, proud', Cornish *bor* 'fat'. Here, however, I suspect that BVRR may be for BARR, 'head', and that an inverted A was read V. My reason is the BARRVS at the beginning and the frequency of pairs like BARRIVENDI FILIUS VENDUBARI;[48] TRENEGUSSI FILI MACUTRENI.[49] Evidently in the early centuries people liked to have one element in the name of the son identical with an element in his father's name.[50] If the *Barrus* is right, then I should expect CONBARR not CONBURR.

[44] With this interpretation cf. LHEB p. 329 n.

[45] CIIC no. 321; ECMW no. 25.

46 *Lap. W.* p. 126, plate 59, fig. 4; [ECMW no. 401].

47 *Lap. W.* p. 86, fig. 5 and p. 192; [CIIC no. 324; ECMW no. 34].

48 *Lap. W.* plate 47, fig. 3; [CIIC no. 368; ECMW no. 150].

49 *Lap. W.* plate 53, fig. 2; [ECMW no. 305. See n. 22 above].

50 Cf. CA line 291 bud*van* vab bleid*van* *Cy.* IX, p. 170; [EWGT pp. 9 ff. (Harleian Genealogies)]: *Catgualart* map *Cat*gollaun map *Cat*man; *Pop*delgu map *Pop*gen; *Cat*tegirn map *Cat*ell; *Cat*gur map *Cat*mor; *Mor*gen map *Mor*mayl.

I The Towyn Inscribed Stone
(By courtesy of the Editor of *Archaeologia Cambrensis*)

## *Chapter III*

# THE TOWYN INSCRIBED STONE

FIRST of all I should like to thank you warmly for the honour you have conferred upon me by electing me President of the Cambrian Archaeological Association.[1] *Diolch yn fawr.* And that is the end of my presidential address!

What I intend to do now is to inflict on you my theory, or rather theories, on the well-known inscription at Towyn, Merionethshire, for as long as you can stand me. The Cadfan Stone, as it is often called, has long been a bone of contention: many and various interpretations have been suggested by various scholars, and it is now my turn to run the gauntlet. We Cambrians cannot leave the problem alone, for, in all probability, the words carved on the Towyn stone are the earliest examples *on stone* of the Welsh language, and it is the clear duty of our association to find out their meaning and date.

It is not an easy task. Westwood[2] gives a brief account of what was known about the stone in 1876, and a summary of the interpretations offered from the eighteenth century down to his own day. These references are brought up to date by Macalister in his second volume of the *Corpus Inscriptionum Insularum Celticarum,*[3] and there is no need for me to recapitulate. To save your time and mine, I shall deal mainly with Sir John Morris-Jones's theory, published as an appendix to his *Taliesin,*[4] which holds the field at the present moment. Can that explanation be corrected and amplified?

The stone itself is just over 7 feet long, 10 inches wide on the two broad sides, much narrower on the other two. On all four sides there are inscribed letters, comparable in form with those familiar to us in manuscripts of the eighth century. Lindsay, in a note to Morris-Jones,[5] says definitely enough: 'The writing on this stone is half-uncial, of much the same type as the writing of the Book of St

[1] The Presidential Address to the Cambrian Archaeological Association, delivered at Harlech, 30 August 1949.

2 *Lap. W.* pp. 158–61. [The inscription is dated by Westwood 'seventh or eighth century', *Arch. Cam.* (1850), p. 95. Cf. n. 7 below.]

3 CIIC no. 1033; [ECMW no. 287 (following the interpretation by J. Morris-Jones), plate xxiii].

4 *Tal.* pp. 260–7.

5 *Tal.* p. 267.

Chad.' The Palaeographical Society editors date this manuscript 'about 700'.[6] The Towyn letters are not quite the same, but of *much the same* type as those in use 'about 700'. So we may start with 'about 750' as a possible date for our inscription, and see how it fits![7]

On two sides of the pillar, near the square head, there are crosses, one on the broad side, the other on the narrow. These mark the beginnings of two separate inscriptions. The first cross is twice as big as the other, and in my opinion was the first carved on the stone. So I label this side *A*, and the one with a small cross *B*. The other broad side is my *C*, and the narrow side *D*. If the pillar were upright, and you stood in front of *A*, then *B* is on your right, *D* on your left, and *C* at the back. The inscriptions on *AB* run downwards, and those on *CD* are to be read upwards. The butt end of the stone is pointed 'as though it had been prepared to stand in a socket', says Macalister. The crosses confirm this: no one would carve them upside down. The end of each arm has a serif, except the bottom of the perpendicular.

Whoever found this pillar, or fashioned it to suit his purpose, had the choice of four sides for his memorial. Why should he choose the narrow side, and leave the broad one empty? That is why I find it hard to accept Morris-Jones's theory that the original inscription began on *B*. When the inscription on *A* had been cut, the carver turned the stone on its side, and carried on along the narrow side *D* finishing at the head of the pillar. He then added a 'footnote', at the socket end of *A*.

The second sculptor was a far better craftsman: his letters are well formed, his spacing is good, and he—or his employer—knew how to arrange his words so as to get a pleasing balance. He too starts with a cross at the top of *B*, carries on down this side a little way, and then stops, leaving plenty of space for the socket. For the rest of his epitaph he has the whole of the broad side *C*: here he arranges his two lines neatly on the smoothest part of the stone, reading upwards. And then he too added what I call a 'footnote' at the socket end of *C*. Compare his workmanship with the lettering of *A* and *D* and I think you will agree with me that the neat lettering of *B* and *C* and the ill-shaped clumsy letters on *AD* cannot be by the same hand.

So we have two main inscriptions to read and interpret, and two 'footnotes' as well. The order is *A–D*, *B–C*, and in that order I shall

6 According to Lindsay, EWS p. 3.

[7] Jackson (LHEB 668 and n.) agrees with Westwood in dating the inscription 'seventh to eighth century', believing this to be implied by the evidence which IW here cites. 'Probably early eighth century would be the nearest it would be safe to go.'

deal with them. I use ordinary type for the Hiberno-Saxon characters, as the exact forms can be seen in the photograph. The loop of the *g* is 'wrong way round' in all three examples on *A*.

*A*

Morris-Jones reads:

tengruin malte(d)gu
adgan

He comments that we seem to have here merely proper names: the *d* in brackets has been supplied from the drawings of Lhwyd[8] (*circa* 1700), who saw the stone before it was broken, leaving a gap here in the inscription. The final *n* in *tengruin* 'is read *ci* by Westwood, and it appears as *ci* in Pennant's drawing; but in Gibson's *Camden* it is given as *n* and Westwood says "it looks like *n*". Clearly it is *n*, and the small circle read as *c* must be accidental'.

This 'accidental circle', however, is not the source of the reading *c*; for that circle in the photograph is in fact a hole nearly three inches deep drilled into the pillar to hold a gate hinge, when a vandal used the stone as a gatepost. There is another one, its mate, halfway between the middle of the cross and the bottom of the perpendicular shaft. Hole no. 1 was bored into the *c* and destroyed most of the letter, except the upper curve, and the tip of the tail. Rhŷs so describes the *c*: Pennant and Westwood read *ci*; the Lhwyd drawing in Stowe MS. 1023, 160, has *ci*; and I can add the testimony of my own eyes, and rubbings! Why then did anyone read *ci* as *n*? Because there is an 'accidental' furrow on the stone, which, in a photograph or rubbing, might be taken as the first stroke of an *n*. The edges of this groove, however, are sharp and rough, very different from the real letters, which are well defined and smooth to the touch. I am sure that if Sir John had re-examined the stone after seeing Rhŷs's second article, he would have discarded his first reading.

[8] See T. Pennant, *The Journey to Snowdon* (Tours in Wales II, 1781), p. 93; 'I find, among Mr. Llwyd's papers the drawing of...two rude pillars, one seven feet high, with the figure of the cross, and an inscription on each side, in old characters'. A drawing of the stone appears in Pennant's second edition (1784), plate V, where Pennant cites his source for Lhwyd's notes as 'Sebright MSS.'. His description of the stone was followed, and the plate copied in R. Gough's *Camden* (1789), II, 541, and plate XIX. The name 'St. Cadvan's Stone' appears first in Gough. No reference to the stone is to be found among Lhwyd's notes to Gibson's *Camden*, in either of its two editions (1695 and 1722)—*pace* Westwood and Morris-Jones (who are evidently referring to the edition by Gough).

Anyhow, *tengruin malted* is obviously wrong, and so there is no need for me to discuss his suggestion that *tengruin* could have become *Egryn*. The middle word is *cimalted*.

**cimalted**. In Old Welsh, *cim-* (cognate with Latin *com-*) corresponds to modern *cyf-*; for instance, the gloss *cimadas* is our *cyf-*addas. The *ed-* is the common termination *-edd*, and *-alt* is the stem of the word. A Celtic *alt-* remained *alt* under the accent in Old Irish, but in Welsh it changes gradually to *allt*, which in turn may become *all*. Meyer gives us five Irish words of this form *alt*, all with different meanings, 'a joint, height, condition, razor, house' (CIL pp. 81–2). The most promising for our inscription is *alt* 'joint', used of joints of members of the body, such as the finger-joint, knuckle, ankle, wrist. As a verbal stem it is seen in the participle *accomallte* 'joined';[9] a gloss on *socius* in the Latin version of Rom. xi. 17 (where the Greek has συνκοινωνός 'a fellow-sharer, a joint-partaker'). The variant *accomolta* explains *coniunctus* and, best of all, *acomoltae* is given as a gloss on *coniunx* 'husband, wife, spouse',[10] just the word we require to make sense of the *A* inscription! Instead of a series of proper names, quite unconnected, here is the familiar formula, '*X coniunx* of *Y*'. Old Welsh *cimalted* equates syllable by syllable with the Irish word: *cim-* (*com-*), *alt* (in both), *-ed* (often corresponds to the *-e* in Irish). The omens are favourable!

Now for confirmation. In Cornish the Celtic *-lt* would become *-ls*, so that *als* must be sought for: in the oldest Cornish document, the *Vocabularium Cornicum*,[11] I found *chefals* explaining the Latin *artus* 'joint'. This answers exactly to a Welsh *cyfallt*, or Old Breton *Comalt*, cf. the Breton gentleman called *Comalt-car*, which means, I hope, that he was a worthy man and loved his wife.[12] A Celtic *comaltios* would give in Welsh *cyfaillt*, and we have it in the medieval form of modern *cyfaill* 'friend', one joined to us by bonds of affection. The Old Welsh *Cimeilliauc* 'Cyfeilliog' must have been a very sociable and friendly person. A Celtic *co-maltia*, on the other hand, would give in Welsh *cyfalledd* by Rhŷs's law[13] (that the abstract ending *-ia* became *-ida*, later *-edd*). A final *-dd* is very unstable, and occasionally dropped even in early Welsh (e.g. *i fynydd* became *i fyny*; *eistedd* became *eiste*, etc.), and *cyfalle* is found in the *Red Book of Hergest* (*circa* 1400) in the Welsh Charlemagne story edited by Stephen J. Williams:[14] Belisent, the emperor's lovely daughter, is given by him in marriage to Otuel, a doughty warrior whom she had never seen before. When she is brought into the hall and sees her future husband, she promptly agrees, saying, 'Ny dyly dyuot ediuarwch ym byth am vy *ghyfalle*'. A literal translation would be, 'Repentance (or *regret*) ought never to

9 GOI p. 75. 10 VKG II, 509–10. 11 B XI, 92.

12 *Chr. Br.* p. 119; W. Stokes, *The Breton Glosses at Orleans* (Calcutta, 1880), p. 57.

[13] See J. Rhŷs, 'Etymological Scraps', RC II (1873–5), 115–19; also IW's account of Sir John Rhŷs in the *Dictionary of Welsh Biography*.

14 YCM p. 64, l. 20. Cf. GPC *cyfalle(dd)* 'a joining together, bond, union, mate, spouse'.

come to me of my *cyfalle*'. Is she using *cyfalle* for 'husband', or for 'marriage', the marriage *bond*? Dr Williams quotes the original French in his notes, 'De tel *mari* doi je bien estre lie'. 'Of such a *husband* I ought to be very proud (or *glad*)'. Repentance is a curious word for a wife to use of her *husband*, though she may regret that she ever *married him*. The French original refers expressly to the husband: Belisent is thinking not of marriage but of Otuel as a husband that she can always be proud of.

Another instance of *cyfalle* occurs in the Book of Taliesin[15] (a chyn *vyghyfalle* ar y llatheu). Here without a doubt *cyfalle* is used of 'laying out' a corpse for burial. We need not discuss the gruesome details! I shall only quote in a similar connexion the use of *cysylltu* 'iungere, copulare', in Canu Heledd[16] where the princess laments '*kyssyllu* y ystyllot du gwynn gnawt Kyndylan'. Here there is no mention of husband, or marriage, only of the act of tying together, binding.

Taking both examples together, I am compelled to translate *cyfalle* as 'joining together': and so I dare not force *cimalted* standing alone to mean husband or wife. The termination -*ed*(*d*) has usually an abstract force (cf. *trugaredd, gwirionedd*).

On the stone, however, *gu* follows *cimalted*. I suggest, therefore, that these letters stand for *gureic* 'gwraig, wife', and do not connect with *adgan* in the lower line to form the husband's name. This carver, on the same side, *A*, uses a similar contraction, as will be shown later. What we have now is *tengrui cimalted-gu*(*reic*) *adgan*. *Cimalted-gureic* can be compared with a compound like *priodas-ferch* (*priodas* 'marriage' and *merch* 'woman'): it is used here to show that *tengrui* was the legal wife of *Adgan*, formally bound to him. It has all the dignity of *coniux* in Latin epitaphs.

**tengrui**. The initial has been read *t* by all who have written on the Towyn stone from Lhwyd to Morris-Jones. They may be right, but I must confess to having doubts about the correctness of this reading. To me, at any rate, the letter looked very like a *c* with a flake chipped away at the top so that it now resembles a Hiberno-Saxon *t*. If the minority by a lucky chance happens to be correct, then the name is *Cengrui*, with *Cen* as the old orthography of *Cein* 'fair, beautiful' (Mod. Welsh *cain, cein*, in names like *Ceinwen*) and *grui*, a derivative of the root *ghrēu-, ghrōu-*, which has given Greek χρόα 'skin, colour'; χρῶμα 'skin, colour' (and 'paint, rouge'!); χρώς 'surface, skin, complexion'. From a form of this root, with *d* added, comes the Welsh word *grudd* meaning 'cheek', but in an old version of Ovid[17] the Latin *occellos* has been glossed *oculos*, and also in an Old Welsh hand *gruou*. There is a slight gap between the *u* and *o*, and above this a crescent-shaped down-stroke has been added which looks more like a thin *d* than anything else. Did the Welsh glossator mistake the meaning of *occellos* (taking it as 'cheeks' instead of 'eyes') and explain it as *gru-ou*, which was later modernized into *grud-ou*? If *grui* in Old Welsh meant 'cheek', then *Cein-grui* 'lovely cheek' conjures up a very

15 BT p. 3, l. 20; RBP 1055, 10–11. 16 CLlH no. xi, 17b.
17 B v, 5 (glosses in Ox. I on Ovid's *Ars Amatoria*).

pleasant picture of a Welsh lady of long ago. In Modern Welsh her name would have become *Ceinrwy*. May I compare *Creirwy*,[18] the name of a medieval beauty? If it is from *crei* 'fresh' and *grwy* (from Old Welsh *grui*) 'cheek', we have another beautiful name to pair with *Ceinrwy*. Etymologies, however, are not proofs, and so I must retain *Tengrui* until someone confirms the reading *Cengrui*.

The husband's name is either *Guadgan* or *Adgan*: my choice is the second. Why should the carver, however stupid he may have been, squeeze the two initial letters of his lord's name into the tail end of the first line, when he had room in plenty on the second? In fact he did his best to spread out *adgan* (*ad ga n*) just below *tengrui* to get a better balance. And *gu*, as suggested already, may go with *cimalted.*

Loth[19] gives us an early Breton name *Adgan*; the prefix *ad-*, however, as he points out, may be from *ate-*, and in an early Welsh inscription one would expect *atgan*, later *adian*, if that were the case. Lloyd Jones explains *adyan* in the Hendregadredd MS. as *adian*, but he has also *addien* 'fine' (from *ad-*),[20] a form which may be related to *adgan* on the stone, if read as *addian*.

My reading of the *A* inscription is 'Tengrui (or *Cengrui*) the wife of Adgan'. With this must be taken the words carved on the *D* side.

## *D*

Morris-Jones divided the letters into *anterunc dubut marciau*(*n*): the (*n*) however is not on the stone, and is not required by the sense. He explains *anterunc* as a preposition or adverb meaning 'between', possibly 'including, together with', a compound of *anter* (a British cognate of Latin *inter* 'between') and *unc*, found in Welsh *rhwng* 'between' (from *per-ong-*, or *per-onk-*). *Dubut* is a personal name, 'either an abbreviation of *Dubutuc*, or a short form without the suffix *-uc*'. He equates *Dubutuc* with Welsh *Dyfodwg*, Irish *Dubthach* (*Duffy*). Rhŷs[21] had identified *Marciau*(*n*) as the Old Welsh *Merciaun*, later *Meirchiawn*, and Sir John accepted this.

Egerton Phillimore[22] saved the philologists from the temptation of reading a final *n* 'which wasn't there' by pointing out that there was in the *Book of Llan Dâv* a man's name *Merchiau,* which suited even better than *Merciaun.*[23] He mentioned the parallel use of *Caiau* (*Cayo*) and *Caiaun*.

[18] For Creirwy see TYP p. 311.

19 *Chr. Br.* pp. 105, 186.

20 G pp. 8, 10.

[21] *Arch. Cam.* (1874), p. 243; *Tal.* p. 264.

22 *Arch. Cam.* (1919), p. 592 and n. Cf. also Phillimore's note, *Cy.* IX, 177, on *Ebiau* in the Old Welsh pedigrees, a possible variant of *Ebiaun*, from whose name is derived *Eifionydd.* [Cf. EWGT index, p. 185.]

23 LL p. 182.

There is another possibility. *Merchiau* and our *Marciau* (to be read *Marchiaw*) may be the pet-name of *Marchiud* in LL[24] a compound of *March* 'horse' and *iud* (later *iudd, udd*) 'lord'. In the *Life of St Teilo*[25] we are told that his name was *Eliud* (i.e. *el-* 'much, many' and *iudd* 'lord'), later written *Eliudd*. The pet-name formed from *Eliudd* was *Eiliaw*, which would become *Eilio* in North Wales (as in Moel *Eilio*) and *Eilo* in South Wales, where the *-i-* is regularly dropped. *Eiliaw* with the honorary prefix *To-* gave *Teiliaw Teilaw*, and at last *Teilo* in one Llandeilo after another. So I suggest that *Marciau* (with *c* for *ch* and *u* for *w*) is *Meirchiaw*, a pet-name for *Marchudd*, or any other compound of *March-*, just as *Suliaw* (*Tysilio*) was formed from *Sulgen* (later *Sulien*). 'In Brittany Tyssilio is known as *Suliau* and *Sulien*.'[26]

You will note that the *El-* of *Eliudd* became *Eil-* when *-iaw* was added to it, i.e. the consonantal *i* affects the *e* in the preceding syllable to *ei-*. It has the same effect on *-a-*; so that *Marciau* on the stone must be a very early form of *Meirchiaw* (or a mistake for it, due to the influence of the formal *Marciud*) and can be accepted without any hesitation as a personal name, and a pet-name. And that is the only thing I am sure of when dealing with the *D* inscription, except this, that there is one other personal name hidden somewhere in *anteruncdubut*! You will find out why, in the discussion on the 'footnotes'.

**anterunc.** My reasons for rejecting Sir John's explanation can be put briefly thus: accepting *anter* as the pre-Welsh or British cognate of Latin *inter*, I should expect the *e* to disappear in Welsh, giving *antr* to begin with, and then later *athr*. We all know that the *athr* in *cyfathrach* 'inter-relationship' can be so explained. In the glosses of the ninth century *ithr* (probably = *ythr*) is found as a preposition meaning 'between'. Thus *athr*, and a variant *ythr*, were available; Sir John admits all this, and yet thinks it possible that the British *anter*, the full parent form from which *athr* and *ythr* derive, might still be in use in the early eighth century. To this 'antique' formation he adds *unc* 'which may be the second element of *rh-wng*', which also means 'between'.

There are two other possible explanations of *anter*. In the ninth century Cambridge Juvencus,[27] *amter*metetic glosses the Latin *semi*-putata; here *anter* corresponds in meaning (and origin) to Latin *semi*. In later Welsh it became *hanner* 'half', cf. also the Oxford gloss *hanther*. Early scribes, both Welsh and Irish, often omitted initial *h-* where the etymology demands it, as here, and on the other hand, inserted it in other words where it was not required. Speakers of modern English sometimes avail themselves of a similar licence. So our *anter* may be Old Welsh for 'half'.

24 LL p. 239. 25 LL p. 98. 26 LBS IV, 297. 27 B VI, 117.

And further, in early and medieval Welsh *wnc* is well attested with the meaning 'near'. Davies (1632) in his Dictionary[28] has *wng, wngc* (and eidd-*wng*) 'prope', i.e. near, close by. Sometimes it has the value of a noun: *yn i wnc* means 'yn ei ymyl', by his side, near him. The verb formed from it in *Pedeir Keinc y Mabinogi*,[29] means 'to draw near, approach'. Thurneysen too[30] explains Old Irish *oc* 'at', by the help of our *wnc*. *Anter-unc* may thus be *hanner-wnc* 'half-near', cf. the way *lled* 'half' is used in *lled dda* (hanner da), *lled agos* 'quite near, not far', *lled ymyl* 'margin'.

The other possibility is that we have here the intensive prefix *er-* (from **per*) with *wnc*, i.e. *er-wnc* 'very near', preceded by *ant*, a possible variant of the *int* in the Juvencus englynion, *int couer*[31] 'yn gywair'; Early Breton *int coucant* 'yn geugant, yn sicr'; *ent* in Medieval Breton and *en* in Modern, e.g. *en mat* 'yn fad'.[32] This particle *int*, modern *yn*, is used with an adjective to form an adverb. Reading *er-unc* as an adjective, we could take *ant erunc* as an adverbial expression 'very near', 'yn agos iawn'. Unfortunately I cannot quote an instance of *ant* with the force of this adverbial *int* (pronounced *ynt*), but I can compare the doublets *ithr* (*ythr*) *athr* referred to above: the medieval pronoun 1st person plural *an* became *yn* in Modern Welsh, and is so pronounced, though the Salesbury orthography *ein* conceals the fact:[33] the prefix *am-* varies with *ym-* (*am*ddiffyn, *ym*ddiffyn; *ambell, ymbell*; *amwnc, ymwnc*; etc.); *canhorthwy* became *cynhorthwy*; *cynnal* is written *kannal* in certain parts of the Book of Chirk.[34] So it is not too risky to consider *ant* in this inscription as a possible variant of *int* (*ynt*), *ent*, *yn*, in an adverbial phrase, where the stress would always be on the last word, the adjective. The choice (for me) is between *anter unc* 'lled agos' ('rather near'), where the *anter* modifies the nearness, and *ant erunc* 'yn agos iawn ('very near'), where the *er-* strengthens the nearness, and we have a full adverbial phrase introduced by *ant*. I am rather attracted by the second alternative.

After an adjective meaning 'near' we expect the preposition *to*, e.g. near *to*, close *to*: in Welsh, agos *i*. It has been shown that the medieval form *wnc* meant 'near'. Is it followed in this example (assuming that *unc* is the same word) by a preposition meaning *to*? In Celtic the preposition cognate with *to* was *do* (Old Irish *do* 'to')[35]. In British/Welsh *do* became *ddo*, later *ddy*: then the initial *dd* dropped, leaving *y*, which later still came to be pronounced *i*. This is our modern preposition

[28] John Davies (Mallwyd), *Antiquae Linguae Britannicae Dictionarium Duplex* (London, 1632), s.v. *wng, wngc*.

29 PKM p. 237. Cf. also CLlH pp. 86, 172–3, CA p. 325; where I have dealt rather fully with early instances of *wnc*.

30 GOI p. 525.

[31] Chapter VII, p. 121 below.

32 B VI, 223–4. [Cf. chapter VII, pp. 111, 114 below.]

[33] On Salesbury's orthography see W. J. Gruffydd, *Llenyddiaeth Cymru* (1540–1660), pp. 59–63; E. Lewis Evans, *Y Llenor* XII, 180–3; J. Lloyd-Jones, *Y Beibl Cymraeg*, pp. 20–2; IW in *Y Traethodydd* (January 1946), pp. 37–43.

[34] *Facsimile of the Chirk Codex of the Welsh Laws*, ed. J. Gwenogvryn Evans (Llanbedrog, 1909), p. 54, line 24; *kanal* p. 4, line 13.

[35] GOI p. 506 and n.

*i* 'to'.[36] In Old Welsh it was regularly written *di*, as *i* had to represent both *i* and *y*. When *u* followed, both *i* and *y* in a preceding syllable were often attracted to it, and became *u*. So instead of *iddu(nt)* 'to them' we find in medieval MSS. *udu* or *udunt* (with *d* for *dd*):[37] *yr un*, or *ir un* became *urun*:[38] *mi hun* became *muhun*, and *di hun duhun*, etc.[39] Cf. the glosses, *cuntullet* (cynnull-), *damcirchinnuou* (plural ending -*iou*): *olin*, and *olunou*: *cihutun* (Welsh), *cohiton* (Breton).[40] The *u* in all these is not Old Welsh *u* = *w*, but medieval *u* which resembled French *u* (or an *i* pronounced with rounded lips): *i*—(*i*) tended to become (*i*)—(*i*), if we may use (*i*) as a symbol for a rounded *i*.

On the stone, *unc* is followed by *dubut*, which I propose to read as *du But* 'to But'; the *du* is Old Welsh *di* 'to' attracted to the following *u*.

*But* is a personal name. Holder[41] gives twenty instances of *Boutius* and *Boutia* as names of Celtic men and women. From either form *Bud* is possible in Welsh. On the stone the *b* is cut 'out of line', and this recalls the way *c* in *cimalted* too is out of line. One is above the normal level and the other below it. May not this be an attempt at word division? In both cases this change of level marks the beginning of a word.

My attempt at the whole inscription on *A–D* is thus:

*Cengrui* (or *Tengrui*) *cimalted gu(reic)*
*adgan*
*ant erunc du but marciau.*

'Ceinrwy wife of Addian (lies here) close to Bud (and) Meirchiaw.' I suggest that Bud and Meirchiaw were the children of Ceinrwy, buried before her in the same holy ground. She was laid to rest as near as possible to her dear ones.

### *B*

On *B* Morris-Jones and others before him have read *CiNgeN celen* 'Cynien's corpse'. On the stone itself, however, I read the fourth letter as a *b*, a fine example of the curving Hiberno-Saxon *b* of the *Book of St Chad*, or the Lindisfarne Gospels. I have examined the stone on several visits, have taken rubbings of this letter, and traced every curve

[36] GMW p. 201, n. 1; LP p. 130 § 226.
[37] GMW p. 60; WG p. 112 (2, viii); p. 407.
38 See the instances quoted in CA p. 163.
[39] PKM p. 143; CLlH no. xi, 27*c* and n. on p. 205.
[40] VVB pp. 92, 94, 199, 71. For *cihutun/cohiton* see now DGVB p. 113; cf. GPC p. 746.
[41] ACS p. 499. Cf. O.I. *buaid* 'victory, profit, excellence', W. *budd* 'profit, gain, blessing', GPN p. 156 and n. 8; DGVB p. 91.

with my finger! It was a *b* when first seen, and it remains a *b*. I have seen it and felt it! So far as I am concerned, this *Cingen* is worse than dead: he never was.

And then *Cinben* worried me much. Was the name *Cynfyn*? The *cinmin* of the *Book of Llan Dâv*[42] and the Bodmin Manumissions with its -*min* instead of -*bin* ruled that out very definitely indeed. The solution, when it came, was simple. Sir John held that the uncial *N*'s of his *ci*N*ge*N favoured an earlier dating of this *BC* inscription than could be given to the one on sides *AD* with its minuscule *n*'s. (No sort of pun is intended!) He consulted Professor W. M. Lindsay on this point, and this is the expert's reply: 'that an inscription with two uncial *n*'s and the remaining *n* half-uncial must be older than an inscription with all the *n*'s half-uncial is not impossible but by no means certain. For scribes found half-uncial *n* an awkward letter sometimes. In particular the combination *in* was so like *m* that some Insular scribes preferred *i*N (with uncial *n*) while others wrote *In* (with tall *i*). In short, if an uncial letter is to show its face in half-uncial script, one may expect the letter to be *n*'.[43]

So N is possible in late inscriptions to save the bother of cutting an *n* with its curving second stroke. But the *BC* sculptor cut three excellent *n*'s: why then did he write *ci*N*be*N? It was not for lack of skill: he revels in curves, as you can see from the illustration.

Furthermore, the *Black Book of Carmarthen* was written five centuries later than the presumed date of our inscription; and a study of the facsimile showed quite a large number of N's, e.g. kyffrediN, vebiN, huN, eituN, GugauN, KadwallauN, prideiN, keiN, maelguN. Evidently N was a favourite for the final position! The Old Welsh boundaries in the *Book of Llan Dâv* provided similar instances, e.g. LL, pp. 173, rudlaN, 174 ceciN, hafreN, 222 bruiN, 246 ElmoiN, 255 pennicheN, 272 bronN. These lists suggested to me that we had here a possible clue to the word division on side *B* and that the *N*'s were to be taken as final letters. Well, this key fitted the lock. *Cinben* dissolved into *Cin ben* very readily.

One other correction in the reading had to be made. Checking up on the stone itself once more I found that the *in* in *Cin* was a ligatured UN, i.e. after cutting U the carver used the second digit of this letter as the first stroke of an uncial *N*, and added a diagonal and the second down-

[42] LL p. 277. On the Bodmin Manumissions (tenth to twelfth centuries) see LHEB pp. 59–60.

43 *Tal.* p. 267.

stroke. The first word is thus CUN, and others had so taken it. To quote Morris-Jones again: 'Westwood took the IN in *Cingen* to be a ligatured UN; and in Pennant's figure the bottom of the *I* is actually joined to the *N*...On the other hand Westwood's drawing shows no connexion, so that it seems safer to read *Cin* as Hübner does. Rhŷs also reads *Cin*'.[44] On the stone, I repeat, the letters *U*N are 'actually joined', and we can with confidence read *B* as

*Cun Ben Celen*

followed by two crescents, to show that the inscription is not complete, and that the continuation is to be looked for elsewhere, i.e. on side *C*. I should like to point out here that *ben* is cut on a higher level than *cun*, cf. above on *cimalted*. This too is a possible sign of word division.

**cun**. As a common noun *cun* occurs frequently in early poetry for lord or chief:[45] *cun* Gwynedd, *cun* Rheged, etc., and the well-known name *Cunedda*. Welsh *u* comes from Celtic *-au*, *-eu-*, or *-ou*, when followed by a consonant, and so we can connect *cun* with such Celtic names as *Caunos*, *Caunae* (used of mountains), *Caunus*, *Counos*, a man's name; *Cauna* (*Caune*), a woman's name.[46] On the Pentrefoelas stone Macalister reads *Brohomagli Iatti Ic Iacit Et Uxor Eius Cavne*.[47] Here we have a certain Brochfael's wife called *Caune*, for *Caunae*, the genitive in the later inscriptions often replacing the nominative. Indeed, this *-e* became the usual feminine ending in Latinized Welsh names, for instance *hancarate* 'Angharad'.[48] This *Caune* bore the same name in the sixth century as the Towyn lady in the eighth (or later), but the British form by then had become the Welsh *Cun*.

I should like to derive *caun-*, *cun*, from the root *keu-*[49] seen in Greek κυέω 'I grow big'; κύριος 'lord'; Gaulish *kauaros*, Welsh *cawr* 'champion, giant', etc.

**ben** 'wife, woman', Old Irish *ben*, Cornish *ben-en* 'wife', Greek γυνή, English *queen*; Welsh *ben-yw* 'female'. I know of no other instance of *ben* in Welsh, so that this is specially welcome.

**celen**. The *e* in the final syllable, as elsewhere on this stone, is equivalent to *y* in Modern Welsh, so that *celen* corresponds to our *Celyn*, now used for 'holly' only. In the medieval period it could also be used as a man's name, as for instance *Celyn son of Caw*,[50] cf. *Coll*, *Collen* 'hazel', with the saint's name in Llan-*gollen*;

44 *Tal.* p. 262.

45 G p. 186. [On *Cunedda* < **Couno-dagos* 'good lord' see PT p. lxv; LHEB p. 498; TYP p. 312.]

46 ACS I, 868, 1150.

47 CIIC no. 401; *Lap. W.* p. 202 has *Iam* for *Iatti*.

48 LL p. xlvii.

49 Alois Walde, *Vergleichendes Wörterbuch der Indogermanischen Sprachen*, herausgegeben von Julius Pokorny (Berlin und Leipzig, 1930), I, 365.

50 RM p. 107, l. 16 = WM col. 461, l. 39.

*Gwern* 'alder' and a boy's name in the Mabinogion; so also *Gwernen*; *Onnen* 'ash', and a girl's name as well; *Eithin* 'gorse', *Eithinin*, a warrior of the Gododdin tribe. Holder has *Betuus*, *Betua* as masculine and feminine personal names, though *bedw* is used only of the *birch* nowadays. With the diminutive ending seen in *Eithinin*, we have *Celynnin* as a man's name. There is a Llan-*gelynnin* quite close to Towyn, and it is tempting to identify the Celyn of the stone with the 'little Celyn' of the church, cf. Llan*sadwrn* in Anglesey, with the *Saturninus* of the old inscription inside, 'Sadyrnin'.[51] If it be argued that our Celyn had a wife and therefore could not be a saint, my answer would be that marriage might have made him one. And what of the *sancta coniux* 'holy wife' of *Saturninus* commemorated at Llansadwrn? Anyhow, nothing is known of the Towyn *Celyn* and nobody can tell how many men called *Celyn* lived their lives, saintly and otherwise, in this district. Does the name, I wonder, survive in a local place name, a charter, or other early document? Later generations might easily have made a 'holly bush' of his name.

Early examples of *e* = *y* occur in the Juvencus englynion of the ninth century, with *leder* (llyther); *remedaut* (rhyfeddawd), *celmed* (celfydd); Ox. I[52] *emedou*, plural of *emed* 'efydd', written *emid* in *Martianus Capella*.[53] So *Celen* may be a ninth-century form of *celyn*, though *i* is the common symbol for our *y* in that period. I cannot prove that *e* was written for our *y* in the eighth; it may have been, but I have no dated document to prove that it was.

The rest of the epitaph is on side C.

## C

**tricet nitanam.** I wish I could translate these two words 'May she rest in peace'! But Sir John is surely right[54] in taking *tricet* as a 3rd sing. pres. indic., not a 3rd sing. imperative 'let her stay' like *triged* nowadays. In early Welsh the 3rd pres. indic. often ends in -*it*, -*yt*,[55] when it begins a sentence, so that *trigyt* would be normal here. We have already found *e* = *y* in *celen,* so *tricet* may be for later *trigyt*, Modern Welsh *trig*. Morris-Jones translates the whole inscription 'Cynien's body *lies beneath*', for he takes *nitanam* as *ni* 'under': *tan* as Welsh *dan* in *o dan* 'under': and -*am* as an adverbial ending.

Against this interpretation one may stress the irregularity of having the long form in -*et* (-*yt*) in the middle of the sentence: and further, *trigo* to my knowledge never means 'lie', but 'stay, remain, dwell'. I should prefer to take [*lies here*] as something understood, and begin a new sentence with *tricet*, as the syntax demands. What that new sentence is to be, I am not so sure!

At the moment my best guess is that *nitanam* may be the subject of *tricet*; it can be explained as a compound of synonyms, *nit* and *anam*. *Nit* can be the cognate of the

[51] CIIC p. 323; ECMW no. 32 (following IW's reading and interpretation in AMCA pp. cix ff.).

52 VVB p. 117.

53 VVB p. 118.

[54] *Tal.* p. 263.

[55] Cf. GMW p. 119.

Old Irish *nith* 'a mortal wound': Modern Irish *nioth* (*níoth*, *nith*) 'mortal wound, loss, affliction', so Dinneen.[56] *Anam* 'anaf' (cf. Old Welsh *anamou*, gloss on *mendae*)[57] is explained by Dr Davies as *mutilatio*,[58] by Anwyl as 'blemish, defect, wound': Old Irish *anim*, Modern Irish *aineamh* 'blemish, defect'; the adjective is *aineamhach* 'blemished, maimed'. Combining *nit* and *anam*, we have in both elements the meaning 'wound, hurt', but *anam* 'anaf' stresses that it is a wound that maims: it is a *mutilation*, an essential limb has been lopped off.

If *nid-anaf* is the right analysis, then *tricet nit-anam* means 'the pain, the hurt, and the sense of loss remain'. Cun has passed away, but the cruel loss remains, the mortal wound can never be healed. Such a contrast would be in keeping with all we know of Early Welsh poetry: the primitive bards, the *Cynfeirdd* and *Gogynfeirdd*, delighted in such contrasts, which they expressed with masterly brevity and force. The compound noun and compound adjective were an integral part of their technique. No chieftain's household in the old days was complete without a bard: in Celyn's hall there was, I think, a true poet.

I read the whole inscription on *B–C* then as

*cun ben celen : tricet nitanam*
Cun, wife of Celyn : grief and loss remain.

## THE 'FOOTNOTES'

The two main inscriptions are thus fairly straightforward. Two 'footnotes'—if I may use the word—were added, one on *A* and one on *C*, both at the foot of the pillar. Though *A* is certainly the earlier, that on *C* must be tackled first, for a correct interpretation of it is essential, if we are to make sense of the cryptic letters on *A*.

The *C* footnote is nicely cut in rounded lettering. At the beginning, four points have been arranged thus, ❖. Then follow

mozt
cicpe
tuar

Rhŷs read this as *moltcic petuar*.[59] The last word is obviously Old Welsh for *pedwar* 'four', and he took the *molt* he saw in the first line to be *mollt* 'a sheep', and *cic* in the second to be *cig* 'meat, flesh'. Combining the two he evolved his *molltgig*, 'which means either "the mutton flesh of four", or "a wether (is) flesh of or for four"'. He goes on: 'I need hardly say that I have considerable misgivings as to this

56 P. S. Dineen, *Foclóir Gaedilge agus Béarla: An Irish–English Dictionary* (Dublin: Irish Texts Society, 1927).

[57] VVB p. 39.

[58] D.; s.v. *anaf*.

59 *Arch. Cam.* (1897), p. 145.

stone. Perhaps inscriptions 1 and 2 (= *B* and *A*) are genuine; but I can hardly think the rest is so, or divine its meaning. The former may have served as models for the lettering of the rest.' The 'mutton flesh' evidently disagreed with him—and no wonder.

Morris-Jones read *mol*, and identified this with *moll* in an obscure poem in the *Black Book of Carmarthen*,[60] which he thought might mean 'tomb'. He then took the following *t* to be the initial of *Tegryn* (*tengrui*), *c* the initial of *Cynien* (his *cingen*), the *i* as 7, the symbol for *et* 'and', and the following *c* as *ceteri*. His interpretation of the whole is 'the tomb of Tegryn, Cynien, et ceteri four (and four others)'. 'The four others would be *Malted*, *Guadgan*, *Dubut*, and *Marciaun*, leaving *anterunc* as a connective.'[61]

I challenge the reading *molt*. The third letter is not an *l* but the *r* found in early MSS. after round-backed letters like *o*. The first element of *R* was a curving downstroke, and the scribes in order to save space occasionally made use of the last curves of *o* and similar letters as the first element in *R*, and added what was left of the *R* (closely resembling the figure 2). I suggest that the author of this footnote wrote *o2* (=*or*) in the copy he made for the stone cutter. What the latter made of it was *o* and something which looks like *z*. Rhŷs indeed remarks that the *l* on the stone has become 'almost a *z* in the word *molt*'. If he had only recognised this *z* as the *r* symbol, he would have been rid of his 'mutton for four', and his misgivings about the authenticity of the inscription. Lindsay, in his *Early Welsh Script*, has a facsimile of the Cambridge Univ. Lib. Ff.4.42, Juvencus (dated ninth century by Bradshaw),[62] plate VI, p. 51. You will see there a good example of the *r* symbol (mentioned above) at the end of line 7, *cruore*. Plate VII gives the top of the first folio of this MS.; the third line from the bottom begins *cōmorat*: after the *o* here too we get a fine example of this *r*. On the *Martianus Capella*, dated the end of the ninth century, Lindsay remarks, 'The by-form of *r* normal after *o* (really a majuscule *r* without the shaft) is used not only after *o* but after *e* in this MS.' He notes this as favouring a later date, not mid-ninth but late ninth century.[63] In our inscription, the *r* 'normal after *o*' occurs in *mort*. How early this *r* was introduced, I cannot tell. The Juvencus was written about 850, and we started with a vague idea that the lettering of the Towyn inscriptions suggested a date about 750.

[60] BBC p. 20, l. 8: *kin muill moll mud*; *Tal.* p. 265. [61] *Tal.* p. 266.
[62] See chapter VII below. 63 EWS p. 22.

**mort cic** or **mortcic**. The *t* stands for *th* (cf. *c* = *ch* in *marciau* above). After *r* in Welsh *t* and *c* are aspirated, becoming *th*, *ch*. The final *c* corresponds to modern *g* as a rule in our early documents, but in the *Book of Llan Dâv* -*c* sometimes varies with *ng*. Archenfield in Herefordshire (*Ariconium*) is given in Welsh as *Ergin*, *Ercic*, *Ergic*, *Ercicg*, and *Ercig*.[64] So *mortcic* may be *morthgig* in later Welsh, or *morthging*, or *morthgin*. Or even *mort c.x* (for *crux*!).

I hope to deal with *mortcic* in full later on, so I will only say this now: *mort* may be connected with Latin *mort*- 'death' (*mors*, *mortis*, *mortuus*), or be from the same root as *mor* in Latin *memor*; *morthcin*(*g*) could be a borrowing from Latin *morticina*;[65] *cic* may be *cig* 'flesh', or the *cing* in *gweilging*, *perging*, *Erging*. This bunch of linguistic problems calls for a very full, detailed (and boring) discussion, which we can postpone until another day. So I shall content myself now with just giving my opinion, that *mort cic* must mean either 'death pillar' or 'memorial stone' or 'mortal remains', and with your permission I shall use *memorial* for it—until another example turns up on vellum or stone, to correct me.

So I read *mortcic petuar* as 'the memorial of four', viz. *Ceinrwy, Bud, Meirchiaw* and *Cun*.

Now, we can go back to the untidy footnote on *A*. This, with the help of Lhwyd's drawings, can be read

mc
Ertri

The *mc* is certain. The first letter of line 2 looks to me like an uncial E with the mid-horizontal used as part of a following *r* (*er* ligatured), but it may be *a*; so *Er* or *Ar*. Then *t* from Lhwyd's copy: the curve at the bottom of the downstroke is all that remains of it, beyond the break in the stone. Then *r* is clear. After that I see a faint *i*. These letters are of the same type as those in the main *A* inscription, and are as badly arranged as the rest.

It has been suggested above that *gu* on this *A* face is an abbreviation or suspension of *gureic*. I am quite convinced that the cryptic *mc* too is a similar abbreviation of *mort cic*, the compound you have permitted me to translate for the nonce as *memorial*.

If *ertri* be read, the *er* can stand for the definite article, usually written *ir* in Old Welsh (even before consonants), our *yr* (with the *r* dropped before consonants). If *artri* be read, *ar* too may be a variant of *er* (*yr*); cf. above on the *ant* (= *ynt*) in *anterunc* and on *e* = *y* in *celen*.

[64] See LL index, p. 398.

65 Cf. Ir. *mortchend*, English *morkin*; Llwyd, *Parochialia* (supplement to *Arch. Cam.* IX (1909); part I, North Wales), 40, Llysvaen, an urn found 'at Pwlh *Morkyn*'.

*tri* is our *tri* 'three'. And so the meaning of the *A* footnote whether we read *mc er tri,* or *mc ar tri,* is 'This is a memorial of the three', viz. *Ceinrwy*, *Bud*, and *Meirchiaw*.

Why was it added? Was it because the *A* sculptor found that he had left out the conjunction *ac* 'and' after *But*? He wanted to make it quite clear that this was a memorial of the THREE, hence the postscript, untidy, but well-meant. After Cun's burial, the second craftsman had no option: he had to cut in his turn another footnote to emphasise that the *mortcic* was now the memorial of *four*, not of *three*. The two footnotes supplement one another, and the later helps to explain the earlier: *mc er tri* 'a memorial of the three'; *mort cic petuar* 'a memorial of four'.

This is the best I can make of the writing on the Towyn Stone.

## *Chapter IV*

# THE EARLIEST POETRY

I HAVE been asked to talk to you this evening on the earliest forms of Welsh poetry, and as the subject bristles with controversial topics of all sorts, I must tell you that I have found it very difficult indeed to compose a short sketch which could fairly be described in the opening word of the third gospel as 'a declaration of those things which are most surely believed among us'.[1] We have an old Welsh proverb that two Welshmen never agree. Well, once in a while they do, but Welsh scholars never, or hardly ever.

Two thousand years ago a Celtic language with close affinities to Latin was spoken over England and Wales, parts of Scotland, the whole of France, and parts of Spain. We call it British,[2] but that is just insular conceit, for which I ask pardon. Latin, as you know, changed gradually in the course of centuries, and became French in France, Italian in Italy, and Spanish in Spain. Similarly, British changed in the lowlands of Scotland, Cumberland,[3] and Wales to Cymraeg or Welsh, and in the Cornish peninsula to Cornish. Emigrants from Britain carried it over to France, where it survives as Breton.

When did British become Welsh? I think that the Roman occupation of Britain in the first four centuries is the most likely period, for it provides suitable conditions for such a change.[4] Latin at that time

[1] The Gospel according to St Luke i. 1.

[2] Sir John Rhŷs employed the term 'Brythonic', Kenneth Jackson uses 'Brittonic'; IW throughout his writings uses 'British' (Welsh *Brythoneg*) for the parent language out of which Welsh, Cornish, and Breton evolved. These names are, however, all synonymous (LHEB p. 3).

[3] The Welsh spoken in Strathclyde and Cumbria may not have differed greatly from the Welsh of Wales. According to Jackson, if the Gododdin was composed in 'Cumbric'—the speech of north-west England and the Lowlands of Scotland—this northern dialect 'cannot have been so fundamentally different from Primitive Welsh that the metre of the poem would be destroyed in the process, unless indeed the "translation" were a very free adaptation into Welsh'; LHEB p. 10, cf. OSPG p. ix. He concludes that Cumbric may have survived as a living speech down to the early eleventh century; LHEB pp. 9–10, 219. The only written remains of Cumbric, apart from place names, are three legal terms preserved in the so-called *Leges inter Brettos et Scottos* (probably early eleventh century); on these and their date see Jackson's article 'The Britons in Southern Scotland', *Antiquity* XXIX (1955), 88.

[4] The argument that the Roman occupation was the formative period which saw the

became the official language in southern Britain, the language of trade and commerce in the ports, market towns, garrison towns, and great cities, and so British died out in these centres of Roman civilisation. The Britons of the towns and plains became Latin speakers, long before the Angles and Saxons invaded these shores. In the hilly districts of Wales and Cumberland the tribesmen lived their lives in the old way, under their own chieftains, with their own tribal laws and customs, and their language was still British; but not the old fully inflected British. For twelve generations their Celtic tongue had remained without honour or repute; and rapid linguistic deterioration took place in consequence. Then the Romans left; Latin lost its prestige, and the daughter of the ancient British, the new Cymraeg, became a language of honour and culture, spoken not merely by rustic tribesmen, but by officials, nobles, and kings in royal halls. Its special guardians were the bards, as the Celtic poets were called. They developed it into a fitting instrument for their craft. A bardic tradition of standard Welsh was formed, and transmitted with vigorous loyalty by a close guild of artists in song from generation to generation for a thousand years. And even today a good deal of the technique they evolved is still employed by the master-poets who sing in the ancient strict metres. It is a remarkable testimony to the stubborn conservatism of the Celt.

About the year 796 a young Welshman, whose name is Latinised into Nennius or Nemnivus,[5] wrote in Latin a short account of Britain and the Britons, or rather he compiled a little volume of selections or quotations from earlier authorities. His library was small, his learning meagre; his Latin is elementary, and often very inaccurate and strongly flavoured with Welsh idioms. But in spite of all its faults and deficiencies his short *Historia Brittonum* is the main source, if not the only

evolution of Welsh out of its parent Brittonic was forcibly presented by J. Morris-Jones in his monumental study 'Taliesin', *Cy.* XXVIII (1918) (here abbreviated *Tal.*). In LHEB Jackson argues in detail for a slightly later date—*circa* A.D. 450–600—and this view is commonly accepted as a working hypothesis at the present time. Cf. GMW p. xvi; Ceri Lewis, *op. cit.* p. 150.

[5] On Nennius and the *Historia Brittonum* see below chapter VI, pp. 72–3, and n. 8. 'Nennius' is the form of this name which has received the sanction of most frequent usage, though in his 'Notes on Nennius' in B VII, 380–1, IW followed Thurneysen (ZfcPh. XX, 97–137) in asserting that 'Nemnius' or 'Nemnivus' was the correct form, on the basis of a passage in Bodleian MS. Auct. F.4.32 (Zeuss's *Oxoniensis Prior*) fol. 20*a*, which alludes to a certain 'Nemniuus', who is credited with having invented a Welsh alphabet. Both IW and Thurneysen conclude that this 'Nemniuus' is the same as the chronicler: Thurneysen believed that he was also the scribe of *Oxoniensis Prior*.

source, of much of our knowledge of early British history. We are greatly in his debt.

Among the curious collection of materials he had gathered together there was an early list of Northumbrian kings, a very important document. This he inserted bodily into his *Historia*, for these Northumbrian kings were the men who invaded and conquered great tracts of British territory from the Humber to the Forth, all along the east coast and far inland as well, during the second half of the sixth century. Their leader, between 547 and 559, was Ida, the founder of the Northumbrian royal line. When Nennius reached his name on the list he added some extremely valuable details from Welsh tradition. First of all he states that, 'At that time a British king called Eudeyrn fought bravely against the Angles.'[6] (Nothing is told elsewhere of this warrior king.) He then goes on in words of vital importance to the historian of Welsh literature:

Tunc Talhaern tat aguen in poemate claruit, & neirin & taliessin & bluchbard & cian qui vocat*ur* gueinth guaut simul uno tempore in poemate brittannico clarue*runt*. ['At that time Talhaearn Tad Awen (i.e. the father of the muse) was famous in poetry, and Neirin, Taliesin, Blwchfardd, and Cian who is called Gweinthgwawd, at one and the same time were renowned in British poetry.'][7]

[6] HB chapter 62. The MSS. give *Dutigirn* as the name of this British king. In B VII, 387–8, IW showed that this name must be a mistake for O.W. *Outigirn* (> *Eudeyrn*), a form actually attested in the *Harl. Gens.* (no. 10), and as *Eutigirn* in LL pp. 140, 245. IW points out that 'the person mentioned in Pedigree 10 (EWGT p. 11) is far too early to be the opponent of Ida in the mid-sixth century, but this early instance of the name in a Northern pedigree is not without significance.' In early Welsh script, *o* and one of the forms of *d* were easily confused.

[7] HB chapter 62. These are the famous *Cynfeirdd*, or 'Early Bards'. On their names and epithets see LEWP p. 75 n., CS p. 29. All are preserved in O.W. orthography: *Neirin* later became *Aneirin* by the growth of prosthetic *A-*, which occurred before *N* in some words in Ml.W. (cf. GMW p. 12); CA pp. xv, lxxxvii, TYP pp. 271–2; see chapter VI, p. 76 below. *Talhaern* became *Talhaearn* 'Iron Brow'; *Talies(s)in* means 'beautiful brow', *Bluchbard* is perhaps 'beardless (or bald) poet' (cf. Breton *blouc'h* 'beardless, bare', and EWGP p. 43), *Cian* 'puppy'. Cian and Talhaern are mentioned by name in the poem *Angar Kyvyndawt* (BT pp. 19–20), but no extant poem is attributed to either of them. Cian's epithet is obviously corrupt: *Guaut* (*gwawd*) originally meant 'song', and *Gueinth* has been variously interpreted. If it represents *guenith* 'wheat' the two words together could mean either 'wheat of song' or (less probably) 'of the Wheat Song'. IW's note in LEWP suggests some other possibilities, including *gwenid* or *gweinid* which could be an old 3rd sing. pres. indic. (or a noun of agency?); cf. the verb *gweini* 'to serve', and such phrases as *gwennwawd weini* (H p. 41, l. 7), and the epithet *Adar Weinidawc* (BD p. 222) 'bird-server' (i.e. on corpses). Or the medial *-n-* could represent *-r-*, giving possible associations with *gweirydd* 'pledges' or *gwerth* 'value'. Yet another possibility is that suggested by W. J. Gruffydd (*Cym. Trans.* (1937), p. 265), who takes *gueinth* as a

Talhaearn, of whose poetry not a line has been preserved, gets a sentence to himself. He is given a definite date—the reign of Ida, so just after 550—and a significant epithet, *Father of the Muse*, like Chaucer in the long line of English poets.[8] Talhaearn is in the still longer line of Welsh poets. Chaucer, before 1400, Father of the English Muse; Talhaearn, 550, Father of the Welsh Muse. Then comes a group of four contemporary poets, *Neirin*, in later spelling Aneirin, *Taliesin*, and two of whom we know nothing, *Blwchfardd* and *Cian*.

Nennius then gives the names of the sons of Ida who ruled after him, and adds the names of four British kings who fought against them, giving special prominence to Urien, the greatest war leader of all, who before he fell, deserted by his allies, cooped up the invaders for three days and nights in the island then called *Metcawd*, now known as Lindisfarne.[9]

Nennius, as I have said, wrote in 796. These British poets sang, and these British kings fought 200 years earlier. How was their story preserved and how did it reach Nennius? There is just a possibility that he had before him a chronicle or other record compiled in a Welsh monastery.[10] If so, it would have been in Latin, and a Latin source would not have given him the Welsh epithets of Talhaearn and Cian, or the uncomplimentary Welsh nicknames of some of the Anglian kings. Therefore it seems to me much more likely that his source was the oral tradition of the Welsh bards, handed down by these professional guardians of past history, in the form of sagas or long tales which they used to tell in the halls of their chieftains,[11] interspersed with songs of

corruption of *gwreith*: this could be a noun or an old 1st sing. pret. of *gwneuthur* (G pp. 695–6, 708; CA pp. 75, 260, 263). If it represents the old pret. 3rd sing. *gwneith* the meaning would be 'he (who) made a song'.

[8] It was Dryden who in 1700 first called Chaucer 'the father of English Poetry' in his *Preface to the Fables*. Morris-Jones compared the epithet with *Tad Awen*, given in this passage to Talhaern, and meaning 'the father of (poetic) inspiration'. He adds 'Obviously, it must be for the same reason: the one is the earliest Welsh poet, the other the earliest English', *Tal.* 32. On the meaning of *awen* see AP[2] note to line 107.

[9] See chapter v, p. 52 below.

[10] Nennius claims to have been a *discipulus* to 'Elvodugus', who is commonly identified with the *Elbodg(u)* described as *archiepiscopus Guenedote regionis*, whose death is recorded in 809 AC. It has been suggested, therefore, that Nennius's documentary sources may have been in the possession of the monastery of Bangor in Arfon, and it may have been there that he compiled his chronicle. See SEBC p. 44; and cf. CS pp. 21–62.

[11] In his lecture 'Hen Chwedlau' *Cymm. Trans.* (1946), IW deduces from the style and idioms of Nennius's Latin that an O.W. source underlies much of his work. In particular, he argues that Nennius was reproducing a native tale or *cyfarwyddyd* concerning Gwrtheyrn (Vortigern). A poetic source in O.W. has been advocated more than once as most probably underlying Nennius's account (HB chapter 56) of Arthur and his

their own composing in praise of their own patrons. They also used to recite poems by earlier bards to the heroes of the past. Indeed it was a regular part of their bardic training to memorise and recite ancient poetry. They held competitions, where the honours went to the bard who remembered more than his fellows of the old songs. Poems of old were composed to be sung, not to be read. They lived on for generations not on vellum, but on the lips of living men. When one of the early Welsh bards died, or fell in battle, his library perished with him, unless he had in his lifetime stored his wealth in the retentive memories of disciples who survived him.

Luckily, some of these pupils distrusted their memories, and wrote on vellum, or perhaps got a monk to write for them, what they had learnt by word of mouth.

But even vellum does not last for ever. The royal dwellings were of wood; so were the early churches and monasteries. Halls and monasteries were often burnt down both in peace and war.[12] And books, like poets, became dust and ashes. Welsh monasteries were repeatedly attacked and burnt by the pagan Danes. Indeed, the Danes in Wales and Ireland had a habit of throwing manuscripts into rivers and lakes, so that the magic letters they dreaded might be washed away. So, by fire and water, helped by greedy bookworms or the gradual fading of poor ink, the great store of Welsh verse was steadily diminished, and much was lost irretrievably. Scraps and fragments, however, at last found sanctuary in the stone-built abbeys of the Norman period.

Providentially three or four manuscripts written in the thirteenth century have preserved for us specimens of much earlier poetry. I have only time to mention two, the *Book of Aneirin*,[13] written in 1250 or

battles; see ALMA pp. 7–8, SEBH p. 124, and especially Thomas Jones, 'The Early Evolution of the Legend of Arthur', *Nottingham Mediaeval Studies* VIII (1964), 9–10.

[12] Cf. IW's remarks in his introduction to *Gemau'r Gogynfeirdd* (ed. A. Hughes, Pwllheli, 1910), pp. xiii–xiv, where he raises the question: what has happened to the work of the poets who lived between the period of the Cynfeirdd and that of the twelfth-century court poets—the bards of Rhodri Mawr, Hywel Dda and Gruffudd ap Llywelyn? 'Perhaps at that time the poets were not accustomed to write down much of their compositions, but entrusted them instead to oral preservation. And even if we were to suppose that they composed a great deal and wrote down their poems, where could there be found a dry place to preserve them from the onslaught of the enemy? The courts of the chieftains were houses made of wood, and they were quite frequently burned to ashes. There was no protection for them even in the churches and the monasteries, which were made of wood in early Wales. Monasteries and courts alike were burned by the Danes, without sparing books and parchment, so that it is no wonder that the records are so brief.'

[13] Cardiff. MS 1.

thereabouts, and the *Book of Taliesin*,[14] written about the year 1275. As their names show, these two manuscripts contain poems believed to be or pretending to be the work of two of the sixth-century bards mentioned by Nennius in 796, *Aneirin* and *Taliesin*. Between them they contain about 5,500 lines.

This brings one up against the hard core of our problem. Nennius can be cited as a credible witness in support of the case that two poets, Aneirin and Taliesin, composed Welsh poetry some time between 550 and 600. That by itself is a big enough claim. Accepting it for a moment, what guarantee have we for adding to it that the poems ascribed to them in 1250, 1275, are authentic, and genuine products of the sixth century? Between the poet in 575 and the oldest copy we have of his work in 1275 there is a gap of seven hundred years—to put it mildly, a considerable interval! Can we bridge the gap?

Yes, in part. In my study of the *Book of Aneirin*, I discovered plenty of evidence of confusion in the text, due to oral transmission, and much corruption due to misreading an original written in the Hiberno-Saxon characters used before the Norman conquest. Scores of words were written in the orthography of the early ninth century, exactly like the Welsh words quoted by Nennius about 800, and exactly like the Welsh phrases and sentences to be found in an Oxford manuscript written in 820.[15] I found that one out of every five stanzas in the long Gododdin poem ascribed to Aneirin occurred twice over in the manuscript, once in the regular orthography of 1250, and then at the end in another hand, giving a text teeming with forms current in 800–50. In other words the first scribe gave the accepted text in the spelling of his own day, and then a second scribe found a ninth-century copy which he in part modernised, and in part preserved in its early form.[16] Thanks to him we know now that there was a written copy of at least one-fifth of the Gododdin in the ninth century. The gap between poets and poems is not really one of 700 years but of 250 or 300 at the most.

[14] Peniarth MS. 2. N. Denholm Young has argued for a later date for the *Book of Taliesin* (? second quarter of the fourteenth century), *Handwriting in England and Wales* (Cardiff, 1954), p. 44.

[15] Bodleian MS. Auct. F.4.32; named *Oxoniensis Prior* by Zeuss (*Grammatica Celtica*, pp. 1054–9), and this name has since obtained general currency. The glosses were edited by IW in B v, 226 ff., vi, 112–15. See also LHEB pp. 47, 53–4. Cf. chapter v, p. 51 below.

[16] On the two texts of the Gododdin contained in the *Book of Aneirin*, one in an archaic orthography (the 'B' text) and one in a contemporary hand ('A' text), see CA p. xiii, OSPG pp 41 ff.

Now for the evidence of date offered by the subject matter. This is even more satisfactory. There is no earthly reason that I can think of why any Welshman should have composed the poem in 800 or 850. The setting is in the North and the poet claims to be a North Briton. He sang in Welsh, but his home was not in Wales at all, the land we now call Wales, but somewhere in the neighbourhood of Edinburgh, the southern shore of the Firth of Forth. The British tribe called the Gododdin are known to have held that very district in the first centuries of the Christian era. And they held it between 550 and 600. One of their chief fortresses was called Caer Eiddyn, or Din Eiddyn;[17] the Gaelic form of the latter, *Dunedin*, is still used for Edinburgh, which is merely a Saxon translation of it, and has nothing to do with the Northumbrian king Edwin, as some have held. The British lord of Edinburgh, or Dineiddyn, according to the poet, had collected a retinue of three hundred young warriors of noble birth, every one a skilled fighter, famed for valour, every one of them wearing a golden collar or torque, the decoration of a Celtic champion. He feasted them right royally for a full year. A warrior's pay in those days was plenty of mead and ale and wine. These were well paid. In return for their mead, they were expected to be faithful to their lord, even unto death. They had been gathered together for a special purpose. News had reached Dineiddyn that the English invaders, the Angles or Saxons of Northumbria, had pushed far inland and captured Catraeth, Richmond, or Catterick, on the Roman road leading northwards. The road to the north was thus open to the enemy. Catraeth had to be recovered at all cost. And the lord of Dineiddyn sends his noble three hundred to recover it. They had drunk his mead, and they gave him full value for it. As Aneirin sang, 'They paid with their lives for that feast of mead.'[18]

> Warriors went to Catraeth, ready were they.
> Fresh mead their feast: poison it proved.

[17] The value of the medial consonant in this name is left ambiguous by the various medieval spellings. IW favoured *-dd-* as representing the original pronunciation; K. Jackson argues that the original name for Edinburgh was *Caer Eidyn* with *-d-* and not *-dd-*; *The Anglo-Saxons: Studies Presented to Bruce Dickins*, ed. Peter Clemoes (London, 1959), pp. 39–41; also OSPG pp. 75–8. This was also the opinion of Morris-Jones, *Tal.* pp. 77 ff. But considerable uncertainty continued to be felt as to the value of this medial consonant, as may be seen from the treatment of the names *Mynydawc Eidyn*, *Clydno Eidyn*, *Llawgat trwm bargawt Eidyn* in the successive copies of TYP written at various dates.

[18] *Gwerth eu gwled o ved vu eu henaid*; CA line 356.

Three hundred by command in order of battle,
And after the merry shouting, there was—silence.
Warriors rose up; they gathered together.
With one accord they charged forward.
Short was their life; long their kinsmen mourned them
Seven times their number of the Saxons they slew.
There were tears in the eyes of many mothers.
The war-band of Gododdin on shaggy-maned horses,
Of the colour of swans, their armour drawn tight,
They fell on the foe, on the front of his host.
  Shields were shattered.
  Swords flashed down on pale faces.
It was not shame they won, these intrepid warriors.
Three hundred wearing gold torques set forth
To defend their land—sad was their fate.
Though they were slain, they slew.
Honoured they shall be till the end of the world.
Of the band of kinsmen that set out,
Alas, only one returned.[19]

Perhaps I have quoted enough to show the main theme of the Gododdin. Aneirin sang, not to celebrate a great and glorious victory, but to honour a company of noble youths, who in loyalty to their lord fought gallantly against heavy odds, to the bitter end. And died, as befitted a royal bodyguard, rather than surrender. Short was their life; long their kinsmen mourned them.[20] The last glimpse we have of them is given in one line:

Scattered weapons; ranks broken; unyielding.[21]

Their story was told and sung at many a royal feast, and by many a camp-fire, from the seventh to the ninth century. The original poem in process of time attracted to itself stanzas of similar form from other early war-songs. Current terms were substituted for words which had become obsolete, and so on. Granting all that, many lines, many stanzas, still preserve for us a good deal of the ancient poem that won

[19] This passage combines extracts translated from various stanzas of the Gododdin: CA stanzas viii, lviii, xcv (B text), xc (B text).

[20] *Byrr eu hoedl, hir eu hoet ar eu carant*; CA line 670.

[21] *Aryf angkynnull, agkyman dull, agkysgoget* CA lines 258–9.

for Aneirin the title of High King of the Bards,[22] a poem that must have been composed just before or just after 600.

Of the *Book of Taliesin* I have only time to say that it is a pretty mixed bag.[23] Most of the poems in it belong to the ninth and tenth centuries. They have their value, and their special interest. Amongst them, however, some ten or twelve short pieces seem to be of much earlier date, and are comparable in antiquity to the Gododdin itself. These are the poems to Urien and his son, Owain.[24] Urien is styled in them the lord of Catraeth, so we may date them a few years before the Gododdin, say about 575–90. One is to a certain Cynan ap Brochfael, whose son called Selyf fell in the battle of Chester in 615. His ancestor Cadell, the founder of the royal line of Powys, is mentioned by Nennius in his *Life of St Germanus*, and can be placed in the fifth century. So his pedigree is all in order. As for the language of the poem, I may say that it bears many marks of undoubted antiquity, as I hope to show in detail elsewhere.[25]

I have had to omit all reference to the early nature poetry, and to the delightful stanzas of the Llywarch Hen saga of the ninth century.[26] In the time allotted to me, I thought it would be more useful to try and show briefly what grounds we have for accepting the early date of some, at any rate, of our Old Welsh poems. You see, if I have managed to prove my point, then next to Greek and Latin, Welsh poetry is the oldest in Europe.[27]

[22] The epithet *Aneirin Gwawtryd Mechdeyrn Beird* ('A of Flowing Verse, High King of Bards') is bestowed upon Aneirin in a triad, TYP no. 33. Cf. also RBP p. 1050, ll. 3–5, *Aneirin gwawtryd awenyd.* With the epithet *gwawtryd* J. E. Caerwyn Williams compares *clotryd* 'freely praising' (or as a noun 'eulogist'), applied to Urien Rheged by Taliesin, PT p. 45.

[23] For the 'mixed' contents of the *Book of Taliesin* see LEWP pp. 51 ff.

[24] Morris-Jones accepted as authentic the nine panegyrics to Urien and Owain (including two poems describing their battles), and he edited six of them with translations, *Tal.* pp. 156 ff. He also accepted as authentic the two poems to Gwallawc and the poem to Cynan Garwyn, also contained in the manuscript, *Tal.* p. 199. These twelve poems were accepted by IW and edited by him in CT (English edition in PT). But IW rejected the so-called *Marwnad Cunedda*, BT p. 69, which Morris-Jones had edited in the belief that it was an elegy for Rhun ap Maelgwn. For IW's reasons for this rejection see PT p. xxiii.

[25] PT pp. xxviii–xxxv, and Poem I. A translation and discussion of this poem is given by Idris Foster, PEW pp. 228–30. Saunders Lewis has recently expressed doubt as to whether the poem to Cynan Garwyn is not the work of some other early poet, rather than of Taliesin himself, *Cymm. Trans.* 1968, p. 298 n.

[26] Chapter VII below.

[27] This concluding sentence was omitted from *The Welsh Review*, but is supplied here from the abbreviated form of this article printed in *The Listener* for 12 June 1947, p. 919.

## *Chapter V*

# THE GODODDIN POEMS

IN the Free Library at Cardiff there is a small, but beautifully written manuscript known as the *Book of Aneirin*. Experts say that it was written about the middle of the thirteenth century, *circa* 1250; and that originally instead of 38 pages as at present it must have had at least 44.[1] The size of the page is only $6\frac{3}{4}$ inches by 5, so that it is quite a small manuscript. Yet, if this little book had disappeared before the sixteenth century, like so many other Welsh manuscripts, all knowledge of the Gododdin poems in honour of the men who fought and died at Catraeth in the days of long ago would have perished also, for every known copy derives from this *Book of Aneirin*, and from it in its mutilated state.

Now, what does it contain? First of all comes a rubric. 'This is the Gododdin: Aneirin sang it.' Then comes a series of short rhyming stanzas, called *Odleu*; three longer poems (lines 64, 15, 72) called *Gorchaneu*; then an extra *Gorchan* of 89 lines, which claims to be the work of Taliesin, a contemporary of the bard Aneirin. From this to the end of the volume, some of the earlier *odleu* are repeated, together with some hundreds of new lines, but all in a much more primitive orthography than that of the first part. Indeed, the orthographical peculiarities of this *Appendix*, as I have called it, prove that it is a copy of a Welsh manuscript written in the same period as the glosses of the ninth and tenth centuries.[2] Certain scribal errors in the first part, also, can best be accounted for by assuming a pre-Norman exemplar. As you know, the script usually known as Hiberno-Saxon dropped out of use in Wales in the twelfth century.[3] In it certain letters were liable to be mistaken for one another, for instance *n* and *r*, *t* and *g*, and as several

[1] The *Book of Aneirin*, Cardiff MS. 1, is described by Gwenogvryn Evans, *Rep.* II, 91; see also OSPG pp. 41 ff. The manuscript is fragmentary, having lost six (or more) pages at the end; see the note by Gerald Morgan on the five (incomplete) gatherings of which it is composed; B XX, 12 ff.

[2] Cf. chapter IV above, and n. [15] to chapter IV.

[3] N. Denholm-Young, *Handwriting in England and Wales* (Cardiff, 1954), pp. 13–14 and *passim*; Lindsay, *Early Welsh Script*. 'Insular' is the term now commonly used in place of 'Hiberno-Saxon'. The evidence which proves the *Book of Aneirin* to have been copied from an exemplar in O.W. orthography is fully discussed CA pp. lxvii–lxxiii; see also Denholm-Young, *op. cit.* p. 41.

instances occur of this particular type of mistake in the first part of the *Book of Aneirin*, it is safe to postulate a pre-Norman original for this section also.

The verse is written continuously like prose. I have arranged it into 102 stanzas and four Gorchanau, a total of 1,468 lines. Of the 102 stanzas, 27 are repetitions. The Taliesin poem must be subtracted (69 lines). So the Gododdin proper just falls short of making 1,400 lines.[4]

We have thus to deal with poems written down in 1250, for the most part in twelfth-century orthography, but bearing unmistakable traces of a ninth- or tenth-century manuscript source. The scribes have modernised all they understood. Where they failed to understand the old forms they copied them as they stood, thus providing very valuable material for a critic hunting for evidence of date. What the earliest possible date for this original may be I cannot say. The earliest bits of Welsh I've seen—excepting a page or so in the *Book of St Chad*, now at Lichfield[5]—belong to the early ninth century, about 820:[2] and the orthography of the earliest forms in the Gododdin is of the same archaic character.

I now come to the poet, Aneirin. In the Harley 3859 version of the *Historia Brittonum* usually ascribed to Nennius, there are several interesting additions to the section known as the Saxon Genealogies. The most famous of all comes in the list of Northumbrian kings: a passage which has proved a very juicy bone of contention. There is still plenty of marrow left, and quite a number of prickly points of very hard bone. You will not expect me to solve the Nennian problem today. With your permission I shall merely quote the statement, and leave it to you to decide what value must be attached to it. Ida, son of Eobba, is said to have reigned twelve years. Then comes the addendum:[6]

[4] In CA this figure is increased to 103 stanzas, 1,275 lines; so also chapter VI, p. 76 below. These are followed by the four 'Gorchanneu' (*gorchan* 'great song', but also 'counsel, teaching' see G). Of these the last, *Gorchan Maeldderw* (CA p. 55) is attributed to Taliesin in the prose note which precedes it in the manuscript. See further OSPG pp. 51–3, 153 ff.

[5] The O.W. marginal entries in the *Book of St Chad* have been edited by W. M. Lindsay in his *Early Welsh Script*, p. 46 and plate I; by J. Rhŷs and J. G. Evans, LL pp. xliii–xliv; and by Morris-Jones, *Tal.* pp. 269 ff. Morris-Jones believed the earliest of these entries, the so-called 'Surexit Memorandum' to be a copy of a document originally written in the time of the sixth-century St Teilo. In LHEB pp. 42–6 Jackson argues against quite so early a date for the exemplar of this passage, believing its language to belong to the eighth century, and to the latter rather than to the earlier part.

[6] For the passage concerning the early poets, see chapter IV, p. 43 above, and pp. 76, 124 below; and n. [7] to chapter IV.

'At that time Outigirn fought bravely against the tribe of the Angles. At that time Talhaern, Father of the Muse, was famous in poetry: and *Neirin* (our Aneirin), and *Taliesin*, and Bluchbard and Cian called Gueinth Guaut, at the same time, in the same period were renowned in Welsh poetry.'

Ida ruled from 547 to 559 according to Bede.[7] So the above statement bears witness at least to a tradition that a group of Welsh poets flourished as early as the middle of the sixth century.

Further on, five sons of Ida are named as ruling in succession, the last being Hussa. 'Against him four kings fought, namely, Urien, Rhydderch the Old, Gwallawg, and Morgan.' Then comes *Deodric* or *Theodric* (572–9); against him Urien and his sons fought bravely. At that time sometimes the enemy, sometimes the 'citizens' (so he calls the Britons) were conquered. Then in the usual muddled Latin of Nennius, 'And he himself (*ipse*) shut them up for three days and nights in the island of *Metcaud*, and while he was on that campaign, he was killed, Morgan planning it through envy, because in him was the greatest valour in waging war.' The *ipse* must refer to Urien; the island *Metcaud* or *Medcaut*, the *Inis Metgoit* of Tighernach,[8] must be Lindisfarne, for in a later passage Nennius states that bishop Cuthbert died there (687).[9]

Hussa ruled from 585 to 592 according to Dr Lloyd.[10] His opponent, Urien, in poems ascribed to Taliesin, one of the bards mentioned above, is called the Lord of Catraeth.[11] If he fell through treachery in the Lindisfarne expedition, one can understand why the British alliance broke up; the men of Deira then advancing, and capturing Catraeth or Catterick before the end of the sixth century, and then later Edwin attacked the British kingdom of Elmet, near Leeds, subdued it and

[7] HE v, 24. For Ida and his sons, see n. 10 below, and cf. chapter vi, p. 76 below.

[8] *Ann. Tig.* s.a. [630]; RC pp. xvii, 182.

[9] HB chapter 65. According to Bede, HE iv, 29, St Cuthbert died on Farne Island, and his body was brought to Lindisfarne to be buried. But this minor discrepancy need not weigh as evidence against the identification of *Metcaud* with Lindisfarne; see Hunter-Blair, SEBH p. 151 n., and Jackson, CS p. 31.

[10] HW p. 163. A new assessment of the evidence by Dr D. P. Kirby proposes that Hussa's dates should be put slightly earlier, 579–86, and that his reign preceded that of Theodric, during which Nennius states that Urien was slain; 'Bede and Northumbrian Chronology', EHR lxxviii, 525 ff. Cf. LHEB pp. 707–8; OSPG p. 9 and n.; Hunter-Blair in SEBH pp. 149 ff. (quoted PT p. xii).

[11] *Gweleis i lyw katraeth tra maeu* 'I saw the lord of Catraeth beyond the plains', PT no. viii, line 9. Cf. chapter vi, n. [39] below.

drove King Ceredig from his throne.[12] It is worth noting that Urien is not mentioned even once in the Gododdin poems, or for that matter any of the three other kings named by Nennius as opponents of Hussa. Catraeth seems to be securely held by the men of Deira and Bernicia. Was the Battle of Catraeth in reality an attempt to recover Catterick, after the death of Urien in the closing years of the sixth century?[13]

This tradition about Aneirin and Taliesin cannot be later than the date of Harley 3859, say 1100.[14] If Zimmer be correct in ascribing the editing of the *Historia* by Nennius to 796, and the Saxon Genealogies to 685–6,[15] and a still more important *if, if these passages were already incorporated in these earlier forms of the Historia*, we get much nearer to Aneirin's *floruit*. But who dares be positive in such a matter? I'll just say that Welsh tradition puts Aneirin in the last half of the sixth century, and leave it at that.

The next point is the name given to the Aneirin poems, *Gododdin*.

According to Ptolemy, in the second century A.D. a British tribe occupied the east coast from the Firth of Forth down to the Tyne (or the Tees?) whose name is given in most of the manuscripts as ωταδηνοι or ωταδινοι. In Nennius, the district near Edinburgh, round Slamannan and Clackmannan, is called Manaw *Guotodin*, which would give in modern Welsh Gododdin. So, as Rhŷs suggests,[16] the ancient form was probably Ουοταδινοι. To give initial *gw-* in Welsh, one must postulate an initial *w* in the old form. Rhŷs also discovered that the headland over against Fife was called in Irish documents *Fothudan*, which agrees except in its termination with the *Guotodin* of Nennius, for initial *w* in Irish developed into *f-*, and medial intervocalic *t* into *th*.

Plummer in his edition of Bede[17] says in a note on the name *Uetadun* 'This place was identified by Smith with *Watton* in the East Riding of Yorkshire, which is nearly half-way between Driffield and Beverley.'

[12] AC ann. 616: *Ceretic obiit*; ann. 617: *Etguin incipit regnare*; HB chapter 63: *E(t)-guin filius Alli regnavit annis decem et septem et ipse occupavit Elmet et expulit Certic regem illius regionis*. Jackson points out that this event would be quite unknown but for the mention by Nennius; CS p. 46. See also HW p. 183. On the identity of 'Certic' see n. [49] to chapter VI below.

[13] CA p. xlvi. The argument is repeated OSPG p. 11.

[14] On this manuscript, which combines the O.W. Genealogies, AC, and the oldest text of Nennius's recension of HB, see LHEB pp. 48, 56. See chapter VI, n. [9] below.

[15] H. Zimmer, *Nennius Vindicatus* (Berlin, 1893), p. 78.

[16] J. Rhŷs and D. Brynmor Jones, *The Welsh People* (London, 1900), p. 98 n.; Rhŷs, *Celtic Britain*² (London, 1884), p. 155. Cf. CA p. xviii, OSPG p. 5.

17 C. Plummer, *Venerabilis Baedae Opera Historica* (Oxford, 1896), II, 275.

In Folcard's Life of Bishop John it appears as *Betendune* with a variant reading *Yatadini*. McClure, in his *British Place Names*[18] adds 'There seems to be in this name a reminiscence of the people called *Otadinoi*'. This may be so, but Watton is rather far to the south. It may, however, mark the site of a settlement by the Votadinoi in the territory of the *Brigantes*, the British tribe who once occupied the whole of Yorkshire and Lancashire as well. Instances occur also in Wales of small settlements by one tribe in the territory of another.

Another suggestion advanced by Rhŷs was that the *Bernicii* of Bede, Anglo-Saxon *Baernicas*, 'appears to have been the English pronunciation of the Welsh equivalent *Breenych* or *Brenneich*: and this in its turn is to be traced to the same origin as the name of the *Brigantes*. Thus the term *Bernicii* would seem to have meant the people of the Brigantian land'.[19] This seems to me to be a very risky proposition, although Lloyd, Plummer and others accept it without demur. I am equally doubtful of his explanation of Deira. He starts from the form *Deifr* in thirteenth-century manuscripts—suggests an original form *Debria* or *Dobria*, 'the latter if connected with the Welsh word *dwfr* "water", would lead one to suppose that the district got its name from its south-eastern portion being nearly surrounded by water'.[20] Why should one start with the

18 McClure, *British Place Names in their Historical Setting* (London, 1910), p. 188.

19 *Celtic Britain*², p. 114. [In LHEB pp. 701–5 Jackson rejects the derivation of *Bernicii* < **brĭgant*, as proposed by Rhŷs and others, on both phonological and geographical grounds. The oldest forms of this name are those given by Nennius: *Berneich* HB chapters 61, 63; *Birneich*, *Bernech*, chapter 61. Jackson offers the alternative derivation from a stem **bernā* or **birnā* which appears in O.I. *bern* (cf. *ebyrn* CLlH pp. iii, 40*c* and n. 137) 'gap, mountain pass', and he interprets the early forms as derived from **Bernăccī* or **Birnaccī* 'the people of the land of the mountain passes'; which, as he says, would be 'a very good name for the Pennines'. This gave by metathesis the Ml.W. forms *Brenneych*, *Brennych*, *Bryneich* which are found in CA, and elsewhere in early poetry. Further, he points out (OSPG p. 81) that 'the land of the Brigantes ends precisely where that of the Bernicians begins'.

More recently D. A. Binchy has challenged this interpretation in his discussion of the etymology of *brenin* (O.W. *breenhin* < **brigantīnos*) 'king'. He revives the etymology from **brigant-* first proposed by Rhŷs (*Celtic Britain*², pp. 282–3), and interprets the name by reference to the goddess **Brigantī* (> *Brigid*) 'the Exalted One'. The tribal name of the Brigantes would then perpetuate the name of the tribal goddess: an idea widely paralleled in early Irish sources, and for which it is arguable that there are parallels in some Gaulish tribal names such as *Bituriges* which could mean 'the people of the god **Bitu-rīx* ("world-king")'. See his *Celtic and Anglo-Saxon Kingship* (The O'Donnell Lectures for 1967–8; Oxford, 1970), pp. 12–13.]

[20] Nennius again gives this name in its oldest written form as *Deur*, HB chapters 61, 63. The forms *deor*, *dewr* in CA (see below) are indistinguishable from the adj. *dewr* 'bold', and the alternative *Deivyr* in the text of CA could represent a purely scribal

late form *Deifr*? Nennius has *Deur* and *Berneich*: he preserves the *b* in *Urbgen, Catgabail, Atbret, Ebrauc.* Why drop it in *Deur*? In the archaic Appendix to the *Book of Aneirin* the expression *teulu Deor*[21] occurs—everybody has taken it to be the Welsh *dewr* 'brave': it may be a survival of the Nennian *Deur.* Harley 3,859 at any rate is a reliable witness to the form in 1100. Bede, who lived in the district, uses *Deiri* and *Deri*[22] with no trace of any labial. Then think of the localities. The twelfth-century Life of Oswald says that the kingdom of the Deiri reached from the Humber to the mouth of the Tyne: and of the *Bernicii* from the Tyne to the Forth.[23] Between the Tyne and Tees was waste land, and as Plummer says, this explains why some authorities place the northern frontier of Deira at the Tees, others at the Tyne.[24] If Bernicia had been the southern half of Northumbria, one could understand how the name of the Brigantes survived as *Bernicia* for that district, but how and when did they oust the Votadini from the northern half and give their name to that district? I can't follow at all.

To return to the Gododdin poems. Many theories have been formulated to account for them. The Reverend Edward Davies in the *Mythology of the Druids*[25] asserts that their theme is the massacre of the Britons at Stonehenge in 472: Gododin (*sic*) is not the country of the Ottadeni, but derives from *godo* 'a partial covering', and *din* a fence: Gododin and Cattraeth are synonymous, and convertible terms. Yet Cattraeth is not the name of a place, but a contraction of *Cadeiriaith*, 'the language of the chair of presidency', whatever that may mean, and is used naturally enough for the great temple at Stonehenge!

G. D. Barber, in the *Ancient Oral Records of the Cimri*, 1855,[26] in a volume dedicated to Queen Victoria, is much more interesting and entertaining. He saw a translation of the 'Gododin' into English by

innovation. See OSPG pp. 80–1, LHEB pp. 419 f., where Rhŷs's derivation from **dubro-* 'water' is rejected. The origin and significance of this name remains a problem: Jackson proposes that Bede's *Deiri* is a borrowing from Primitive Welsh **Deir*, LHEB pp. 419–20.

[21] CA line 1216; see n.

[22] HE II, 1 etc.

[23] *Life of St Oswald*, cited in Plummer's notes to HE, II, 120.

24 Plummer, *op. cit.* II, 120.

25 *The Mythology and Rites of the British Druids* (London, 1809).

[26] The full title of G. D. Barber's exotic work is *Ancient Oral Records of the Cimbri or Britons in Asia and Europe, recovered through a literal Aramaic translation of the Original* (London, 1855). The book is described in some detail by IW, with further extracts, in his review of Gwenogvryn Evans's 'emended text' and introduction to the *Book of Aneirin*, *Y Llenor* IV, 49 ff. Cf. IW's remarks p. 58 below, and n. [35].

Ab Ithel;[27] translated it into Aramaic, changed all the vowels, and translated this new text back again into English, with the following results:

'The reader is here presented with an Aramitic composition, which purports to have been delivered orally at a school meeting in Wilts, at some time before the Christian era.' There are 6,000 puns, 'very cleverly maintained' in the 'Gododin'. 'The poem gives scenes of Aram, Ararat, or Armenia. *Hud*, the patriarch of the Arabs, and the *Abram* of the Hebrews, is the hero of the Cimri, at their original site near Lake Van. The irruption of the Hindus from Coshier, here also styled Gododin, Anak, and Rooken, is given in plain and distinct terms. The Gododin, Battle of Catraeth, now appears to have for its subject the Game of Chess, of which it gives general descriptions in successive stanzas, assigning it to a Hindu inventor, Caw of Gomer, as in Ferdushi.' This is a specimen:

*Lech* is joined. Here's *la*. La is weary.
What is Gododin?
What? A trifle to Cherubim.
Cast at it quickly! Give it up! Turn it over!
Consider! Rest! Hurry on! Stand still! Go back.
A pleasant games of games.
Gododin, deep hole!...
Neighbours, enjoy Gododin, the Hindu people's game—
The fat Chinese heroes have skill to find out little marks.

This is more to the point:

The game bears a likeness
To blows, blood and armies.
I wish for rest at intervals,
Extended wisecraft weakens the too weary head.

[27] *Y Gododin: A Poem on the Battle of Cattraeth by Aneurin, A Welsh Bard of the sixth Century, with an English Translation, and numerous Historical and Critical Annotations*, by the Rev. John Williams ab Ithel, M.A. (Llandovery, 1852).

The spelling *Gododin* is used commonly by the older writers; e.g. by Evan Evans in his *Specimens of the Poetry of the Ancient Welsh Bards* (1764), p. 64. The value of the medial -*d*- is ambiguous in manuscripts of the date of the *Book of Aneirin* (cf. chapter III, n. 16 on *Eidyn*, *Eiddyn*). But IW showed that in this instance medial -*d*- is proved by the derivation of the name, CA, pp. xvi–xviii). Ptolemy gave the name O(*u*)*otadinoi* (his rendering of Brit. **Votadini*) to a tribe whose territory stretched from the southern shore of the Firth of Forth, including Edinburgh, across the Lothians and as far south as Co. Durham. The Brittonic form developed regularly into O.W. *Guotodin* (HB chapter 62), and later *Gododdin*. See further OSPG pp. 5, 69–70.

I say Amen to that, and wonder what Queen Victoria thought of the 'Gododin'.

Ab Ithel in his edition[28] explains Catraeth as the Catrail, a deep ditch in Roxburghshire. The battle took place between the Welsh and the English in 570.

Villemarqué puts it in 578:[29] on the banks of the River Calder in Lanarkshire.

Stephens:[30] an expedition of the Ottadeni against Catterick, or Cataracton. The battle was the battle of Degsastane in 603, between Aidan, king of the Dalriadic Scots, and Ethelfrith, King of Northumbria.

Nash:[31] the battle between Oswy and Penda, king of Mercia, at Winwaedfield in 654, the *Strages Gai Campi* of Nennius.

Skene[32] divides the poem into two parts.

Part I tells how Aidan, king of Dalriada, helped by the Britons, fought against the half-pagan Picts of Manaw Guotodin, near Edinburgh (the Slamannan district) and the pagan Saxons; this is the 'Bellum Miathorum' of Adomnan, fought in 596.

Part II is later than 642, for it contains a reference to the ravens

[28] *Op. cit.* pp. 4–5.

[29] Theodore Hersart de la Villemarqué, *Les Bardes Bretons du sixième siècle* (Paris, 1860), p. 242.

[30] Thomas Stephens, *The Gododin of Aneurin Gwawdrydd: An English Translation, With Copious Explanatory Notes*, ed. Thomas Powel (London: Hon. Soc. Cymmrodorion, 1888), p. 30. But Edward Williams (Iolo Morganwg) had already identified Catraeth with Catterick. In his *Poems Lyric and Pastoral* (London, 1794), II, 16, he wrote that Catraeth 'was probably Cataractonium in Yorkshire, for the battle was fought near the river Derwenydd, or Derwent'. Iolo seems to have been the first person to make this identification (cf. G. J. Williams, *Iolo Morganwg* (Cardiff, 1956), p. xliv n.). Lewis Morris in his *Celtic Remains* (ed. Silvan Evans (London, 1878), but written in the mid-eighteenth century) has merely 'Cattraeth or *Cad Traeth*, some place in Scotland where a battle was fought by Mynyddawc Eydyn' and quotes the triad TYP no. 31 in support. For the identification with Catterick see CA pp. xxxii ff., OSPG pp. 83–4, and a note by O. G. S. Crawford based on a letter from IW in *Antiquity* XIII (1939), p. 34. IW suggested that the fort *Cataractonium* may have derived its name from the original name of the river near which it stands: the river *Catar(r)acta* later becoming known as the Swale. Crawford queries whether the name may not have been originally applied to 'a native hill-fort situated on the site of the medieval castle of Richmond' (which is near the waterfall or *cataract* on the Swale), and that it was here that the battle was fought, rather than in the vicinity of the Roman fort itself, which by *circa* 600 would have become derelict in all probability. This suggestion is followed in PT p. xxxvii.

[31] D. W. Nash, 'On the History of the Battle of Catraeth and "The Gododin" of Aneurin', *The Cambrian Journal* (1861), pp. 1–16.

[32] FAB I, 233; II, 369–70.

devouring the head of Domnall Brecc, killed in the Battle of Strath*cauin* or *cairinn*[33].

For his identification of the first battle, Skene relies on Adomnan's account of the Bellum Miathorum, in his Life of St Columba.[34] By his prophetic gift the saint, far off in Iona, was enabled to see King Aidan rushing on the enemy, and at last gaining the victory. He tells his disciples 'Now the barbarians are put to flight, and to Aidan, the victory, though hapless, is granted'. He even told the number of slain in Aidan's army, 303 men. Skene comments on this. 'The allusion to the three chiefs and three hundred slain at Cattraeth seems unmistak-able.' But is it? The figures I've seen in the Gododdin are 299 and 359, not a single reference to 303. If the figures are significant, something is wrong somewhere.

The latest editor of the Aneirin poems,[35] Dr Gwenogvryn Evans, disregarding all the linguistic evidence of early date, and the con-sistency of the tradition ascribing the poems to an early period, came out with an astounding theory that the Battle of Catraeth was really the Battle of Anglesey Sound, fought between the two Norman earls, Hugh the Fat of Chester, and Hugh of Shrewsbury, on the one hand, and Gruffudd ap Cynan of Gwynedd, helped by Magnus Barefoot, King of Norway, on the other. The date is 1098. He secured plenty of

[33] CA stanzas lxxix A and B; OSPG pp. 98, 147. See chapter VI, pp. 79–80 below, and nn. 37, 38.

[34] *Adomnan's Life of Columba*, ed. with translation and notes by A. O. and M. O. Anderson (London, 1961), p. 226, and cf. p. 41.

[35] *The Book of Aneirin*, revised and translated with notes by J. Gwenogvryn Evans, II (Llanbedrog, 1922). What follows in the above paragraph is a condensed *résumé* of IW's review of this book in *Y Llenor* IV (1925), 49–52, in which he pays deserved tribute to the excellencies of the facsimile edition of the text, previously published by Gweno-gvryn Evans (*The Book of Aneirin*; no. VIII in the *Series of Old Welsh Texts*, Pwllheli, 1907), but exposes in some detail the absurdities of his interpretation of the poem, as arbitrarily emended by himself (cf. IW's remarks on Barber's book, pp. 55–6 above, and n. 26). Here it seems just to quote from IW's appreciation of Gwenogvryn's achievement in the *Dictionary of National Biography* (Supplement 1922–30, p. 293): 'For over forty years, in spite of great bodily weakness, he toiled over manuscripts and proofs, and even set type with his own hand, in order to provide scholars with texts as perfect as possible in every detail and absolutely reliable as a basis for linguistic research. It was his devotion and indomitable courage which kept him to his task... Unfortunately, in his introductions and notes to the Taliesin and Aneirin poems Evans left his own field and ventured to formulate theories as to their nature and date which were uncritical and even fantastic.' More recently, N. Denholm-Young has spoken of Gwenogvryn's 'unrivalled knowledge of the manuscripts and remarkable flair for deciphering them' combined with his 'equally remarkable ignorance of the value of evidence and quite illogical habit of thought' (*Handwriting in England and Wales*, p. 40).

support for this really amazing theory, by inserting wholesale references to Anglesey, Penmon, the Menai Straits in the poem, and by changing ruthlessly the personal names found therein and substituting the names of eleventh-century Welshmen and Normans in their stead—with convincing results. He pushes the two earls into the verse, very effectively, by reading *Hugh*, wherever the old Welsh preverbal particle *hu* occurred in the text.[36] And then, arguing nicely in a circle, he quotes his own insertions as unchallengeable evidence of an eleventh-century date. I am afraid that it is impossible to take Dr Evans seriously any more than Mr G. D. Barber. Until you have compared his 'amended text' with the original, you will find it difficult to believe that my criticism is a fair one. It is really incredible that a scholar should treat old texts in this preposterous manner.

Now, what can be the reason for this medley of contradictory explanations? The reason, I think, is simply the difficulty of getting at the real meaning of the old vocabulary. Don't be too hard on the old editors. Very little is known of pre-Norman Welsh. Our manuscripts date from the twelfth century, at the earliest, and for the old Welsh period we have to work back from twelfth- and thirteenth-century forms, with all the errors natural to such a risky method. The only checks are a few hundred glosses in ninth- and tenth-century manuscripts and a dozen stanzas written in a copy of the Juvencus paraphrase of the Gospels, in a ninth-century hand.[37] Our task would be really hopeless, were it not for the rigid conservatism of the Welsh bards. Hundreds of poems are extant, dating from the twelfth to the fourteenth centuries, and a good deal of prose as well—all in practically contemporary manuscripts. A comparison[38] of the prose and verse shows that the bards, as is their wont even now, revelled in every type of archaism in form and construction. There is sufficient evidence to prove that every bardic disciple was trained to model himself on the language of the early poems. Even in the little *Book of Aneirin* we find a very suggestive rubric, to this effect:

[36] The same feat had been performed earlier by Iolo Morganwg, in his search through the *corpus* of Old Welsh poetry for references to his mythical 'culture-hero' Hu Gadarn (see R. Bromwich, *Trioedd Ynys Prydain in Welsh Literature and Scholarship* (Cardiff, 1969), p. 22 and n.). On the particle *hu(d)* 'as, so' see B VIII, 237–8.

[37] See chapter VII below.

[38] The bulk of the panegyric poetry composed by the bards of the twelfth and thirteenth centuries is contained in two manuscripts—the *Red Book of Hergest* (*circa* 1375–1425), and NLW MS. 6680 C, or *Llawysgrif Hendregadredd* (fourteenth to fifteenth centuries) —here abbreviated RBP and *Ll.Hen.* For details see GMW pp. xxv ff.

Every stanza in the Gododdin counts as "one singing" in a bardic contest. Each of the additional poems, the Gorchaneu, counts as 363, because they mention the number of the men who went to Catraeth. Any more than a man should go to battle without arms, no bard ought to go to a bardic contest without this song.'[39]

So they had bardic contests in the thirteenth century, and there are references to some in the twelfth,[40] and in these the competition was meant to find out which bard could recite most of the early songs. In the *Book of Taliesin* (*circa* 1300) there are several difficult old poems, with a number added to the title, occasionally the phrase in full, 'It is worth 24', or 'It is worth 300'[41]—a reference which is explained by the rubric in the *Book of Aneirin*. If these twelfth-century bards were trained to memorise the old songs, and were expected 'to show off' their antiquarian learning in their own compositions, it follows that their archaisms in vocabulary and constructions may help substantially the student of the real archaic poems.[42] But it makes it very difficult to prove beyond cavil that a certain form is definitely Old Welsh. If we only had a number of manuscripts belonging to the ninth or tenth century, whose authenticity was beyond challenging, then we could discover definite canons for Old Welsh as compared with Early Medieval. As it is we have to be content with the glosses—and furious controversies are the result.

Another reason for our difficulties is the vagaries of scribes, who copied these old songs, modernising them ruthlessly, where they understood them, or thought they did—changing the orthography, and substituting modern terms for old. Sometimes they forgot to modernise, or frankly gave it up in despair, and copied what was before their eyes, and then we pounce on these old forms with holy or unholy glee, to back up our own theories, or to smite one another hip and thigh.

What I have discovered is this: editors have a remarkable fondness for changing words unknown to them into place names, and then

[39] CA p. 55. On the meaning of *gorchan* see n. 4 above. On the prose note, and the evidence which it provides for bardic contests, see OSPG p. 52.

[40] One such twelfth-century bardic contest was that between Cynddelw Brydydd Mawr and Seisyll Bryffwrch for the office of *pencerdd* or Chief Poet at the court of Madog ap Maredudd of Powys, which took place before 1160. (*LlHen* pp. 180–1.) But the tradition of such contests goes back to the ninth or tenth centuries in both Wales and Ireland: for a summary of the evidence see R. Bromwich, *Tradition and Innovation in the Poetry of Dafydd ap Gwilym* (Cardiff, 1967), pp. 15–16 and n.

[41] BT pp. 30, 31, 34, 36, etc.

[42] IW has repeatedly emphasised his debt to the vocabulary of the Gogynfeirdd for interpreting that of the Cynfeirdd, by reason of the archaisms which they preserved and cultivated. On this aspect of bardic learning and practice see TYP pp. lxx ff.

hunting in the Ordnance maps for names with a similar form, and they always find them, for any chance resemblance will do. For instance:

> O lychwr i lychwr luch bin
> Luchdor i borfor bererin.[43]

which means, 'From twilight to twilight, from night to morn, there were flaming pine torches, and a shining open door to the purple clad wanderer'—i.e. there was feasting all night in a brightly lit hall, with the light streaming out to welcome the bard or another guest. Stephens translates geographically, 'From Lucker to Lockerby Lochmaben, there is an open door, i.e. From Lucker in Northumberland to Lockerby near Lochmaben in Galloway.'[44]

The poet in one stanza evidently refers to a well-known incident in the life of his hero.

> A ddalwy mwng blaidd heb brenn
> Yn i law, gnawd gwych nawd yn i lenn.[45]

'He who seizes the mane of a wolf without even a cudgel in his hand, must have a brave heart beneath his mantle.' Stephens renders the second line, 'And customary is hospitality in the cloister.'[46]

Skene, as I've said, divides the stanzas into two poems. The division comes at a stanza which he takes as a description of the bard in his grave.[47] 'These old poems', he says, 'are frequently added to and continued by later hands, and when the continuation is written in the person of the original author, the machinery is introduced of his being called from the tomb for this purpose.' This is his rendering:

> My knee is stretched.
> My hands are bound,
> In the earthen house
> With an iron chain
> Yet of the mead from the horn
> And of the men of Catraeth
> I Aneirin will compose
> An elaborate song.[48]

[43] CA stanza lv A, lines 645–6; OSPG pp. 137–8.
[44] T. Stephens, *The Gododin* p. 265.
[45] CA stanzas xliv A and B; OSPG pp. 101, 133.
[46] *Op. cit.* p. 245.
[47] FAB II, 361 (in ref. to CA stanza lv A). E. Anwyl also believed that the Gododdin was 'not one poem, but composed of portions of several poems', 'Prolegomena to the Study of Old Welsh Poetry', *Cymm. Trans.* (1903–4), p. 69.
[48] FAB I, 390 (Skene's stanza xlv).

The original runs:

Ystynnawc vyg glin
en ty deyeryn.[49]

'Stretched out is my knee (or leg) in the earthen house.' But Skene has added, 'My hands are bound'. Where did he get this? In late sixteenth-century copies, just here, the words *a bundat y* have been inserted, and every editor has wrestled with these difficult words. Silvan Evans, Skene's translator, comments in this manner: '*bun*, "a hand". It is not at all improbable that the bard's hands as well as his legs or knees were confined, and that that is the particular part of his person that is here intended'.[50]

But *bun* never means 'hand', and on examining the *Book of Aneirin* I failed to find a trace of this *a bundat y* anywhere—until I came to late copies. At last, on looking at the manuscript I noticed that the letter *y* occurs six times in these two short lines, and the solution hit me in the face. Somebody had noticed this before me, and jotted down in Latin, as was their wont in the old days, in the margin or between the lines, *abundat y*, 'there is a lot of *y* here', and this innocent remark has been twisted into Old Welsh and forced into the stanza where it makes no sense and spoils the metre.[51]

But in any case, Skene's explanation of the whole stanza is to be rejected. No one fastens iron chains round the knees of the dead. At any rate, it seems rather unnecessary. Living captives were often confined in this manner, even in underground prisons, and what the bard is trying to tell, surely, is his experience as a prisoner in the hands of the enemy after the battle. In the next stanza[52] he tells how Cenau, son of Llywarch, the champion of the North, the bold and brave, rescued him by the might of his flashing sword. 'From that cruel earthen prison he brought me, from that place of death, in a hostile land.' There is not the slightest suggestion that he is being brought back like Persephone, from the other world. And so the main part of Skene's argument falls to the ground.

Leaving the editors and their theories, what of the poems themselves? A certain number of stanzas can be linked together in one poem, I think, but I also think that stray pieces of early stuff have from time to

[49] CA lines 542–3.

[50] FAB II, 76, 382.

[51] CA pp. lii–liii. IW notes that Edward Davies in 1798 had already pointed out, after examining a proof-sheet of the *Myvyrian Archaiology*, that these words must have originated as a gloss on the text.

[52] CA stanza xlix.

time been added to the original kernel, simply because they happened to be in the same kind of metre and diction generally. Amongst these additions one must place a stanza referring expressly to the death of Aneirin the bard,[53] also an englyn or verse from a totally different type of poetry, the Llywarch Hên Saga,[54] which has slipped in, probably from the margin, and lastly a delightful song to a child, which has nothing whatsoever to do with the Battle of Catraeth. A mother might have sung it, or an old bard, with the child on his knee.

> The mantle of Dinogat is of many colours, of many colours.
> From the skins of martens I made it.
> When thy father went a-hunting
> With spear on shoulder and cudgel in hand
> He would call his big dogs,
> Giff, gaff: Catch, catch! Fetch, fetch!
> In his coracle, he would spear a fish,
> Striking suddenly like a lion.
> When thy father went up the mountain
> He would bring back a roebuck, a wild boar, a stag,
> A spotted grouse from the mountain,
> A fish from the falls of Derwennydd.
> As many as thy father caught with his spear,
> Wild pigs, and foxes, and ——
> None would escape, except those with wings.[55]

This is the earliest Welsh nursery rhyme known to me. From the margin of an empty page, where somebody had jotted it down, at the next copying it was merged in the war poems. If a verse of this character could get in, why not others, of a much more warlike character? That is how I would account for the Domnall Brecc reference.[56]

As for the main body of war-songs, I find it almost impossible to make an intelligible summary. There is no connected account of the fighting: you must infer the story from scattered references. What you do get is stanza after stanza praising individual warriors in the way that

[53] CA lines 653–5. With the tradition of Aneirin's death, cf. TYP nos. 33, 34 and nn.

[54] CA stanza xlvii; cf. OSPG pp. 47, 134.

[55] CA stanza lxxxviii; cf. OSPG pp. 46, 151.

[56] CA stanza lxxix A and B. This interpolated stanza heads the B text of the poem; see OSPG pp. 98–9. On the reference to Domnall Brecc see chapter VI below, pp. 79–80.

became a convention with the later school of Welsh poets; with an occasional verse to the whole group. The centre of it all is a chief called Mynyddawg of the Great Treasures.[57] His home is called Ysgor Eidyn, or the Fort of Eidyn. Caer Eidyn, and Din Eidyn, are mentioned, and I can see no reason to doubt that these names survive to this day in Edinburgh. Carriden on the Forth, and Dunedin.[58] In the Capitula of Gildas's work[59] the northern Roman wall is said to start from *Kair Eden civitas antiquissima*, about two miles from the monastery of Aber-cunrig 'which is now called Abercorn'—a variant of Bede's note, HE I. xii. Skene quotes from a life of St Monenna, '*Dunedene* que Anglica lingua dicitur Edineburg.'[60]

Woe to us for grief and lasting sorrow,
When the warriors came from the region of Dunedin.
The picked warriors of all lands,
The Retinue of the Gododdin, on horses with tossing manes,
Of the colour of swans, with harness drawn tight,
And in the van of the host, charging the enemy,
Defending the cornlands, and the mead of Eidyn.[61]

Every chief had his retinue or war-band, noble youths who lived at his table, and fought his battles. Mynyddawg gathered a war-band of champions in his hall at Eidyn, and feasted them royally for a full year. A warrior's pay in those days was plenty of mead and wine to drink. And these were paid in advance.

They drank mead, yellow, sweet, ensnaring,
For a year, and many a minstrel made merry.
The men who went to Catraeth, famed were they,
Wine and mead from cups of gold was their drink,
For a year, in noble fashion.[62]

And not from golden cups alone:

White was the drinking horn in the hall of Eidyn.
Though we drank clear mead, by rush light
Though sweet was the taste, the bitterness lasted long.[63]

[57] On Mynyddawg's epithet *Mwynfawr* 'wealthy' see IW's note in B II, 129–30; and for some other characters to whom it is attached in early sources, TYP p. 465, EWGT p. 227.

[58] On these places see further OSPG pp. 77–8.

[59] *Gildae De Excidio Britanniae* (London, Hon. Soc. Cymmrodorion, 1899), p. 12; ed. Th. Mommsen (*Monumenta Germaniae Historica Auct. Antiquiss.* XIII, i, Berlin, 1894), p. 18.

[60] FAB I, 85.

[61] CA stanzas xciv, xcv.

[62] CA lines 92–3, 235–7.

[63] CA lines 156–7, 168–9.

This is the burden of the whole series:

> Gwerth eu gwledd o fedd fu eu henaid.
> 'They paid with their lives for that feast of mead.'[64]

Over and over, we get the same idea: 'they deserved their mead'. Most people have read into this that they were drunk on the battlefield,[65] but that is not the meaning. Mead was their pay, and they earned it. If you'll think of the connexion between salary and salt, you will get the right meaning here. In an old poem in the earliest Welsh manuscript known, the *Black Book of Carmarthen*, a chief calls on his men, 'My war-band, after mead, incur not shame.'[66] After drinking his mead they were bound in honour to follow him to the death.

The first stanza of all is something like this: one of the retinue or war-band, a mere lad, is setting forth. In curt sudden little phrases the poet describes him:

> A man in strength, a boy in years,
> Famed for valour.
> His steeds were swift, long maned,
> Handsome was the youth.
> A shield light and broad
> Lay on the crupper of his swift slender horse.
> Blue and bright were his swords,
> Gold fringes to his mantle.

Yet,

> Before his wedding feast
> His blood streamed to the ground.
> Before we could bury him
> Food for ravens was he.
> It was a shame to leave him under the ravens.[67]

[64] CA line 356.

[65] This interpretation was invariably placed upon the poem by the earlier commentators, including Sharon Turner and T. Stephens, and by IW himself in his earliest published article on the poem, *Y Beirniad* (1911), p. 55. In his discussion of the point in CA pp. xlviii–xix, IW acknowledges his debt to Professor Bruce Dickins for pointing out to him that the repeated references in the poem to *talu medd*—the payment for mead-drinking—are to be interpreted in the light of the *ethos* characteristic of a heroic warrior society in other early literatures, in which 'mead' typified all the material support which a chieftain gave to his personal warband or *teulu*, and in exchange for which he expected—and received—faithfulness to the death. Professor Dickins drew attention to a closely similar allusion in the Anglo-Saxon poem *The Fight at Finnsburgh*. See further OSPG pp. 36–7; A. O. H. Jarman, HI pp. 199–200.

[66] BBC p. 92, ll. 14–15; CLlH no. vii, stanza 19.

[67] CA stanza 1.

Wearing a diadem, always in the very front of the fight,
But breathless before a maiden. He deserved his mead.
Pierced was the face of his shield, when he heard the battle cry,
He gave no quarter to those whom he pursued.
He never drew back from the fray until the blood flowed.
Like rushes he hewed down those who fled not.
The Gododdin tells, on the floor of the great houses,
Before the tent of Madog when he returned,
There was only one man out of a hundred that set forth.[68]

Further on, he is called Madog *Elfet*.[69] Though there is an Elfed in South Wales, it seems more reasonable to suppose that this shy warrior came from the Leeds district, where names like Shirburn in *Elmet* and Barwick in *Elmet* preserve the old form of the name to this day.

The number of this famous retinue is given as 300.

Of the retinue of Mynyddawg, alas,
Of three hundred only one man returned.[70]
Of 300 champions that set forth
To Catraeth, sad it is that only one returned.[71]
Of the retinue of Mynyddawg,
Only one man escaped.[72]
Three hundred, wearing gold torques, set forth,
And of that host of kinsmen
Sad it is that only one man escaped.[73]

But elsewhere there is talk of a war-band of 363.

Three men and three score, and three hundred,
Wearing torques of gold,
Of the number that set forth from the feast,
Only three escaped by their courage in the fight,
And I was spared because of my holy muse.[74]

In the rubric already mentioned, the number is given as 363. Has there been a later confusion of two accounts, one giving 300 and the other 363, or did they reckon 120 to the 100? The other possibility

[68] CA stanza II.
[69] CA line 1179. On Elmet see chapter VI, p. 82 below, and nn. 49, 50; PEW pp. 222, 228; TYP pp. 375–7.
[70] CA lines 693–4. For a collection of refs. see CA pp. liii–liv.
[71] CA line 707.
[72] CA lines 699–701.
[73] CA lines 706–7.
[74] CA lines 238–42.

is that two parties set out for Catraeth, one of 300, and one of 363.[75]

Whether 300, or 363, the odds against them were heavy, 'nine score to one', says one stanza; 'a hundred thousand fought with three hundred', says another. It was evidently a kind of forlorn hope, or if you will allow me to call it so, another 'Charge of the Light Brigade'. The chief gathered his war-band from all parts; men of North Wales are mentioned, and men of the extreme north, beyond the Bannog Mountains, wherever they may have been; one came from Elmet, one from the south. He feasted them, and then after mead, and in return for mead, he set them the hopeless task of riding through the enemy to Catraeth. Every man obeyed, and proved that he was worth his mead: and all fell except the bard and three others. The bard was spared, and thrust into an underground prison, whence he was rescued by another prince of the North.[76]

The warriors went to Catraeth: ready were they,
Fresh mead was their feast, and bitter poison it proved.
Three hundred by command set forth in battle array,
And after the joyous shouting, there was utter silence.
Though they went to churches to do penance,
True is the tale, death got them.[77]

The enemy were the men of Deira and Bernicia; these are mentioned more than once. 'Seven times their number of the men of Lloegr did they slay;[78] 'in Lloegr', says another line, 'men were cut down before the three hundred chiefs.'[79] Lloegr is never used of Scotland: so that Catraeth need not be looked for north of the Roman Wall. It always

[75] The problem of the discrepancy between the variant statements made in the poem as to the number of Mynyddawg's war-band (300 or 363) is discussed in detail CA pp. liii–lviii. Finally the figure of 363 is rejected by IW as the invention 'of a man who cared more about triads than about the exact truth'. See further OSPG pp. 13–16. The point is important for its bearing upon the date of the various accretions which have been made at later dates to the text of the poem.

[76] The single survivor, in addition to the poet, was Cynon son of Clydno Eidyn, CA p. lviii. According to the later *Stanzas of the Graves* (ed. Thomas Jones, PBA (1967), pp. 120–1), Cynon's grave was not in North Britain, but was identified in Wales. The reference made here to the 'three escapers' belongs properly to the variant tradition of the war-band of 363 (stanza xxi). The poet's imprisonment appears to be referred to in stanza xlviii.

[77] CA stanza viii.

[78] *Seith gymeint o loegrwys a ladassant*, line 671.

[79] *En lloegyr drychyon rac trychant unben*, line 481.

means England in Welsh literature.[80] That is one reason why I cannot accept Skene's idea that Catraeth was close to Edinburgh. One stanza says that the hero's grave was over the border of the Gododdin.[81]

For many years I have been convinced that Stephens was right in identifying Catraeth with Catterick.[82] It fits all the facts known to me. It is over the border of the Gododdin; it is on the Roman road from the north, and the war-band could ride their white horses down through Bremenium or Ribchester, by way of Corbridge and Lanchester, down to Catterick. If that road was in the possession of the enemy, they had the optional route through Carlisle, Brougham and Kirkby Thore.

The best commentary on the Gododdin, in my opinion, is a song by a Welsh prince, Owain Cyfeiliog, who ruled over southern Powys, N.E. Wales, from 1160 to 1197. In this ode[83] he tells how he sent his war-band on a foray into English territory, and on their return he gives the survivors a royal feast. He calls on the cupbearer to take the long blue horn, full of mead, to each warrior who has distinguished himself. His praise is the old phrase, *Talasant eu medd*, 'they have deserved their mead'. He then goes on:

I have heard of a host who in return for mead rode to Catraeth,
Loyal of purpose, with weapons sharp and keen,
The retinue of Mynyddawg, renowned in battle.
Their fame was sung, these fierce battle champions,
But they did not achieve as much as my men did
In the hard fight of Maelor,
The rescue of a prisoner, etc.

This reference is some 80 years earlier than the date of the *Book of Aneirin*; further, the ode is full of echoes of our poems. A twelfth-

[80] Cf. AP p. 45, where IW speculates as to whether the name *Lloegr*, whose origin is obscure, may not have originally designated the men of Mercia, since Mercia was the midland kingdom which bordered on Wales. It may have spread thence to become a more general term for the English, as it is in the poems of Aneirin and Taliesin. But see also OSPG p. 7 and n.

[81] *byt orfun gododin bed*, line 923; cf. note.

[82] See n. [30] above.

[83] RBP cols. 1432–5, the *Hirlas Owein*. This poem can be dated closely to the year 1155, since it states specifically that the purpose of the raid which it commemorates was the freeing from imprisonment of the poet's brother Meurig ap Gruffudd (col. 1434, ll. 32–7): an event which is noticed in *Brut y Tywysogion* under the year 1155–6; see B XVI, 188–9, TYP pp. 468–9. On the poem see further J. Lloyd-Jones, *The Court Poets of the Welsh Princes* (PBA 1948), p. 14; CA p. xxiii; T. Gwynn Jones, 'Catraeth and Hirlas Owein', *Cy.* XXXII (1922), 1–57; A. Conran, *The Penguin Book of Welsh Verse*, pp. 114–16.

century Welsh prince sends his men on a desperate expedition right into England, and when they come back, covered with blood and glory, 'with the sun shining gloriously on every long ridge and in every hollow', as he says, he can only praise them worthily, by saying that they have done more even than the famous war-band of old who rode to Catraeth. He is nearer the old tradition than we are, and his words show how the Welsh of his day regarded these Gododdin poems. All through the centuries they had been sung by many a camp-fire to spur the warriors to a similar loyalty to their lords, 'Remember the men who went to Catraeth.' In the course of time the text of these oral songs would be greatly modified, and contaminated by intermixture with other war-songs. But the core remained. This was put in writing at any rate as early as the ninth or tenth century, and what we have in the *Book of Aneirin*, if I had leisure to go into the matter in detail, is three[84] different versions of these songs, gathered together by a bard, who wished to memorise them for the regular bardic contest in the old lore. And his copy is the only one that has survived. I will end by quoting just two lines. This is one:

> Byr eu hoedl: hir eu hoed ar eu carant.
> 'Short lived were they; but long the longing for them in the hearts of their kinsmen.'[85]

And this is the other, the simplest line in the whole of the Gododdin:

> Llawer mam a'e deigr ar ei hamrant.
> 'There were tears in the eyes of many a mother.'[86]

What they did we do not exactly know, further than this, they were loyal and brave, and true; their mothers wept for them, their kinsmen sorrowed for them, and their countrymen have remembered them for over thirteen hundred years.

[84] This is the only mention by IW, as far as I know, of a suggestion that the *Book of Aneirin* incorporates parts of *three* (as opposed to *two*) versions of the Gododdin. It is probable that he had in mind the problem raised by such stanzas as CA xlv and li, each of which has three variant versions, and lxiii (lines 717 ff.) which has no less than five variants. Behind such a stanza there must lie a complicated textual history, as has been indicated recently by Idris Foster, 'Rhai Sylwadau ar yr Hengerdd', *Ysgrifau Beirniadol* v, ed. J. E. Caerwyn Williams (Denbigh, 1970), p. 28.

[85] CA line 670.

[86] CA line 673.

## *Chapter VI*

# WALES AND THE NORTH

WHEN Welshmen in the old days spoke of the North without qualification or definition of any sort, they always meant the northern borders of England together with south Scotland, in particular the district between the two Roman Walls. The Men of the North (*Gwŷr y Gogledd*) were the British tribes inhabiting the region between Glasgow and Edinburgh, and down to mid-Lancashire on the west and south Yorkshire on the east.

You will not expect me to tell you in this short talk everything about Wales, and it would be arrant folly on my part if I should try to teach this assembly of Northern experts anything about the North.[1] That would be really and truly carrying coals to Newcastle. My safety lies in confining myself to the middle term of my subject, namely the word *and*, which, I am told, is a conjunction. My task is to touch lightly on the connexion or connexions between the people of Wales and the Men of the North in the early centuries.

The Saxon invaders, from the second quarter of the fifth century to the second quarter of the seventh, by hard fighting took possession of the eastern coasts of Britain and the Midlands from the Firth of Forth down to the English Channel. Their advance divided the British territory (like Gaul) into three parts. The North-Western district, Strathclyde, got its name from the *strath* (our *ystrad*) or plain of the Clyde, but the term came to be used for the whole district extending from the mouth of the Clyde down to Lancashire. Further south came our Wales, with its eastern border running from the Dee near Chester to the mouth of the Severn. Further still to the south lay the third district, which embraced Devon and Cornwall: this was the weakest of the British territories for it was early enfeebled by the mass migration overseas of a good part of its population, to form a Little Britain, a Brittany, in North-West France. Naturally enough the links between Cornwall and Brittany were much closer than those with Wales and the North. Cornishman and Breton were not only members of the same nation but

[1] Read at the Annual General Meeting of the Cumberland and Westmorland Antiquarian and Archaeological Society, Carlisle, 30 August 1950.

of the same tribes.[2] They were in frequent contact with one another. Their dialects differed but slightly, and intercourse was easy.

The Men of Wales on the other hand turned elsewhere for alliance and help. Their deliverers were expected to come from the North, the breeding ground of British heroes in legend and saga.

The dwellers in the three British districts called themselves Britons (*Brython*); so did the men of Little Britain in France, who are still known as Bretons.[3] The Britons of Wales and Strathclyde, however, for some reason or other, began to call themselves also *Cymry*,[4] the plural of *Cymro*, a compound of *com-* a prefix meaning 'together', and *bro* 'border, coast, district'. The earlier form of *bro* was *mrog-*, a cognate of the Latin *margo*, English *march* 'border'; so *Cymro* means one who dwells within the same border as you do, a fellow countryman. Cornishmen were never known as *Cymry*, but the people of *Cumberland* were; as you all know, Cumberland means 'the land of the Cymry'. We Welshmen also call ourselves *Cymry*, though the Saxon preferred to describe us as *Welsh* 'foreigners', and our country as *Wales* 'the foreign land', just as the Germans use *Wälsch* and *Wälsch-*

[2] The tribes of the *Dumnonii* and *Cornovii* gave their names to two of the three early tribal divisions of Brittany—Dumnonée and Cornouailles—as they did to our Devon and Cornwall. See LHEB pp. 12 ff.

[3] The name *Brittones* continued to be employed throughout the Middle Ages by all the Brittonic peoples in reference to themselves, just as they used *Britannia* both of Great and of Lesser Britain, making no distinction in the use of these names (cf. LHEB p. 13 n. 4): a fact which sometimes gives rise to ambiguity. *Brython* is the Welsh equivalent of *Brittones*, and was used frequently by the Welsh of themselves, throughout the literary tradition down to the seventeenth century; see GPC, and cf. the following note.

[4] The earliest occurrence of *Cymry* in reference to the Welsh is probably that in the *Moliant Cadwallon* (see pp. 85–6 below, and n. 71). It occurs also in the Llywarch Hen poetry, and in *Armes Prydein*, though it is not found in the poetry of Aneirin and Taliesin, who invariably employ *Brython*. In reference to the inhabitants of Cumbria the earliest occurrence is in Ethelwerd's Chronicle (*circa* 1000), which speaks of the ravaging of *Pihtis Cumbrisque* by the Danes in 875, where both Asser and the Anglo-Saxon Chronicle refer to 'the Picts and the Strathclyde Welsh'. See E. Phillimore, *Cy.* XI (1892), 95–101, who cites further references in the Anglo-Saxon Chronicle to *Cumbra(land)* in the tenth and eleventh centuries. *Cumbria* is the equivalent of 'the Old North' (*yr hen Ogledd*) of Welsh tradition, and it originally encompassed a large area of north-west England (Cumberland, Westmorland, and north Lancashire), and Strathclyde as far as the Forth–Clyde line in Scotland. Since the name of 'fellow countrymen' united the Britons of the North with those of Wales, it must have originated before Cumbria and Wales became separated in the seventh century. In older Welsh usage *Cymry* denoted both the country and the people; later *Cymru* came to be the name for Wales, and *Cymro*, pl. *Cymry* the name for the people of the country. On the original extent of 'Cumbria' see P. A. Wilson, *Trans. Cumberland and Westmorland Antiq. and Arch. Soc.* LXVI (1966), 57–92.

*land* for *Italian*, and *Italy*. In the name of all the gods of philology, I maintain that we have the right in retaliation to label the whole of England as *Wales*! It seems absurd to use it of our own little corner.

Anyhow, the name *Cymry* is the common heritage of the Britons of Cumberland and of the Britons of the country now known as Wales. We are fellow countrymen in a very special sense. At one time we spoke the same language, *Cymraeg*; many of your place-names are identical in origin and meaning with ours.[5] They have survived in spite of successive invasions by Angles, Saxons, Scots, and Norsemen, and their centuries-long settlement in your midst. Purity of race we cannot claim, either in Wales or in Cumberland, but *Cymry* is still a title we rightfully share. We belong to the country, and we belong to one another.

The next point of contact is historical. A Welshman called Nemnius, whose name is usually given as *Nennius*,[6] compiled a short Latin history of the Britons, about the year 796. His *Historia Brittonum* in spite of its form, or lack of form, in spite of its crude Latin and numerous blunders, linguistic and historical, is of considerable value, if one uses it fairly. Nennius did not pretend to be an author—he realised acutely his own limitations—but only a mere compiler: *Aliqua excerpta scribere curavi*, 'I have taken the trouble of writing certain excerpts'.[7] He made selections, extracts. His little *Historia*, in spite of its title, is not an original work, but a collection of excerpts from earlier works. He wished to rebut the charge of slothful ignorance brought against his people, and that they had no knowledge of their past; and so, he says in his preface, 'I have collected together everything I found in the annals of the Romans, the chronicles of the Holy Fathers, the annals of the Irish and Saxons, and also in the tradition of our own elders.' The sources he used were thus partly literary, partly oral. To the best of his ability he made selections from documents and also from saga material or tradition. He admits frankly that he is a poor critic, and describes

[5] Examples: *Lanercost* 'the glade of Augustus' (as was shown by IW, *Trans. Cumberland and Westmorland Antiq. and Arch. Soc.* (1952), pp. 67–8), *Tallentire* 'the end of the land', *Triermain* 'the village of the Rock', *Penrith* 'the head of the ford'. On the Brittonic elements in Cumberland place-names, see K. Jackson, 'Angles and Britons in Northumbria and Cumbria', *O'Donnell Lectures* (Cardiff, 1963), pp. 60 ff.

[6] In B VII, 380–2, IW endorsed the opinion previously advanced by R. Thurneysen (*ZfcPh.* XX, 97–137), that *Nemnivus* or *Nemnius* was the correct name of the early ninth-century 'editor' of the *Historia Brittonum*, though 'Nennius' has continued to be the form which has obtained general currency. See chapter IV, n. [5] above.

[7] Nennius's preface to HB (ed. Lot, p. 146).

himself as just a *garrula avis*, a chattering bird, singing songs not his own. That may be true. (I am afraid that it *is* true.) Nevertheless, it seems rather ungrateful on our part to stress the poverty of his library, and the contradictions and incoherences of the little volume he produced with such toil and labour. He has preserved for us the earliest traditions of the Britons, in so far as they were available to him in a North Wales monastery at the end of the eighth century.[8] Let us bless him for that. His extracts, luckily, are from documents dating from a much earlier period that 796, and they have provided the historian with much valuable information. We could have done with a few more garrulous birds of his type.

In chapter 14 he tells us that the sons of *Liethan* (an Irish tribe) had taken possession of Dyfed (Pembrokeshire, South Wales) and other districts as well, in Gower and Cidweli, until they were expelled by Cunedda and his sons from all British territory. Who this Cunedda was we are told in Chapter 62, after a reference to Maelgwn, the great king of Gwynedd in North Wales, during the first half of the sixth century: 'His ancestor (*atavus*) Cunedda (*Cunedag*) with his eight sons had come here from the North, from the region known as Manaw Gododdin (*Guotodin*) 146 years previous to Maelgwn's reign, and they expelled the Irish from those regions with great slaughter.' In a Chronicle usually known as *Annales Cambriae*, which is preserved in Harley MS. 3859,[9] immediately following the best copy of Nennius's *Historia*, Maelgwn's death is noted under the year 547. We don't know when he began to rule over Gwynedd, and so must subtract 146 from this 547, which gives us 401, and then suggest *circa* 380 as a possible date for the coming of Cunedda.

Such a guess, alas, is not strongly supported by the early pedigrees. In the tenth-century collection in Harley MS. 3859, the royal line of

[8] The 'Elvodugus', of whom Nennius claims in his preface to be the disciple, has been identified with the *Elbodg(u)* or Elfoddw, *archiepiscopus Guenedote regionis*, who died in 809 AC. It is therefore a reasonable guess that he and his 'disciple' were both associated with the cathedral church of Bangor in Arfon; see SEBC p. 44.

[9] *Harleian MS. 3859*, written *circa* 1100, contains the early text of AC, combined with the early Welsh dynastic genealogies and Nennius's recension of HB. The annals and the genealogies were edited by Phillimore, *Cy.* IX, 141 ff., and again by A. W. Wade-Evans, *Nennius's History of the Britons* (SPCK, 1938), pp. 84–114. Phillimore showed that these documents were brought together in the mid-tenth century, perhaps at St David's. The most convenient edn. of the genealogies is now EWGT. See further LHEB, p. 56; H. M. and N. K. Chadwick, *The Growth of Literature* I (Cambridge, 1932), pp. 140 ff.

Hywel Dda is traced back to *Maelgwn* son of Cadwallon Lawhir, son of Einion Yrth, son of *Cunedda* and on and on to Anna, the cousin of the Virgin Mary.[10] We will not go quite so far. Our present problem is ample for tonight. Are the three generations of Maelgwn, Cadwallon and Einion sufficient to fill the gap between A.D. 380 and 547, between the coming of Cunedda (with eight warrior sons) to Wales and the death of Maelgwn his great-grandson? The pedigree, being official, may be accepted as correct, and even in the Wales of long ago warrior princes sometimes managed to keep alive for quite a time. But I must confess to having doubts about the Nennian figure of 146 years. Nennius used Roman numerals, and they were easily mis-copied, as is well known. I think that cxlvi (or cxlui with a square *u* not *v*) might well be a scribal error for cxuii (117) or even cxiiii (114). If either of these figures were substituted for 146, there would be no need to over-stretch the generations between Cunedda and Maelgwn, and the coming of Cunedda could be roughly dated between A.D. 400 and A.D. 410.[11]

Without wasting more time on the exact figure, we can say that the latest stage of the Roman occupation seems likely to fit the Irish settlements in Wales. Raiding operations are a different matter, but the settlement of Dyfed[12] in South Wales and of the peninsula of Lleyn in

[10] *Harl. Gen.* no. 1; EWGT p. 9.

[11] The date of Cunedda's migration from Manaw Gododdin to North Wales is extremely uncertain, and cannot be determined on the basis of Nennius's reckoning—which in any case has presumably been incorrectly transmitted, though it is by no means clear how his figure of 'cxlvi years' should be emended. The two intervening names which are all that the genealogy gives between Cunedda and Maelgwn are insufficient to span the gap of 146 years, especially since other indications suggest that Cunedda was advanced in years when the expedition took place. Since IW wrote this paper, opinion has tended to favour a slightly later date for the migration, following the view put forward by H. M. Chadwick, *Early Scotland* (Cambridge, 1949), pp. 4 n., 148, that it 'can hardly have taken place before 450'. P. Hunter-Blair puts it 'towards the middle of the fifth century', *The Origins of Northumbria* (Newcastle, 1947), p. 36; see also Jackson, 'The Britons in Southern Scotland', *Antiquity* XXIX (1955), 79–80; SEBC pp. 34–5. The argument is that the Irish are not likely to have established themselves in North Wales in any strength until some years had elapsed after the Roman garrison had withdrawn in 383, and according to a triad, TYP no. 62, Cunedda's grandson (and Maelgwn's father) Cadwallon Lawhir was still engaged in fighting with them in Anglesey *circa* 500, see TYP p. 168. The evidence points therefore to the first half of the fifth century for the migration, but it is impossible to be more precise.

[12] The dynasty which ruled Dyfed down to the tenth century was of Irish origin, being sprung from the tribe of the *Deisi*, who had emigrated from Co. Waterford in the third or fourth century. They seem to have maintained a connexion with their parent stock at least as late as the eighth century, down to which date the names of the kings of Dyfed

Caernarvonshire[13] (so named from the *Lagin* of Leinster), alike testify to these Irish migrations in force, and suggest a serious weakening of the Roman power in Britain.

On the other hand, the transfer of a part of the Gododdin tribe from Manaw Gododdin near Edinburgh (where the Gaelic or Irish form corresponding to British *Manaw* survives as *Manann*, Mannan, in *Clackmannan* and *Slamannan*), a border district, where they formed the advanced defence on the East against the Picts and Scots, and moving them in a body down to Wales—such a transfer obviously calls for a central power to direct and order it. Chadwick's theory that this central power may have been Vortigern or Coel Hen does not appeal to me at all.[14] Nothing is known of Coel, and too much is known of Vortigern's genius for doing the wrong thing.[15] Cunedda has a Welsh name, meaning 'good chief',[16] but his father, grandfather and great-grandfather bore Latin names (*Eternus*, *Paternus*, *Tacitus*), as did three of his sons.[17] His father was a Romanised Briton, but he gave his son a British name,[18] a sign that the Roman element was weakening, and the British element growing more and more conscious of itself. Cunedda marched south to Wales leading troops armed and trained to

listed in *Harl. Gen.* I can be matched by the names given in the Irish tract *The Expulsion of the Deisi* (EWGT pp. 4–8 and n. p. 124; *Cy.* XIV (1901), 104–35; *Ériu* III (1907), 135–42). For the Irish in Dyfed, cf. chapter I n. [26] above, and HW pp. 97–8.

[13] *Llëyn* (di-syllabic) developed from **Legyn* < **Legin* < **Lageni*, which in Irish gave *Laighean* 'Leinster'. J. Lloyd-Jones remarks 'It is impossible to doubt that Irishmen from Leinster occupied Lleyn over a long period', *Enwau Lleoedd Sir Gaernarfon* (Cardiff, 1928), p. 6. Cf. T. F. O'Rahilly, *Early Irish History and Mythology* (Dublin, 1946), pp. 113–14, n.

[14] H. M. Chadwick, *Early Scotland*, pp. 148–9, followed by P. Hunter-Blair, *The Origins of Northumbria*, pp. 46–8, suggest that Coel may have been based on York, and may have been directly responsible for bringing the Saxons to North Britain. The derivation of *Coel* from *Caelius* advocated by these writers has been rejected by Jackson, on the grounds that Latin *-ae-* did not give Welsh *-oe-* (LHEB pp. 335–6; 'The Britons in Southern Scotland', p. 80). On Coel's epithet *Godebawc*, see chapter I above, n. 25.

[15] For an important recent discussion of the role of Vortigern (W. *Gwrtheyrn Gwrtheneu*) see D. W. Kirby, 'Vortigern', B XXIII, 37–59. On the Welsh traditions of Gwrtheyrn see IW 'Hen Chwedlau', *Cymm. Trans.* (1946), 44–55; TYP pp. 392–6.

[16] Cunedda < **Couno-dagos* (*Tal.* 92 n.; TYP p. 312). The form *Cunedag* of HB chapter 62 is archaic and 'not likely to be later than the middle of the eighth century at latest, very probably earlier' according to Jackson, CS p. 30.

[17] *Harl. Gen.* I (EWGT p. 9) gives *Eniaun girt map Cuneda map Aetern map Patern pesrut* ('red tunic') *map Tacit.* The names of Cunedda's nine sons are listed in *Harl. Gen.* no. 32 (EWGT p. 13); of these Rumaun (< *Romanus*), Dunaut (< *Donatus*) and Etern (< *Aeternus*) are the ones here referred to.

[18] O.W. *En(n)iaun Girt* > Ml.W. *Einiawn Yrth.* The epithet *Gyrth* means 'harsh, fierce, strong' (G).

fight in the Roman manner. Their language however was not Latin but British. They drove out the Irish,[19] settled down, and in due course their language, Late British or Early Welsh, spread over the whole of the country. Cunedda gave us a Welsh royal family, a Cymric dynasty;[20] and for 900 years his descendants ruled in various parts of Wales.

Leaving history for literature, here too I find that we are much indebted to the Men of the North. One of Nennius's sources was a tract giving the genealogies of the early Saxon kings. Amongst them is that of Ida who ruled for twelve years in Northumbria (547–59).[21] Then follows the most important Nennian comment of all, at any rate for the student of early Welsh literature: 'At that time Talhaearn Tad Awen was famous in poetry. Also Neirin, Taliesin, Bluchbardd, and Cian called Gweinth Gwawd, were famous together at the same time in British poetry.'[22] *Neirin* is the poet whose name later on developed an *A* before the initial *N* and became *Aneirin*. Much later still a pedantic misspelling *Aneurin* became current. In a manuscript dated 1250 known as the *Book of Aneirin*, a long Welsh epic poem has been preserved, called the *Gododdin*, and is said to be by Aneirin. In my arrangement of it, there are 1,275 lines, divided into 103 stanzas.[23] Of these there are variants, usually in a much earlier orthography, of 22 stanzas.[24] For

[19] With the allusion to Cunedda's expulsion of the Irish from North Wales (quoted above, p. 73) cf. the triad TYP no. 62 *Tri hualhogeon deulu* which refers to the fighting between Cunedda's grandson Cadwallon Lawhir and the Irish in Anglesey; and HB chapter 14 which similarly records the 'expulsion' of the Irish from Dyfed by Cunedda's sons. Cf. also n. [12] above.

[20] I.e. the royal line of Gwynedd; the dynasty of Maelgwn, Cadwallon, and Cadwaladr, of Rhodri Mawr (by the distaff), and of the two Llywelyns. The territories ruled over by Llywelyn's 'sons' (or perhaps his military commanders?) and by the dynasties founded by them, are claimed to have extended from the Dee to the Teifi. See HW pp. 117–18; TYP p. 313; Chadwick, *Early Scotland*, pp. 147 ff.

[21] These are the traditional dates, as based upon the *Moore Memoranda*. But see chapter v above, n. 10: according to the revised dating proposed by Dr Kirby, Ida would have reigned 558–70.

[22] Cf. chapter IV, p. 43 above, and n. [7]; chapter v, p. 52, chapter VIII, p. 122.

[23] This is the arrangement as given in CA. At an earlier date before the edition was completed, IW gave a larger estimate of the number of lines (chapter v, p. 51 above). In the interval he evidently decided on a longer line-length in a number of the *awdlau*; and this, as he explained, is entirely a matter of choice. The metrical unit may frequently be taken as composed of a half-line of four to five syllables, or alternatively as a combination of two such halves. In the arrangement of the poems in PT, IW preferred the longer line-length of nine to ten syllables to the shorter one which is exemplified in the first stanza of the Gododdin, and the reason for his choice is explained in the introduction, PT p. lxiii. The metrical unit is the same in both instances.

[24] See chapter IV, p. 46 and n. [16].

various reasons I have been compelled to reject outright four of these:[25] probably several others ought to be excluded. Close on 1,000 lines remain, after rejects and repetitions have been omitted. Their theme is a valiant but vain attempt by the bodyguard of Mynyddawg, lord of Dineiddyn (Edinburgh)[26] to recapture Catraeth (Catterick, or Richmond)[27] in Yorkshire from the men of Northumbria (Deira and Bernicia), just before A.D. 600, or soon after. This royal war-band or retinue numbered 300 men.[28] All perished except one.[29] The poet sings to the individual warriors in turn, though occasionally a full stanza is devoted to the host, the noble three hundred, the pattern for every retinue, serving their lord faithfully, loyally, to the bitter end. He gave them mead: they paid him for it with their lives. Aneirin, however, preferred to praise one warrior at a time. They were his kinsmen, his comrades, and he knew each one intimately.[30] Evidently this sixth-century poet, Aneirin, was himself one of the Gododdin tribe, a native of the Edinburgh district, the *Manaw Gododdin*,[31] from which Cunedda had set forth two centuries earlier to deliver the Cymry of Wales from their enemies.

The Gododdin poem (or series of poems) was preserved at first by oral tradition in the halls of British chieftains; our 1250 text, however, shows clear traces of a written version, which can be dated in the

[25] On the 'interpolations' in the text of the Gododdin, see chapter v, p. 63 above; OSPG pp. 46–51.

[26] See chapter v, p. 64 above, and n. 58; and cf. TYP pp. 467–9 on *Mynyddawg (Eidyn)*.

[27] On the site of the battle of Catraeth see chapter v above, n. [30].

[28] For the ambiguity in the text with regard to the number of Mynyddawg's war-band, see chapter v, pp. 66–7 above, and n. [75].

[29] According to the poem, Cynon fab Clydno was the sole survivor of the war-band; cf. chapter v, n. [76].

[30] Cf. IW's remarks in LEWP p. 69, 'Each stanza (stresses) some characteristic quality or outstanding achievement. One fought a wolf with bare hands. Another always rode bay horses. One was generous to churches and to minstrels. As for another, though his father was not a king, yet his words were always listened to at every council. One was the poet's staunch friend. Another was courteous and kind, loved by everybody. But all had one virtue in common, loyalty to their lord: they deserved their mead.'

[31] In CS p. 31, OSPG pp. 71–5, Jackson has argued that this name is to be interpreted as 'Manaw *of the* Gododdin', to distinguish it from the other Manaw (the Isle of Man), and that the name refers specifically to the northern part of the Gododdin kingdom, round Stirling and the north shore of the Forth, clearly marked as *Manau* on IW's map, CA p. xvii. He makes the point that Aneirin always calls the kingdom by its full name, Gododdin. The combination *Manaw Gododdin* (in O.W. *Manau Guotodin*) occurs nowhere else but in the one instance in HB chapter 63.

eighth or ninth centuries by a comparison with the forms and orthography of Old Welsh glosses found in Latin manuscripts of those centuries.[32] In early Welsh manuscripts too, references occur to bardic contests where the prize went to the one who could recite more than his fellows of what was even then called the Old Poetry (*Hengerdd*). Marks (!) were given for every stanza of the Gododdin,[33] as one would expect. A significant rubric in the *Book of Aneirin* must be quoted here: 'No bard should go to a contest without this song any more than a warrior should go to battle without weapons.'[34] But where did the competitor learn to say his piece? Did he learn it from his own bardic teacher? Or by poring over an ancient vellum manuscript, dim with age, and much handling by generations of pupils? Or by frequent listening to bards competing in earlier contests? Or by all three methods? One can well believe that in the course of more than six centuries of such oral transmission, the text may have changed considerably. Old Welsh forms would be gradually modernised, and obsolete words replaced by later terms, sometimes to the detriment of metre and consonance. A study of the variant versions of Gododdin stanzas provides plenty of instances of such changes. The written text too would suffer at the hands of blundering copyists. Scribes sometimes misread the original: sometimes they incorporated in the text comments from the margin, or poems by other authors added on blank pages in the old manuscripts they were copying. The prolific family of scribal errors in all its branches has many representatives in the pages of the *Book of Aneirin*.[35]

This brings me to stanza lxxix, on page 20 of the manuscript with a variant on page 23 in another hand.[36] The first version (*A*) runs as follows:

Gweleis y dull o benn tir adoyn.
Aberth am goelkerth a disgynnyn.
gweleis oed kenevin ar dref redegein.
a gwyr nwythyon ry gollessyn.
gweleis gwyr dullyawr gan awr adevyn
aphenn dyvynwal a breych brein ae cnoyn.

[32] See chapter IV, p. 46 and n. [15].
[33] See chapter V, p. 60 and cf. notes [40], [41].
[34] Cf. chapter V, p. 60 and n. [39] on this passage in the *Book of Aneirin*
[35] See chapter V, pp. 60, 62 above, and n. [51].
[36] On the two hands in the *Book of Aneirin* who wrote the *A* and *B* texts, see chapter IV, p. 46 above; CA p. xiii; OSPG pp. 41 ff.

And this is the *B* version:

> Gueleys y dull o bentir a doyn
> a berthach coel kerth a emdygyn.
> Gueleys y deu oc eu tre re ry gwẏdyn.
> o eir nwython ry godessyn.
> Gueleys y wyr tylluavr gan wavr a doyn
> a phē̄n dyuynwal vrych brein ae knoyn.[37]

I wish we had many more to help us to discover what the original text was like, for though this six-line stanza is an obvious intruder in the Gododdin, it has a special interest of its own for us tonight: in my opinion it is a fragment of a poem by a Strathclyde or Cumberland poet in A.D. 642. In metre and diction it resembles the Gododdin songs; that is why a scribe incorporated it in the Gododdin, rejoicing much, we may be sure, that he had discovered a stray sheep from that fold. He failed to see that the subject matter had no connexion at all with the theme of the Gododdin, the battle for Catraeth, but with another battle, a generation later. In the year 642 (641, in the Annals of Ulster) Domnall Brecc, king of Dalriada in the Argyll region of Scotland, was killed in the battle of Srath Caruin (probably the valley of the Carron in Stirlingshire) by Hoan, king of the Britons of Strathclyde.[38] *Domnall* equates with *Dyfnwal* in Welsh: and *brecc* is the cognate of our *brych* 'freckled'. The stanza can be read as three couplets, each beginning with *Gweleis* 'I saw'. The first line is easy, 'I saw a host coming from *penn tir*' or 'from Pentir'. *Penn* 'head' is *cenn* in Old Irish; *tir* 'land', is common to both Welsh and Irish. As a compound, *pentir* means 'headland, promontory'; here it may well be the promontory known as *Kintyre, Cantyre*, in Domnall Brecc's territory. Omitting the second couplet for a moment, and combining the readings of *A* and

[37] CA stanzas lxxix A and B. This interpolated fragment from a poem which refers to the death of Dyfnwal Vrych, king of Scottish Dal Riada, is discussed by Jackson, OSPG pp. 47–8, 98. It evidently belongs to a bardic panegyric on Owain fab Beli, king of Strathclyde (listed in *Harl. Gen.* x as *Eugein map Beli*). The undoubted interest and significance of this stanza is that it provides evidence for the continuation of poetry composed in the style of the Gododdin poem in still-independent Strathclyde not long after the fall of the Gododdin kingdom itself.

[38] Domnall Brecc was killed by Owain fab Beli (= *Hoan*) king of the Britons of Strathclyde at the Battle of Strathcarron, near Falkirk in Stirlingshire, in the year 642 or 643. 'Domnall Brecc was apparently attempting to hold southern Manaw (which his grandfather may have subjugated) not against the Northumbians, but against the Britons', A. O. and M. O. Anderson, *Adomnan's Life of Columba* (Edinburgh, 1961), p. 49.

*B*, I read: 'I saw mighty warriors (*B*; arrayed for battle, *A*) coming with the dawn (*B*; with a battle cry, *A*) and the head of Dyfnwal Vrych, the ravens devoured (*B*; the head and arm of Dyfnwal, *A*).' The *A* scribe had never heard of Dyfnwal the Freckled, *brych*; so he changed the adjective to the noun *breich* 'arm': *B* preserves the original reading without a doubt. The reference to the victory over Domnall Brecc in 642 is clear, and the *Gweleis* 'I saw' thrice repeated, suggests a Strathclyde warrior-bard as the author, one who saw[39] with his own eyes the victory of the Britons of the North. This is just a scrap of his song of triumph, a poor copy, alas, even of that. But what we have shows that the poets of Strathclyde in the West and those of the Gododdin in the East made use of the same poetic forms and conventions.

I have already had cause to mention the tenth-century collection of early pedigrees tacked on to the *Annales Cambriae* in Harley MS 3859. Professor Loth has shown that Pedigree V[40] is a Strathclyde royal pedigree, and that the *Eugein* (Old Welsh for later *Ewein*, *Owain*, now *Owen*) son of *Beli* son of Neithon in it must be the *Hoan* of the Irish annals. This Owen was the grandson of *Neithon*: version *A*, line 4, has *a gwyr nwythyon* 'and the men of Nwythion'; *B*, *o eir nwython* 'by the word of Nwython'. If we amend to *ac ŵyr Neithon* 'and the *grandson* of N.' *ry godessyn* will give a good sense as the past tense third plural of *coddi* 'to offend, to anger',[41] and the whole line will run 'with the

[39] The formula *gweleis i* 'I saw' occurs with significant frequency in early Welsh poetry; see Idris Foster 'Rhai Sylwadau ar yr Hengerdd', *Ysgrifau Beirniadol* V, ed. J. E. Caerwyn Williams (Denbigh, 1970), pp. 21–3. Professor Foster cites a number of instances from the oldest poetry, and also from the twelfth- and thirteenth-century Court poets. He compares the recurrent formulas *atchíu* and *atcondarc* 'I see' and 'I have seen' in early Irish sources, where these frequently introduce prophetic statements attributed to characters in the tales. He compares Proinsias mac Cana's remark (*Celtica* VII, 81) that 'the verbal form *atchíu* in particular is redolent of prophecy and may well have been the first word spoken by the seer in his divinatory trance'. Whatever the original mantic function of these and other comparable formulas (*co cloth ní* is here compared with Welsh *kigleu*, as in PT I, 24), they developed similarly in both languages as recurrent devices in the poetic diction of the bards.

[40] For *Harl. Gen.* V see EWGT p. 10, and n. p. 126. This pedigree does not occur in any other source. It lists the kings of Strathclyde down to the ninth century. 'The pedigree of the royal family of Strathclyde, which is much longer than all the others, is almost certainly a genuine family tradition from the start, handed on by the royal bards; it can be checked at various points from reliable historical sources', K. Jackson, *Antiquity* XXIX, 79; ibid. 'Angles and Britons in Northumbria and Cumbria', *O'Donnell Lectures* (Cardiff, 1963), p. 62.

[41] IW emphasises that this interpretation is purely conjectural. Owing to the normal ambiguity of the value of medial -*d*- in Ml. Welsh manuscripts, *ry godessyn* can

grandson of N. they were wroth'. I suggest this rendering, as a possibility only. When one has to deal with a text where an adjective is twisted into an arm[42] there is always a temptation to emend and amend very freely indeed! Pedigree XVI begins with the name Run map *neithon*.[43] Geoffrey of Monmouth mentions a Rhun son of *Nwython*.[44] There is however a son of *Nwython* in another stanza of the Gododdin,[45] so it is somewhat risky to assume the identity of *Nwython* and *Neithon* everywhere. Let us flee from temptation.

Why was this Cumbrian pedigree included in the Harley MS. collection? Probably to amplify and explain certain entries in the preceding *Annales*,[46] where we find under the year 722, *Beli filius elfin moritur*: and under 760, *Dumnagual filii teudubr moritur*. No further details are given under these years to show who these notables were when they were alive. Pedigree V gives both in their proper setting, and sequence: it starts with Run map Arthgal (killed in 872),[47] and then follow these names, Dumnagual m. Riderch m. Eugein m. *Dumnagual* m. *Teudebur* m. *Beli* m. *Elfin* m. *Eugein* m. *Beli* m. *Neithon* and so on to *Ceritic guletic* and beyond.

To return to Nennius. Besides Aneirin, he also mentioned Taliesin, as one of the sixth-century Welsh bards. In Chapter 63,[48] he states that four kings fought against Hussa son of Ida, namely Urbgen, Riderch Hen, Guallauc and Morcant. Urbgen and his sons also

equally well represent the 3rd pl. pluperfect of either of two verbs—*coddi* 'to offend, anger, rebuke' or *codi* 'to arise'. Jackson prefers the second (OSPG pp. 98–9), and suggests that the line should read *a gwyr wyr Nwyth(y)on ry godessyn* 'and the men of the grandson of Nwython had arisen'—giving a line of the normal length of nine syllables.

[42] I.e. following the evident corruption of the B text (above), *dyvynwal a breych* (*braich* 'arm').

[43] EWGT p. 11.

[44] *Historia Regum Britanniae* IX, 12 (trans. Lewis Thorpe, *Penguin Classics* 227, *Run map Neton*), BD p. 158 *Run uab Noython*, RBB p. 200, *Run uab Nwython*. It may be pointed out that Geoffrey of Monmouth's source for this and many of the other names in this passage was a document giving a text closely resembling the genealogies in Harl. MS. 3859—if it was not this very manuscript. See article by Stuart Piggott, *Antiquity* XV (1941),

[45] CA line 1207. [269.

[46] I.e. the oldest text of AC, contained in the same manuscript, Harl. 3859. See n. 9 above.

47 J. Loth, 'Une Généalogie des Rois de Stratclut' (RC XLVII, 177) refers to the assassination of Arthgal in 872, according to the Annals of Ulster. [Rhun married the daughter of Kenneth mac Alpine of the Scots, and their son Eochaidh (who ruled 878–89) is the last member of this dynasty whose descent can be traced (see K. Jackson, 'The Britons in Southern Scotland', *Antiquity* XXIX, 85).]

[48] On this passage in HB, and on the chronology of the Northumbrian kings here referred to, see chapter V, p. 52 above, and n. [10].

fought valiantly against Deodric or Theoderic, son of Ida. Lloyd gives these dates for Theoderic, 572–9, and 585–92 for Hussa. In the Welsh manuscript called the *Book of Taliesin* (written *circa* 1275), amongst later material, a dozen early poems have been preserved, mainly songs in praise of Urien (the later form of *Urbgen* in Welsh) and his son, Owain; also of Gwallawg. The latter is placed by Taliesin in Elfed,[49] the district near Leeds where the name lives on in its early form *Elmet.*[50] Urien was lord of Catraeth (Richmond–Catterick) and other regions as well, the most important being Rheged. That is why he is called Urien Rheged in our old sagas.

The location of this Rheged has long been the subject of discussion and debate. Possibly the name survives in *Dún Raggit* in Galloway (cf. the *Dún Reichet* of the Calendar of Oengus).[51] Chadwick[52] sees it too in the *Roch* of Rochdale, the *Recedham* of Domesday Book. Ekwall,[53] however, hesitates between Old English *reced* 'hall, house', and a British compound of *rac* 'in front of' and *coet* 'wood': he gives *Rached* as the original form of the river-name: with *Rached-dale* developing into Rochdale. My criticism of this is that Rochdale is too far from the sea: in the *Book of Taliesin*[54] occurs the phrase *tra merin reget* 'beyond the sea of Rheged' which should be compared with *tra merin Iodeo* in the Gododdin.[55] Iodeo is the British name of Inchkeith in the Firth of Forth,[56] and hence I am emboldened to offer you that *Merin*

[49] PT XII (BT 63) is an elegy to Gwallawg. Line 21 reads *a eninat* (= *a enwat?*) *yn ygnat ac* (*ar?*) *eluet?* 'who was named a judge over Elmet'. Other interpretations are possible for the first word (see n.), but the reading of *ygnat* and of *eluet* is perfectly clear. *Ygnad* (*ynad*) can have the meaning of 'elder, magistrate' as well as of 'judge'. IW interprets this reference as meaning that Gwallawg held authority in Elmet—an interpretation which would gain some confirmation if the *Ceredig ap Gwallawg* named in Triad 41 (see TYP 308) could be certainly identified with the ruler Certic expelled from Elmet by Edwin—but since Ceredig is not an uncommon name, this can only remain conjectural. In accepting the association of Gwallawg with Elmet, I. Ll. Foster (PEW p. 228) compares with the title *ygnat* the *magistratus* of the Penmachno inscription (see chapter I, p. 13 above). Cf. TYP p. 375, and for a different view, Jackson in OSPG p. 24 n. 3; CS p. 31 n.

[50] I.e. in the Yorkshire place-names Shirburn-in-Elmet and Barwick-in-Elmet; Bede's *silva Elmete* (HE II, 14). See A. H. Smith, *The Place-Names of the West Riding of Yorkshire*, IV (*English Place-Name Society*, XXXIII; Cambridge, 1961), 1–3.

[51] *Félire Oengusso Céli Dé*, ed. W. Stokes (*Henry Bradshaw Society*, London, 1905), p. 246, line 14. Cf. PT p. xl; W. J. Watson, *The Celtic Place-Names of Scotland* (Edinburgh, 1926), p. 156.

[52] ES p. 144.

[53] *Dictionary of English Place-Names* (London, 1947), p. 371; (2nd edn 1960, p. 371).

[54] BT p. 78, line 15.

[55] CA line 1209.

[56] There can be no doubt that *merin Iodeo* refers to the Firth of Forth. In PT p. xli, IW renews his identification of the fortress of Iodeo with the island of Inchkeith in the

can mean 'arm of the sea, firth', and that *Merin Rheged* is the British name of the Solway Firth. The district *Rheged* must therefore, if I am correct, be sought for near the Solway Firth.[57]

In the twelfth century a Welsh prince, Hywel ab Owain Gwynedd, who was also an accomplished poet, was exiled, and rode northwards: who or what drove him from his native land we are not told, but in the best known of all his songs he complains of the long journey to Carlisle, which he calls *Caer Lliwelydd*. 'Lord of Heaven and Earth', he sang, 'how far from Ceri is Caer Lliwelydd? I rode my yellow charger day and night all the way from Maelienydd to the *land of Rheged*'. This shows that to Welshmen of the twelfth century Rheged was a district near Carlisle.[58]

Forth (cf. *urbs iudeu* HB p. 64; *urbs Giudi* HE I, 12). A more recent opinion identifies *Iudeu, Iodeo* with Stirling. This view was first put forward by Angus Graham, *Antiquity* XXXIII (1959), 63 ff., and it has since received strong support from K. Jackson, CS pp. 36–8; OSPG pp. 6, 72 n. As Jackson points out in CS, the difficulty about the identification with Inchkeith is that there is no trace there of the remains of any early fortified stronghold; whereas 'in the Middle Ages Stirling was a fortified hill-top town of the greatest strategic importance', and it is reasonable to suppose that the medieval castle was built upon the site of an earlier fortification (*urbs*) which was obliterated by it, as is believed to have happened in the comparable instance of Edinburgh Castle. (The editor recalls a broadcast talk in which IW described how he walked down Princes Street, and looked up at the Castle, believing it to be the site of Mynyddawg's fortress.)

[57] In PT pp. xxxviii ff. IW enlarges further on his belief that the heart of the kingdom of Rheged lay around the Solway estuary, and the valley of the river Eden in Cumberland and Westmorland. (If this were so, it would be reasonable to conjecture that Urien's capital could have been at Carlisle.) This view gained additional support from his detection of a reference to the river Eden in the textually corrupt line PT II, 21, where he interpreted the words *kywym don* as representing *rywin Idon* 'the excessive wine of the Idon' (Ptolemy's *Itouna* gives the river-name in its archaic form which developed regularly in Welsh as *Idon*); see n. Another clue which points in the same direction was his identification of Taliesin's *Llwyfenydd* with the river *Lyvennet* which flows into the Eden, PT p. xlv. This view as to the locality of Rheged seems now to be generally accepted—though the actual boundaries of Urien's kingdom must remain extremely uncertain. See K. Jackson, *Antiquity* XXIX, 82; TYP p. 518, and the Ordnance Survey *Map of Britain in the Dark Ages*. Earlier opinions as to the locality of Rheged are summarised by Morris-Jones, *Tal.* 64–5 (quoted PT pp. xxxviii–xxxix). The internal evidence of the Taliesin poems—where Urien is called 'ruler of Catraeth'—imply that his authority in some form must have extended as far afield as to include Catterick, though IW doubts (*loc. cit.*) that this outlying area could properly have been included within the bounds of Rheged. To the north-west, however, Rheged could well have reached as far north as to include Dunragit near Stranraer in Galloway, as is indicated here. See also n. [59] below.

[58] For the poem, see H p. 316; and translation by J. Lloyd-Jones, 'The Court Poets of the Welsh Princes', PBA (1948), pp. 22–3; A. Conran, *The Penguin Book of Welsh Verse*, pp. 108–9. The lines here referred to are quoted PT p. xxxix. The geographical implications of the passage were first shown by J. Morris-Jones, *Tal.* pp. 66–7; 'Ceri' is a commote situated in Maelienydd (Radnorshire), just as 'Caer

To me, the name recalls tribal names ending in *-et* (later *-ed*) like *Dyfed* in South Wales from *Demetae*: the stem is *rheg*, a word of frequent occurrence in our old poetry as you would expect, for it means 'a gift'. Rheged as a tribal name could be explained as the 'Givers of gifts', the generous ones.[59] In literary Welsh we use the compound *anrheg* for a gift or present, never the simple noun *rheg*. The reason, I take it, is that *rheg* in Modern Welsh means 'curse', and *rhegi* is the usual term for swearing. How has this come about? My guess is that the intermediate stage was the use of *rhegi* in the sense of consigning the offender to the devil, in St Paul's words in First Corinthians, *delivering* him unto Satan! Making a present of him to the Evil One!

One of Urien's allies was Rhydderch Hen,[60] or 'the Old', the Rhydderch ap Tudwal who ruled at Alclud, Dumbarton, a friend of the Irish saint Columba. Of him I must beg your leave to quote Sir John Lloyd's exact words: 'He had many enemies of whom he stood in daily fear, and in his anxiety sent a private message to the prophet of Iona to know whether he was destined to fall by their hands. Columba's answer was that he would escape all their wiles, and die in his own house, *reposing on his couch of feathers*, a prophecy which, according to Adamman, was literally fulfilled.'[61] This Rhydderch is called Rhydderch *Hael* in Welsh legend, or 'the Generous'.[62] Perhaps he cheered up after hearing the good news from the Saint—and kept away from that feather-bed as long as he could.

I put the Battle of Catraeth about A.D. 600. Sometime round 615 Ethelfrith of Northumbria attacked and defeated the Britons at Chester.[63] This fight was preceded by the massacre of the 2,000 British

Lliwelydd' (Carlisle) is in Rheged; and by riding both night and day, the poet made a swift journey from the one to the other.

[59] In a review of B. G. Charles, *Old Norse Relations with Wales* (Cardiff, 1934), published in *Arch. Cam.* LXXXIX, 348–50, IW convincingly disposes of the case for the localization of Rheged in south Wales, a location which was originally proposed by Iolo Morganwg, and was subsequently perpetuated by Peredur Jones, *Cy.* XXXV, 117–56. He showed that *Rheged* in certain place-names (notably *Hewl Reged*, Llandeilo, Carms.) is a dialectal metathesis of *rhedeg* 'to run'. This ambiguity may well have led to the original confusion.

[60] TYP pp. 504–5.

[61] HW p. 166; A. O. and M. O. Anderson, *Adomnan's Life of Columba* (Edinburgh, 1961), p. 238.

[62] TYP triads nos. 2, 43, 54.

[63] AC ann. 613 (= 616) *Gueith Cair-legion* (the Battle of Chester). On this battle see HW p. 181, CS pp. 167 ff., and on the Welsh traditions of the battle, TYP pp. 163–5. F. M. Stenton (*Anglo-Saxon England*, Oxford, 1947) points out that there is nothing in Bede's account of the battle (HE II, 2) to suggest that he regarded it as a turning-point in history, and P. Hunter-Blair characterises it as 'no more than a passing raid into Welsh

monks of Bangor-on-Dee. To some historians the defeat at Chester marks the separation of the Cymry of Wales from the Cymry of Cumberland. Others maintain that Ethelfrith's losses were so heavy that he had to retire northwards forthwith.

Then comes Edwin, who conquered the now isolated little British kingdom of *Elmet* round Leeds,[64] advanced south, invaded North Wales, and over-ran Anglesey, where he had once found refuge as an exile.[65] According to the Welsh Triads he was one of the three oppressors of Anglesey, who were nurtured within the island itself.[66]

It was now the turn of the Welsh to produce a great warrior in Cadwallon, king of Gwynedd (mainly Anglesey and Caernarvonshire). He was a descendant of Cunedda, the deliverer of Wales from the Irish invaders, and in his thirst for vengeance on Edwin he planned and attempted what may be called the march of Cunedda in reverse, nothing less than that the men of North Wales should advance northwards, and repay the kinsmen of Cunedda by driving out their enemies, the Northumbrians, from all the lands between the Humber and Edinburgh. It was a scheme on the grand scale! So in 632 he set out north, secured the help of a Mercian noble, Penda, engaged the army of Edwin and conquered it, killing Edwin and his son in the battle.[67] He then in Stenton's words 'set himself to a deliberate devastation of all Northumbria'.[68] A king of Deira and his army were destroyed. The ruler of Bernicia, a son of Ethelfrith, was put to death when he came to beg for peace, and Cadwallon had for a year or more his full revenge on Northumbria.[69] In the last weeks of 633, according to Stenton, or in 634 according to Lloyd, Oswald, another son of Ethelfrith, after a night march, attacked Cadwallon's camp near Hexham with a small army. Cadwallon was slain, and his host scattered. I now quote Stenton once more, 'Cadwallon was the only British king of historic times who overthrew an English dynasty, and the British peoples never found an equal leader.'[70]

In a fragment of an early Welsh poem, preserved only in a late

territory' (*Anglo-Saxon England*, Cambridge, 1956, p. 36); similarly Idris Foster, PEW p. 222.

[64] See p. 82 and n. 50 above.

[65] On Edwin in early Welsh tradition see HW pp. 182–3; TYP pp. 294, 339.

[66] TYP no. 26. The other two Great Oppressions (*prif ormes*) were an unknown 'Daronwy', and Palug's Cat.

[67] For the Welsh sources relating to Cadwallon see TYP pp. 293–6.

[68] *Op. cit.* p. 80.

[69] HE III, 1.

[70] *Op. cit.* p. 81.

copy,[71] Cadwallon's prowess is praised in more extravagant terms. From what I can understand of this difficult text, the poet is celebrating the expulsion of the Northumbrians from North Wales, which must have preceded the counter-attack on the North. 'The foreigners have fled over the salt sea', he sings, referring probably to the Northumbrians driven out of Anglesey, 'and a multitude of them slain. The honour of the Cymry has been redeemed. Cadwallon's deeds will be remembered so long as heaven remains above the earth. Is there anything higher than thee', he asked his lord, 'except the sky and the stars?' I wonder how he improved on that one when news came later of the resounding victories in the North.

Throughout this poem, the Welsh are called *Cymry*—this is the earliest example known to me.[72] Aneirin and the Taliesin of the historical poems used *Brython*.

Now for a change we will leave the warriors and turn to the saints. A few minutes earlier I mentioned Rhydderch Hen of Dumbarton, Urien's ally against the sons of Ida in the second half of the sixth century. He was the victor in a famous battle at *Arfderydd* (Arthuret, eight miles north of Carlisle) in the year 573.[73] His opponent was Gwenddoleu son of Ceidio,[74] whose name lives on in *Carwinley* (earlier *Karwindelhow*, *Carwanolow*) though Ekwall makes a hybrid of it. In early Welsh it would have been *Cair Gwendolow*.[75]

Rhydderch invited St Kentigern to settle in his Stratchlyde kingdom.

[71] *Moliant Cadwallon* was edited by IW in B VII, 23 ff., from two eighteenth-century copies, Panton MS. 55, and BM Add. MS. 14867. He drew attention to this important poem for the first time, and showed that its manuscript tradition can be traced back at least to the twelfth century. The corrupt state in which the text has been transmitted make the poem difficult to interpret and impossible to translate, but according to IW's belief it may be a contemporary eulogy to Cadwallon composed by one of the Cynfeirdd (? his bard Afan Ferddig). 'If it is genuine it was composed before Cadwallon was killed in 634, since it is evident that it is a living king to whom the poet is singing' are his words. On the poem see Idris Foster, PEW pp. 230–1; and TYP p. 294. See further B XXIII, 309 ff.

[72] On the origin of the name *Cymry* and the early instances of its occurrence see n. 4 above.

[73] TYP pp. 208–10, 379, and refs. there cited.

[74] W. F. Skene first identified the site of this battle with Arthuret, a mile south of Longtown in Cumberland, near which the Carwinelow burn falls into the river Esk. See his important article in *Proceedings of the Society of Antiquities of Scotland* VI (1864), 91 ff., which records local traditions about the battle which were still in existence at that date.

[75] H. M. Chadwick pointed out (ES p. 143) that the old Roman fortress of *Castra Exploratorum*, situated near by at Netherby, would be a likely site for Gwenddoleu's stronghold.

This saint is our *Cyndeyrn*,[76] and is said to have been the son of Owain ab Urien. He may have been. I want him tonight, however, as a contact with Wales. He certainly travelled south and founded a monastery on the bank of the River Elwy where his fame attracted 965 disciples—so it is said.[77] Rhydderch recalled him to the North and Cyndeyrn established another monastery at Glasgow close to Dumbarton, Rhydderch's fortress. He left his favourite disciple, Asaph, in charge of the Llan on the Elwy, hence our *Llanelwy*, in English St Asaph.[78]

His 'pet name' according to Jocelyn was *Munghu* (later *Mungo*) 'carissimus amicus'.[79] One could compare the Welsh *mwyngu* (*mwyn* 'gentle, kind', *cu* 'beloved, dear'). His mother, Tenyw, daughter of a king of *Lleuddin*, the Lothian district,[80] became Saint *Tenoc* (cf. Aed(d)an's pet-name, *Maedoc*)[81] and is still remembered in Glasgow at St. *Enoch's*, the initial *t-* in her name having merged with the final *-t* in *Saint*!

Cyndeyrn was not the only saint with northern connexions who spent some time in Wales, or settled in Wales. Doged, Lleuddad, Eleri, Baglan, Dunawd, Pabo[82] and others could be mentioned. Our patron saint himself, St David, was a descendant of Cunedda, a grandson or great-grandson[83]—his pedigree varies in length in different manuscripts.

[76] TYP pp. 319–21. The statement that Owain ab Urien was the father of St Kentigern (Welsh *Cyndeyrn Garthwys*) is recorded in the genealogies of the saints, which date from the thirteenth century in manuscript, but incorporate much older traditions. *Bonedd y Saint* gives the saint's genealogy as follows: *Kyndeyrn garthwys mab Ewein mab Vryen a Denw verch Lewdwn luydawc o Dinas Eidyn yn y Gogled y vam* 'Cyndeyrn Garthwys son of Owain ab Urien, and his mother (was) Denw daughter of Llewdwn Luyddog from the city of Edinburgh in the North'. Textual variants of this genealogy are listed in full, EWGT p. 56 (no. 14). But the nature of the document is such that, while it may preserve some genuine genealogical material, little credit should on the whole be placed upon the more illustrious descents claimed for the saints.

[77] In the twelfth-century *Life of St. Kentigern* by Jocelyn of Furness (ed. A. P. Forbes, *Lives of St. Ninian and St. Kentigern*, Edinburgh, 1874).

[78] On the saint's alleged association with St Asaph's see K. Jackson, 'The Sources for the Life of St Kentingern', SEBC pp. 315–18, 339, and S. M. Harris, *Journal of the Historical Society of the Church in Wales* VI, 5 ff., both of whom argue that the story is a twelfth-century fabrication.

[79] Forbes, *op. cit.* chapter IV, p. 169.

[80] See n. 76 above.

[81] *Maedoc* < *Mo-aid-oc* is listed as an Irish hypocoristic form of the name of St Aidan of Ferns by Baring-Gould and Fisher, *Lives of the Cambro-British Saints* (London, 1907), I, 116.

[82] The 'genealogies' of all these saints are recorded in *Bonedd y Saint*; see index to EWGT.

[83] According to *Bonedd y Saint*: *Dewi mab Sant mab Kedic mab Keredic mab Cuneda Wledic* (EWGT p. 54; for other refs. see index).

The road to Wales, however, was not a one-way street—the saints have always found it difficult to walk in the same direction—and Welsh saints occasionally travelled northwards. The most famous was Cadog[84] from South Wales: Cambuslang near Glasgow is dedicated to him.

I have no doubt about the worthiness and holiness of these early saints. They spoke the truth and preached the truth. But I find it hard to believe this of their biographers! They give us fairy tales far too often instead of sober fact. They crib from one another shamelessly and wholesale in their eagerness to enhance their own patron's glory above all and sundry. How one would appreciate a simple unadorned unrhetorical account of these men, and their heroic labours and suffering! That would surely be glory enough. The truth and nothing more. As it is we are left in almost complete ignorance about them.

In the past, contacts between Wales and the North were made and maintained by warriors and saints. In our day both classes have been merged into one, the antiquarians of Cumbria and Cambria, men and women eager to discover the truth about the lives of our common ancestors, searching for it in the débris of the wars of long ago, ruins of old forts and castles, walls and ditches, churches and monasteries, inscriptions and tattered vellum manuscripts. It is no wonder then that such a discipline has made it possible for you to listen with saintly patience and heroic endurance to these rough notes of mine.

[84] The life of this sixth-century saint, by Lifris of Llancarfan, was composed in the late eleventh century. Ed. and trans. by A. W. Wade-Evans, *Vitae Sanctorum Britanniae et Genealogie* (Cardiff, 1944). See also SEBC p. 235 and *passim*; H. D. Emmanuel, *National Library of Wales Journal* VII (1951–2), 217–27.

II The Three *Juvencus* englynion
(By courtesy of Cambridge University Library)

## *Chapter VII*

# THE JUVENCUS POEMS

An old manuscript preserved in the Cambridge University Library (Ff.4.42) contains a Latin paraphrase of the Gospels by Juvencus, on which there are a number of Old Welsh glosses.[1] In addition to the glosses, this manuscript contains twelve englynion. According to Whitley Stokes (see below), the Juvencus manuscript itself dates from the eighth or ninth century, and W. M. Lindsay[2] cites the concurrence in this dating of the famous Cambridge librarian, Henry Bradshaw.[3] The edges of pp. 48, 49, 50 were cut away by some vandal of a binder, but mercifully the strips which were cut off have been safely preserved.[4] Three of the englynion are to be found on these strips: according to the authorities these too were written down early in the ninth century. The other nine englynion are inscribed on the first page, and these have been dated as belonging to the tenth century.

The Three englynion were first printed by Edward Lhwyd in his *Archaeologia Britannica* (Oxford, 1707), p. 221; Sir John Rhŷs gave his opinion about them in his volume on the origin of the englyn metre, *Cy.* XVIII, 103 ff.; Whitley Stokes discussed all twelve englynion in the *Transactions of the Philological Society* for 1860–1, pp. 205, 229–32, 288; and in Kuhn's *Beiträge zur vergleichenden Sprachforschung* IV (1865), 385–423; VII (1873), 410–15; see also W. F. Skene, FAB I, 218–21; II, 1–2, 311–14. By the kindness of the University librarian, I received every facility to study the Juvencus manuscript on the occasion of two visits which I made to Cambridge. I am deeply indebted also to my friend Mr Ifor Evans, Fellow of St John's College, for a fine photograph of these englynion, which magnifies them splendidly with regard to size—though unfortunately he was not able at the same time to double them in number.

I shall first discuss the Three, and then the Nine.

[1] Ed. Whitley Stokes, *Trans. Philological Soc.* (1860–1), pp. 204 ff., 288 ff.; Kühn's *Beiträge* IV, 385 ff., VII, 411 ff. Certain of the glosses are discussed by IW in B VI, 115–18. See also LHEB pp. 49–52. The Juvencus manuscript was bequeathed to the Library in 1648.

[2] EWS p. 16. On the two poems, see now LEWP p. 28, LHEB pp. 52–3.

[3] H. Bradshaw, *Collected Papers* (Cambridge, 1889), p. 284. For the variant opinions which have been expressed as to the date of the Nine, see below, p. 100 and n.

[4] Since IW wrote this, the strips have been restored to their original places on the upper margin of the manuscript.

## I. THE THREE

On the margin of the strip containing the first englyn, *Hen Vrythonaeg* ('Old British')[5] has been written in the hand of Edward Lhwyd, and the verses have been numbered by him—1, 2 and 3. Each englyn is written in a single continuous line across the strip, but I have divided them up, and print them below in the usual form of a three-line englyn.

1. niguorcosam nemheunaur   henoid
   mitelu nit gurmaur
   mi am [*franc*] dam ancalaur.

2. nicanãniguardam nicusam   henoid
   cet iben med nouel
   mi amfranc dam anpatel.

3. namercit mi nep leguenid   henoid
   is discirr micoueidid
   dou nam riceus unguetid.

1. I shall not talk even for one hour tonight,
   My retinue is not very large,
   I and my Frank, round our cauldron.

2. I shall not sing, I shall not laugh, I shall not jest tonight
   Though we drank clear mead,
   I and my Frank, round our bowl.

3. Let no one ask me for merriment tonight,
   Mean is my company,
   Two lords can talk: one speaks.[6]

### *Palaeographical notes*

The script is remarkably clear, so there is no reason to doubt the reading, except in the case of one or two letters, as follows:

[5] Edward Lhwyd gave it as his opinion that the englynion are written in the language of the 'old Britons of the North of this Island', and he added that if this was in fact the language of the Picts, then the englynion prove that the Picts must have been Britons. He described the orthography of the englynion as the oldest he had yet seen in the British language.

[6] LEWP p. 29. (This is the final translation which IW made of the Three englynion. I give it here, in preference to the translation originally offered in B VI, 110, as an accompaniment to his discussion of the text. Minor differences between the two are commented upon in the following notes.)

1 a. **nemheunaur** According to Rhŷs, 'The...manuscript should be carefully examined again to see whether the reading it suggests be not actually *nemhénuaur*'. But the distinction in form between the letters *u* and *n* in the manuscript makes it quite impossible to make a mistake, and there can be no reason for any doubt as to the reading given above.

1 c. **am [franc]**. The word *franc* has not actually been preserved in this line. After *am* there follow two dots (:), a sign that a word has been omitted, and supplied afterwards above the line; but since the edge of the page has been cut off, it is impossible to read any of this word, except for the lower part of the letters *fra*. At least, I was not able to do so. Lhwyd read *franc* two hundred years ago, and his reading is confirmed by the corresponding reading of 2 c.

2 a. **cana.** This is the only word whose correct form presents any difficulty. Llwyd read *canil*: at first sight the word looks very like *canil* with a small *l*, as in 1 b, *mitelu*. But on a closer inspection one sees that although *i* occurs 23 times in the three englynion, there is no instance of an *i* similar to the one which is supposed to be here. Nor is it possible to read it as *u*, for in each of the 16 examples found in the poem of the letter *u*, the final stroke is continued straight down, without any hook at the base. It would be much easier to read *canil* than *canu* (with Stokes). After close examination and much hesitation, however, I believe the letter to be an *a* with an open top. That is not the scribe's normal manner of writing *a*, though he does have other examples of it in the poem, for instance the two *a*'s in *calaur* in 1 c, and the first *a* in *anpatel*, 2 c. But the best example is the *a* in *franc* in the same line, where the two strokes proceed straight downwards to the hook at the base, with the second one raised a little higher than the first, just as it is in *cana*. In addition, it looks as if a stroke has been written above the *a*, and a slight inclined stroke is attached to the second stroke of the *a*, exactly as in the plate (no. VII) reproduced from the same Juvencus MS. in Lindsay's *Early Welsh Script*, where *mediã* stands for *mediam* in line 8 from the bottom. If *canã* is the word here, the remainder of the contracted stroke for *m* was lost when the page was cut, as we have seen to have been the case with the word *franc* in 1 c. One must note, however, that the form of the first stroke of the *a* is not a usual one, since it is hooked at the top. It looks as though the scribe had written *nicam* as a mistake for *nicanam*; then he corrected his error by placing a hook at the base of the last stroke of the *m*, and by adding the second half of the open-topped *a*. Then he placed the contraction for *m* above the line. The first binder cut away the rest of this sign, while it remained for the second binder to cut away the whole englyn.

3 a. **namercit.** The reading *namereit* given by Lhwyd and followed by Stokes is quite impossible; so is Rhŷs's *erchit*. The letter *c* is unmistakable.

3 a. **mi.** Lhwyd reads *un*, Stokes *nii*.

3 b. **discirr.** According to Lhwyd *discinn*; Stokes reads *disenirr*, Skene *discyrr*, Rhŷs *discirr*. The cause of the trouble is that the second *i* in *discirr* is prolonged below the line in a wavy, trembling stroke, on which Skene comments, 'The letter

represented by the *y* in *discyrr* is a peculiar letter, which may represent one of the Saxon forms for *y*, or the Irish contraction for *ui*, in which case the word will read *discuirr'*. Cf. the *Book of St Chad*, LL p. xlvii, section 6, the two *i*'s in dim*i*n*i*h.

3 c. **riceus.** The tail of the *s* has been cut off, but the reading is not in doubt.

**unguetid.** Lhwyd read *imguetid*, but there is no doubt about the letter *u*.

## *Linguistic notes*

1 a. **niguorcosam nemheunaur.** The meaning is uncertain, except that *guorcosam* is a vb. 1 sing. pres. indic., following the neg. *ni*. Before deciding on the meaning of this verb, any suggestion one might make as to the meaning of *nem-heunaur* could only be uncertain and premature.

**guorcosam.** The preposition is *guor-*, the root is *-cos-*, and the termination *-am* (earlier form of *-af*). *Cos* could be a mutated form of *-caws-*, but it could not be a borrowing from Lat. *causari*; at least, on the analogy of *laudo*, *llawddaf*, one would expect this to give *cawsaf*, not *cosaf*. *Aw* derived from *ō* or *ā* turns into *o* in the penultimate, but *aw* remains when it is derived from the Lat. diphthong *-au-*, without being mutated to *o*. There is a vn. *cosi* 'to scratch, to tickle', as a noun 'itching'; cf. D. *cosi* 'scalpere, fricare, scabere': *cosi* 'pruritus', Cornish *cose* 'to itch'. This is evidently the word that Rhŷs had in mind when he translated 'I fondle no maiden tonight'. Another suggestion is to translate the word as *gorgysgaf*; thus Skene 'I will not sleep', cf. BBC p. 57, line 15, Na *chuste hun* bore (i.e. 'sleep not a morning sleep'), where *cus* = *cws*(*g*). But there is another *cos* which has not yet been considered, the one which appears in *dangos*: according to WG pp. 188, 269, this *cos* comes from the root *kens-* which is found in the Lat. *censeo*; Skr. *śąsati* 'recites, praises, reports, shows'. According to A. Walde and J. Pokorny, *Vergleichende Wörterbuch der indo-germanischen Sprachen* (Berlin; Leipzig, 1930–2) s.v. *censeo*, the Albanian θom 'I say' comes from the same root (**θosmi*, **kēnsmi*; G. Meyer, *Etymologisches Wörterbuch der albanesischen Sprache* (Strasbourg, 1891), p. 91); and he gives the meaning of the Aryan root as 'autoritativ verkunden, feierlich sprechen'. So also Boisacq, *Dictionnaire étymologique de la langue grecque* (s.v. κόσμος) 'annoncer avec autorité, dire de façon solennelle'; H. Hirt, *Indo-germanische Grammatik* (Heidelberg, 1921) II, 73. This recalls the words of the Judge on the Day of Judgement, in the poem, BT p. 12, l. 19:

nys deubi ryrys
*rygosswy rygossys*
Ac awch bi wynnyeith
gwerth awch ynuyt areith.
kayator y dyleith
arnawch y vffern lleith.

I understand *ryrys* as *ryres*: *rygossys* as *rygosses*; and the line *rygosswy rygosses* as 'he will (or "may") pronounce judgement who has pronounced judgement' (for a similar pair cf. Lat. *dicare, dicere*; and the same root in δείκνυμι 'I show'; Lat. *indico, iudex* 'judge'; *digitus* 'finger'). This example from BT (if I understand it correctly) is nearer than any other that I know of to the Lat. *censeo* 'I estimate the value of, I judge', *censor*, 'a rigid judge of morals, etc.'. There is an interesting example in *Mabinogi Pwyll* (PKM p. 18, last line) 'Ef a gyuodes Pwyll...a pheri dodi gostec y erchi y holl eircheit a cherdorion *dangos*.' In my note (p. 139) I failed to understand it, but I suggest now that this example preserves a trace of the original meaning—to ask the minstrels to declare publicly who they were and what it was that they wanted. I think that the same *cos-* is found in BT p. 61, line 2, 'Ardwyre reget ryssed rieu/ neu ti *rygosteis* kyn bwyf teu'. It is not the later word *cost* (corresponding to the English) which is present here, but *cos-* with the *t* which is found in *ffals-t*, etc. (cf. MA p. 287*b*, line 1 *Traffalst cyn amdo gro a graean*). The Sanskrit shows that the original meaning of the word included that of 'to praise'.

One must therefore decide which of the three possible meanings is the most suitable: (i) *cosi* 'to tickle' (? to provoke, to jest); (ii) *cysgu* 'to sleep'; (iii) the *cos-* in *dangos* 'to declare, esteem, to praise'. I incline towards the last, and remembering how *hoffi* can mean 'to praise' and *gorhoffedd* 'a boast', I understand *ni orchosaf* as 'I shall not boast'. One might even understand it more simply, 'I shall not speak'.

[Cf. PT pp. 79–80. In a note in B XI (1941), 82, IW later compared the *cos* in *costawg*, and postulated a vb. *costaw* 'to watch over', in the light of which he suggested that the meanings of both *guorcosam* and *rygosteis* should be reconsidered. 'I do not keep guard (tonight)' would give excellent sense in the englyn, and would be in line with the translation 'thee have I watched over, guarded' which IW here advocates for Taliesin's *rygosteis*.]

**nemheunaur.** According to Rhŷs, 'a regular mutation of *nep menuaur*, and I guess the latter word to be partly of the same origin as *meinir* "a fair maid"'. But the text will not support either this reading or Rhŷs's explanation. Skene gives 'not one hour'. Stokes's version of the whole line is weak, 'No great company will be with me tonight'; *nem, nemh* 'not-me', *unawr* 'will be united', *guorcosam* 'a great company'.

By taking *guorcosam* as meaning 'I sleep', *unawr* 'an hour' follows naturally as the next word, preceded by a negative (cf. Breton *nemet* 'except'). If, on the other hand, *guorcosam* is a transitive verb, one would expect *nemheunaur* to be the noun which is its object, with the pl. termination *-awr* [GMW p. 30, b], but I do not know of any noun which corresponds to *nemheun*. Since the negative *ni* precedes the verb, one could argue that we have here a form corresponding to *nemawr*, cf. WG p. 314, ny weleiste eto *nemawr* o boeneu uffernn 'so far thou hast seen but little of the pains of hell', Ll.A. p. 154; if so, it would represent *neb-mewnawr*. *Meinoeth* is found for 'midnight', and *meidydd, meinydd, meinddydd* for 'mid-day' (cf. WG p. 93), where *mei* stands for *media*. *Mewn* comes from *meddwn*; cf. Ir. *inmedon*, but I do not see the point of *mewn-awr* 'middle hour'. Because of the Irish linguistic influences on the Welsh of the Juvencus, one should bear in mind the

Irish negatives in *neb-*, *neph*, *nem-*, and especially *nemh-*, e.g. *nem-marbda* 'immortal', *nem-duine* 'no one' (cf. Breton *nemo*, *ne-homo*), *neph-ni*, *neimh-ni* 'nothing'. If so, *nemh-ewn* would be possible as the negative of *ewn*, itself a possible variant form of *iawn* (comparing Eutychius *eunt*, gl. on *aequus*, VVB p. 125 [DGVB p. 169]; *Voc. Corn. eun hinsic* 'justus' for a man of upright course, VKG I, 92; Ml. Br. *eeunn*; cf. AL I, 330 *yaunt*; LL p. 229, *iaun*: AL II, 244, y vrawt *yewna*). For the alternation between *iaw*, *iew* cf. Ll. A. p. 58, *diewl* for *diawl* 'devil'; Llan. p. 2, line 344 *dyewl*; Pen. 3. II. 26. If one were to understand *nemh-ewn-awr* as pl. of the negative of *ewn* 'just, right things' it would mean things which are false or unjust, the empty boasting of warriors at their feasts, such as are referred to as having been made at the court of Hu Gadarn in *Pererindod Siarlymaen* (B V, 213, ymadrodyon drythyll kellweirus, val y mae gnawt drwy veddawt 'wanton jocular speeches, as are frequent under intoxication').

These are only groping suggestions, but perhaps they may be helpful to other investigators. To me, it seems that the meaning of the line must be something like 'I do not boast vain things tonight, i.e. I will not make a false boast in public'.

[The rendering given subsequently by IW in LEWP (see above) indicates that he reverted later to his first suggestion as to the meaning of *nemheunaur*, taking it to be a combination of *unawr* with a negative corresponding to the Breton *nemet* and meaning 'even one hour'. See further a note by Brinley Rees, B XX (1962–4), 125.]

Note that there are nine syllables in the line, if one reads *ewn*; there are 11 in 2a, and 10 in 3a.

**henoid** = *henoeth*, MW *heno* 'tonight', WG p. 113 [GMW pp. 4, 221]. It is clear that the use of *heno* in the *gair cyrch* of an englyn, as exemplified here, was a popular device in early poetry in both Ireland and Wales; cf. RBP col. 1040, lines 22, 24 (= CLlH. III, 30a, 31a), [and cf. TYP p. 340]:

Handit euyrdyl aflawen *henoeth*
a lluossyd amgen.
yn aber lleu llad uryen.
Ys trist euyrdyl or drallot *heno*
ac or llam am daerawt
yn aber lleu llad eu brawt.

In these, the scribe of RBH first copied the old form *henoeth* without altering it, but when he came to it in the second englyn, he recognised what the word represented, and altered it to his own contemporary form *heno*. Then, in defiance of the rhyme, he changed *drallawt* to *drallot*. This example clearly illustrates the methods used by scribes in modernising the *hengerdd*.

For further instances of *heno* in early Welsh poetry, cf. CLlH. XI, 18a, Stauell Gyndylan ys tywyll *heno* (repeated in the first line of a chain of englynion); XI, 34–9, Eryr Eli, ban y lef *heno* [= *Penguin Bk. of Welsh Verse*, pp. 90, 92]. In early Irish, the corresponding form *innocht*/*anocht* 'tonight' is similarly used, as in a quatrain in the St Gall *Priscian*, attributed to the ninth century, Is acher in gaith *innocht*, fufuasna fairgge findfolt 'Keen is the wind *tonight*; it tosses the 'white hair of the ocean' (Stokes and Strachan, *Thesaurus Palaeohibernicus* II, 290; R. Thurneysen, *Old Irish Reader*, p. 39). So also in a poem belonging to the story of Suibhne Geilt,

> Muichnidhe mh'aghaidh *anocht*
> gan giolla is gan longphort.
>
> 'Gloomy is my night *tonight*
> Without serving man, without camp.'

(J. G. O'Keefe, *Buile Shuibhne*, ITS XII (1913), 36; ibid. p. 118, Mor múich attú-sa *anocht* 'I am in great grief tonight', p. 124, Eccáointeach atú-sa *anocht* 'Mournful am I tonight'. Cf. B I, 231.) [See also G. Murphy, *Early Irish Lyrics* (Oxford, 1956), p. 138, and—for a further example, this time from the Finn Cycle—p. 152 Forud na Fiann fas *in-nocht* 'Desolate tonight is the Fian's Look-out place.']

These lines are closely similar in their mood to the Juvencus englynion. Is there not here a suggestion that this device came to be the fashion in sad contexts and in laments? By comparing his unhappy 'tonight' with some joyful occasion many years ago, or perhaps even only a month ago, the poet achieved the kind of vivid contrast at which the *Cynfeirdd* aimed continually in their verse.

1b. **mitelu.** 'my retinue'. For the absence of the nasal mutation, see WG p. 172, and cf. its absence also in BT p. 45, line 24 (= PT p. 1, line 18); *Myg kynnelw o gynan*. In old orthography, *e* stood for *ei*, so *telu* here represents *teilu*, which later became *teulu* under the influence of the following *u*. In meaning it is equivalent to *gosgordd* 'retinue, household troops'; cf. Ir. *teglach* [GOI p. 146].

**nit gurmaur.** 'not very large', which means in fact 'very small' (the figure of *meiosis* was popular among the *Cynfeirdd*). *gur* stands for *guor-*, later *gor*.

1c. **franc.** Cf. RBP col. 1048, lines 27–8 (= CLlH XI, 97) Pan wisgei garan-ma(e)l gatpeis Gyndylan/A phyrydyaw y onnen,/Ny chaffei *ffranc* tanc o'e benn, 'When Caranmael put on Cynddylan's coat of mail and shook his ashen spear, no *ffranc* would obtain (a word of) peace from his mouth'. Neither of these allusions could be to a Norman, since in both instances the englynion are too early. The word *ffranc* corresponds to Ml. Lat. *francus* (see Du Cange, s.v. *franci* 'dicit viri potissimum ex nobilitate, ingenui, ipsique proceres'. I conclude that *ffranc* denotes a foreign mercenary soldier (cf. the use of the Irish word *maccoemh* (> Welsh *mackwy*) for a young boy or 'page' serving in a court). Is the pl. of the word *ffranc* preserved in Nant *Ffrancon*?

[Cf. IW *Enwau Lleoedd* (1945), pp. 33–4, where it is pointed out that in foreign borrowed words medial *-nc-* does not turn into *-ngh-*, and it is suggested that the name Nant *Ffrancon* commemorates a settlement of mercenary soldiers belonging to one of the early rulers of Arllechwedd.

For subsequent remarks on the word *ffranc* by IW, see B VII, 366–8, CLlH pp. 237–8, LEWP pp. 30–1, 72–3. In each instance he reaffirms that the word must have been established in Welsh prior to the twelfth century, and compares the similar Irish term *francamais* 'a foreign mercenary soldier' (apparently a compound of synonyms) used in two early sources (RC XIV, 426 = *Book of Leinster* fol. 111a; *Celtic Review* III, 130); see *Contribb.*, Fasc. F, 401. In B XVIII, 58–9, Brinley Rees reviews the evidence with regard to both the Irish and the Welsh words, and queries whether *ffranc*, *francamais* may not more properly be rendered 'freeman' rather than 'mercenary', since this is evidently the meaning of *amuis* in early Irish law, as attested by a passage in *Críth Gablach* (ed. D. A. Binchy, ll. 578–82).]

**dam ancalaur.** 'about our cauldron'. *dam* (*do-ambi-*); *an* 'our' (the old form of *ein*); *calaur*, Lat. *caldaria*. Apparently the two sat on opposite sides of their vat or cauldron; cf. CA p. 697, gloew dull *y am drull* yt gytvaethant 'in a shining array they feasted together about the wine-bowl'; MA 191a (*Hirlas Owein*) ymgynnull *am drull*; CLlH III, 28, Anoeth byd brawt bwyn kynnull / Am gyrn buelyn, am *drull* 'Difficult till Judgement Day will it be to assemble us, about the buffalo horns, about the wine-bowl'.

2a. **guardam,** *chwarddaf* 'I laugh'. For the spelling, cf. CA 884, *mor guanauc* 'mor chwannog'; 938, *guec guero* 'chweg chwerw'; and the common variation between the forms *chware*, *gware*.

**cusam.** Perhaps the same word as *-cosam* in 1a. The series 'I do not sing, I do not laugh, I do not boast' (or 'speak') seems a natural one. Rhŷs and Stokes translate 'I kiss', comparing OE *cus*, *coss*. But an allusion to kissing without any specified object would seem rather strange. Skene understands it as *cysgaf*: I have nothing to object to this as regards form, but it would give a less appropriate meaning to the sequence of verbs which are followed by the contrasting *cet iben* in 2b. If *cusam* = *cosam* be accepted, cf. Ox. II str*o*tur, str*u*tuguar; Ox. I g*u*tan (= *guo-tan*); Juv. *gurgnim* (= *guorgnim*); *gurmaur* (= *gormaur*) in 1b above; LL p. 242, *trus* (= *tros*).

2b. **cet iben.**, *cyd yfem*, 1st pers. pl. imperf. According to Stokes, Skene, and Rhŷs, *nouel* is a borrowing from Lat. *novellus*. I have not found the Welsh word used anywhere with this meaning, but cf. BT, p. 41, line 8 in the 'Song of Ale' (*Kanu y Cwrwf*), 'Golchettawr y lestri. bit groyw y vrecci. A phan vo *anawell*. dydyccawr o gell. Dydyccawr rac rieu. y keingyfedeu.' ('Let the vessels be washed, let the ale be fresh, and when it is clear (?) let it be brought from the cellar, let it be brought before kings'.) I suggest that *gloyw* 'clear' is the meaning; cf. CA pp. 138–9, ket yvem *vet gloyw* wrth leu babir. ket vei da e vlas y gas bu hir 'Though we drank clear mead by candle-light, though its taste was good, its bitterness was long-lasting'; CA line 351, gwedy *med gloew* ar anghat.

[G p. 26, however, suggests *addfed*, i.e. 'mature' for *anawell*.] In the first example, *ket yvem* corresponds to *cet iben* in the englyn. For the development of *nawell* into *anawell* cf. the pairs *Neirin*, *Aneirin*, *nadredd*, *anadredd* and the like [cf. GMW p. 12].

2c. **patel,** *padell* 'bowl'; here a vessel to contain mead.

3a. **namercitmi:** *na*, a negative prohibition; *m* the infixed pronoun in the dative case; *ercit* imperative 3rd sing. Cf. M. Kyffin, *Deffynniad Ffydd Eglwys Loegyr* (1595) (ed. W. P. Williams, Bangor, 1908), p. viii, *Telid* Duw iddynt ddaed eu cyneddfeu 'Let God repay them for their good actions' = *Taled* Duw, etc.; cf. WG p. 329 [GMW p. 140, b] for various examples of the 3rd sing. imperative in *-id. -mi* is the suffixed pronoun, reinforcing the infixed *-m-*.

**leguenid,** *llawenydd* 'mirth'. Cf CA line 766, *laguen* = *llawen* 'joyful'. The meaning of the whole line is 'Let nobody ask me for laughter (or 'entertainment') tonight'. After losing all his retinue except one, joking is impossible for him. There is no need to follow Rhŷs, and translate *erchit* as *erchwch* on the analogy of the Breton form which has *-it* in the 2nd pl., nor is it possible to take *nep* with *leguenid* as he does.

3b. **discirr.** In order to get a line of six syllables, Rhŷs reads *is discirr mi couid* and translates 'my lay is a wail'; so also Skene, 'my song is a lament'. But if it is necessary for metrical reasons to delete a syllable, I should prefer to discount the syllabic length of *is*, and to read it as *'s*. While recognising that there exists a word *disgyr* meaning 'a scream, a shout' (RBB p. 48, line 15, gan gwynuan a *disgyrein*; RM p. 156, line 4, gan *disgyrein* y gwyr; RBP col. 1047, l. 30; col. 1167, l. 33; col. 1433, l. 22), this is not the meaning which is most appropriate in the present context. In *Sanas Cormaic* (*Anecdota from Irish Manuscripts*, ed. O. J. Bergin, R. I. Best, Kuno Meyer, J. G. O'Keefe, Halle, 1907), IV, 38, no. 455, we find *Dīscir* .i. dis a cōir. .i. bec. The translation is 'little its justice'. Windisch *Wör.* 484 gives *dí-scir* 'fierce'; 464 (under *dairmitnech*) demon *díscir* dairmitnech; *Fís Adamnáin* (ed. Windisch, *Irische Texte* I), 30, *daiscuir*, 495, *dóescair* 'gemein'; *daiscuir* scurra St Gall Glosses 56b; *dóescur-ṡluag* 'a rabble rout' CIL p. 580; iffrind cona *daescor-sluag* 'Hell with its rabble host' *Fís Adamnáin* 3; diabul cona *doescursluag* ibid. 191, 26 (for the devil with his fiends). [Cf. *Contribb. degra-dodelbtha* (1959), p. 141, *díscir* 'bold, fierce, wild, shameless', etc., also 'mean, vile, insignificant', ibid. *dodénta-dúus* (1960), p. 258, *doéscair* 'common, mean, vulgar', etc. *daiscuir* gl. *uulgari* (*conversatione*) Ml. 37b 5 'common epithet of devils'. In a note in the *Journal of Celtic Studies* I (1949), 70, K. Jackson pointed out that the two words *díscir* and *doéscair* are unrelated, and that the last can have no connexion with Welsh *discirr* (apparently only attested with its present meaning in this instance), though he admits the possibility of a connexion between W. *discirr* amd Ir. *discir.* Since the meaning of *doéscair* is irrelevant, he rejected IW's translation 'mean' for W. *discirr.* But the lexicographical material subsequently made available in *Contribb.* shows that Ir. *díscir* (no less than *doéscair*) can bear the meaning 'mean, etc.' and this evidence justifies the rendering of the line originally proposed by IW.] In the light of these examples, one may safely reject the meaning 'fierce' for *díscir*, in favour of its second meaning 'mean, vile, insignificant'; and in conjunction with a word meaning 'host', 'rabble' would be the best possible translation. In the englyn, the word is not 'host' but its equivalent *coueidid* 'company', and the chieftain says that his company is *discirr*. The phrase is parallel to 1b, where it is said *mi telu nit gurmaur*. The noble retinue has disappeared, and only this stranger remains. No wonder that he calls his companions common, mean and abject. I suggest therefore that *discirr* in the text is synonymous with the Irish adjectives quoted above, and that it has nothing to do with the Welsh word *disgyr* 'scream'. It is perhaps worth calling attention to Skene' note (FAB ii, p. 2, n.) 'the letter represented by *y* in *discyrr*...may represent...the Irish contraction for *ui*, in which case the word will read *discuirr*'.

**coueidid.** 'host, company'. Cf. PKM p. 45, llyma *gyweithyd* yn kyuaruot ac wynt o wyr a gwraged. For *d* = *th*, cf. *henoid* above for *henoeth*. For *mi* 'my', see above on 1 b.

3 c. **dou,** *dau* 'two'. This line, and 1 a, are the two difficult lines in the poem. Rhŷs gives as his translation 'One word two ills doth cause', Stokes, 'He to me has not said one word'; Skene, 'Two do not talk to me (with) one speaker'. None of these renderings strikes me as being very happy, but I am not sure that I can improve on them.

**nam.** Rhys: *nam* 'ill'; cf. RBP col. 1143, l. 13, Gwnaetham *nam* arygam ryuu. Skene and Stokes, *na'm*. In the context I prefer to understand the word as *naf* 'lord'.

**riceus.** Very uncertain. *ri* could be the perfective particle *rhy-*, Ir. *ro* [GMW §. 185]. According to Stokes, 'The *-ceus* is probably, as Mr Edwin Norris suggests, identical with the Cornish *keus*, *cows*, which seems to be borrowed from the Latin *causari*, Fr. *causer*'. According to VKG I, 170, however, the Breton *koms*, *coms*, *comps* 'to speak' comes from the preposition *com-*, and *med-tu-*, the root that is in *meddaf* 'I say'; according to Victor Henry, *Lexique étymologique des termes les plus usuels du Breton moderne* (*Bibliothèque bretonne armoricaine* III, Rennes, 1900), p. 75, it comes from *kom-wep-s-*, or from the root *weq*; according to R. Williams, *Lexicon Cornu-Britannicum* (Llandovery, 1865), p. 69, Cornish *cows* is a later form of *cowms*, to be compared with *ymgom* in Welsh. I have failed to find any ancient example of the last (see Lhwyd, *Archaeologia Britannica*, pp. 49, 220 s.v. *colloquium*, *ymgomio* 'to discourse').

Another suggestion was made by Loth, RC XLIX, 220. He suggested that the verb is a pret. 3rd sing. in *-s*, preceded by the perfective particle *ry-*, and that *ceus* comes from the root of *cawdd*, *coddi*. He refers to the *eu* ( = *ew*) in the gloss *toreusit*, and takes *un guetid* as *un gwedydd* 'one speaks'. In a footnote, he suggests that *riceus* could be associated with *rygosswy rygosses* in BT pp. 12, 19 [see above under *guorcosam*], which he describes as 'unfortunately obscure'. He translates the whole line as 'Deux qui ne se sont guère irrités mutuellement, un seul parlant ou puis-qu'un seul peut parler' (for *guetid* explained as 'qui parle' see his later note RC XLII, 363). This explanation does not seem to me at all suitable. [The above reference to Loth's conjectures was added by IW in the form of a note appended as an afterthought to his edition of the Nine englynion, B VI, 224 n.]

We are on more certain ground in comparing Welsh *cyngaws*, D 'causa, dica.

Advocatus, causidicus' *cynghawsedd, cyngheusedd*, 'causa, dica'. T. Lewis, GML pp. 94–5 has *kyghaused*, etc. 'a pleading'; see also AL II, 70, *kygheussedo*; 172, *llyuer kygheussed*, 242, *kygeuseddent*; 244, *kygevsedev*. [On the legal terms *keghaus, keghau-saeth* 'legal argument, or representative of one', see now Dafydd Jenkins, *Llyfr Colan* (Cardiff, 1963), pp. 127, 186, and S. J. Williams and E. Powell, *Llyfr Blegywryd* (Cardiff, 1942), pp. 222, 245.] There is an obvious connexion between *cyngaws* and *cygheusedd*, and it shows that *aw* can mutate to *eu* in the last syllable but one. But it is not an example of *eu* in the *final* syllable. Even apart from that, the ordinary orthography of the ninth century has *ou* for later *eu*, and *eu* regularly represents *ew*.

If, therefore, we read *cews*, cf. 1a above on *iawn, iewn*, etc. The Cornish *cows* would provide an attractive analogy, were it not that the Breton form has *m* (*koms*, etc.) and one would expect some trace of that in the O.W. form. One might, of course, hold that this is a direct borrowing from Lat. *causari*.

One could equally well take *caws* as coming from the vb. *caffael*, WG pp. 343–4 [GMW § 161], since in the same way that we find pres. indic. 1st pers. sing. *cafaf* abbreviated to *caf*, and pret. 1st sing. *cefais* to *ces*, pret. 3rd sing. *cafas* to *cas*, could not *caws* be a variant form of this last, parallel to the pret. 1st pl. *cawsam, cawsom*?

If, however, *cews* is taken as pres. indic. 3rd sing. it will be necessary to understand *ri-* as the *rhy* of possibility, corresponding to the Ir. *ro* of possibility [GMW § 185, c] and look for a different meaning for the verb.

**unguetid.** Rhŷs and Stokes give 'one word'; Skene 'one speaker'. A Breton gloss gives *guet(i)* for *secundum*, VVB p. 137 [DGVB p. 190]. The most probable root is the *gwed-* which is found in *dy-wed-af*, cf. *gwawd*, Lat. *vates*, Ir. *fáith*, 'bard, poet'. The termination *-ydd* commonly denotes the agent, cf. *prydydd, gwarthegydd*, etc., and especially BT p. 52, l. 12, dogyn *dwfynwedyd*; 31, 22, *kyfreu dyfynwedyd*; 19, 9, dydwyth dydyccawt o *dyfynwedyd gwawt* (34, 22, treded *dofyn doethur*); 20, 2, *Doethur* prif geluyd...am doleu dynwedyd, am gwyr *gwawt geluyd*. But *-ydd* is found also as a termination with abstract nouns, cf. *llawenydd*.

The meaning of BT p. 87, Dydyccawt *ynwet*, tra merin reget, is not clear, so we must be satisfied with *un* + *gwedydd*, with *un* 'any' as in un*dyn*, un*gwr*; or else an emphatic *un* 'one' in contrast to *dou* 'two' at the beginning of the line; or as *un* in VVB p. 227 (Martianus Capella) *uncenetticion*, gl. on *solicanae* (in reference to the Muses singing by themselves), or *un* meaning 'the same'. Since it is fully in accord with the style of the early poets to favour antithesis and contrast, I incline towards rendering *un* as 'one'.

[In a note on his later translation (reproduced above) of the Three englynion, LEWP p. 30, IW concluded finally that *guetid* is 3rd sing. pres. indic. of the root of which *dywedyd* 'say' is a compound, and he compared the meanings of the O.I. vb. *fethid* (which Thurneysen had shown to be a cognate of (*dy*)*wedyd*, *ZfcPh*. XIII, 303–4) 'watches, observes, pays attention to' (cf. *Contribb*. F-fochraic (1950), where the other meanings given for *fethid* as an intrans. vb. 'waits, remains, endures (?)' may also be relevant to the Juvencus context). On this final rendering he commented 'The solitary chief can make observations, remarks. He can lay down the law, but free and pleasant conversation is impossible. There is none who dares answer back! To make matters worse in this story, the only other person present is a foreigner...']

## II. THE NINE

The Nine englynion are written upon the upper margin of the first page of the manuscript. Because this has been much soiled and rubbed, a number of words and letters have become so faint that they are impossible to read. Lindsay gives a photograph (EWS plate VII), and this is accompanied by Bradshaw's transcription. According to Lindsay (ibid. p. 16), the Nine englynion were written in the tenth century and the Three in the ninth. I cannot myself see that there is much difference in the form of the letters between the one and the other,[7] but it is fair to remember that Bradshaw held that the same hand wrote all the notes in Latin, both grammatical and theological, which fill the rest of the page; and according to Lindsay, the abbreviation *tn̄s* is consistently employed in these [i.e. in the main body of glosses] for *trans*, but in the Juvencus text itself the regular abbreviation is *t̄s*. (*Notae Latinae*, 310.) This may be accounted for by a difference in the school of orthography, but it does not necessarily imply the difference of a century in date.

In my transcription I have placed in italics the letters of which I am not perfectly certain, with an asterisk to represent the place of a letter which is either completely lost, or of which only a part is visible. I have used italics also in 4a, 8a, to expand the contractions *ihu* 'Ihesu' and *psen* 'presen.'. I have put brackets round the *i* which has been added beneath the word *clus* in 6a. I have placed square brackets round any letters which I have added myself. In the manuscript, each englyn is written as a single line, so that I am responsible for dividing and numbering the stanzas. The last half of the first englyn has been cut away by the binder, leaving only the bottom half of the first letters in

[7] On this dating, see now LHEB 52, where Jackson points out that Lindsay does not explain how he arrived at his estimate of the lapse of a century between the Three englynion and the Nine. On p. 16 of EWS he appears to ascribe this opinion to Bradshaw, though its expression is not traceable anywhere in Bradshaw's *Collected Papers*. It appears most likely, therefore, to be Lindsay's own opinion, rather than Bradshaw's. In his later statement (LEWP p. 28) that the Nine are written 'in a similar hand' to the Three, IW seems to have returned to Bradshaw's published view (*op. cit.* pp. 454–5, 484) that all twelve englynion date from the ninth century. Jackson himself (LHEB p. 53) considers the ninth century to be more likely than the tenth.

III The Nine *Juvencus* englynion
(By courtesy of Cambridge University Library)

line 2. By examining the manuscript under a microscope, I came to the conclusion that it was a palimpsest: that there had been earlier writing on the page, and that it was only by rubbing this out that room had been found for the Welsh englynion (and likewise for the theological notes). Lindsay's reproduction shows how crooked the lines are in which these are written. I mention this because in attempting to establish the text, my eyes were repeatedly deceived by ghost-letters: I was not able to feel certain whether the letter which I saw, or thought that I saw, belonged properly to the englynion or to something which was inscribed on the page earlier. In one place, also, there are words between the lines in a faint ink (perhaps later glosses?).

1. omnipotens auctor tidicones
   adi_am_*_r_**[1]........

2. nit arcup betid hicouid   canlou[2]
   cet treidin[3] _gu_el[4] haguid
   t**e—rd_u_tou _t_i[5] guird****.[6]

3. dicones pater harimed[7]   presen
   isabruid icinimer[8]
   nisacup nis[9] arcup leder.

4. dicones ih_es_u dielimlu[10]   pbetid
   aguirdou pan[11] dibu
   g_u_otiapau_r_[12] _oime_r _di_du[13]

5. gur dicones remedau[t]   elbid
   anguorit anguoraut
   ni guor[14] gnim molim trintaut.

6. it clu(i)s [it] _di_bān[15] iciman   guorsed
   ceinmicun u_cn_ou·[16] ran
   ueat_iu_taut[17] beant_rid_ent.[18]

B stands for Bradshaw's text, EWS p. 52: Sk. for Skene, FAB II, 1–2: St for Stokes, _Transactions of the Philological Society_ (1860–1), pp. 204–6, 288.

[1] St. _adiamor_: Sk. _adiamor p_, B. _adiamor pre._ [2] St. Sk. B. _canlon._ [3] Sk. _cetticeidin._ [4] Sk. _gui-_, B. _gue:._ [5] There is a hole in the parchment in the middle of the word. Sk. _uor-rdutou ti_, B. _guor_ (? _guei_) _dutoutit._ [6] Sk. _guirdoned_, B. _guirdonid._ [7] St. _harinied_, B. _harimed_ (? _harmied_). [8] Sk. B. _icunmer._ [9] Sk. _m-._ [10] B. _dielimlu_ (? _dielmilu_). [11] Sk. _pen._ [12] Sk. B. _guotcapaur._ [13] Sk. _anmer-adu_, B. _dimer didu._ [14] Sk. B. _niguru._ [15] Sk. B. _inban_, St. _biban?_ [16] Sk. _ucmout_, B. _ucmon_ (? _ucinou_). [17] Sk. _ucatrintaut_, B. _ucatritaut._ [18] Sk. _bean trident_[_an_], B. _beantiudent::._

7. it cluis it humil inhare*d* celmed
rit pucsaun mi ditri*nt*aut[19]
gurd meint icomoid[20] imolaut.

8. rit ercis *d***raut[21] inadaut p*re*sen
piouboi·[22] int groisauc
inungueid guoled trintaut.

9. un hamed[23] *h*apuil[24] haper
uuc nem isnem intcouer[25]
nitguorgnim[26] molim map meir.

1. Almighty Creator, thou hast made...

2. The world cannot express in song bright and melodious, even though the grass and the trees should sing, all thy glories (miracles, riches), O true Lord!

3. The Father has wrought [such a multitude] of wonders in this world that it is difficult to find an equal number. Letters cannot contain it, letters cannot express it.

4. Jesus wrought on behalf of the hosts of Christendom [such a multitude] of miracles when he came (? like grass is the number of them).

5. He who made the wonder of the world, will save us, has saved us. It is not too great toil to praise the Trinity.

6. Purely, without blemish, in the great assembly, let us extol...

7. Purely, humbly, in skilful verse, I should love to give praise to the Trinity, according to the greatness of his power.

8. He has required of the host in this world that belong to him, that they should at all times, all together, fear the Trinity.

9. The one who has both wisdom and dominion above heaven, below heaven, completely; it is not too great toil to praise the Son of Mary.

## *Notes*

*Metre.* The final englyn has three rhyming lines of seven syllables each, so that it is an englyn *milwr* of the old type. Numbers 2–8 are all englynion *penfyr*, but it is difficult to be certain of the metre of the first englyn. In the englynion *penfyr* there are ten syllables in the first line in

[19] St. *ditrintaut*, Sk. *detrintaut*, B. *ditrimaut.* [20] St. Sk. *iconidid*, B. *icomcuid* (? *iconioid*).
[21] Sk. *o-raut*, B. *oraut.* [22] Sk. B. *pioubui.* [23] Sk. *hanied*, B. *hamed* (? *hanied*).
[24] St. Sk. B. *napuil.* [25] Sk. *nitcouer.* [26] B. *nitguorgnau.*

nos. 2, 3, 7, 8, but nine syllables in nos. 5 and 6, and eleven syllables in no. 4. In all the seven there is a *gair cyrch* [a word or phrase standing in caesura at the end of the line] of two syllables following the main rhyme.[8] The length of the second line in each one of them is six syllables (since one can ignore the *is* in 3 b, and the *mi* in 7 b). In 2, 4 and 6 the text of the third line is uncertain; in 3 c, 7 c the third line has eight syllables, in 5 c and 8 c it has seven syllables.

What is the metre of no. 1? If *auctor* carries the main rhyme, the *gair cyrch* (*ti dicones*) would have four syllables. If we read *adiamor* in the second line, this gives a rhyme in -*or* in the fourth syllable of the second line, to match with auct*or* in the first. But if the words *tidicones* are understood as belonging instead to the second line, the length of the first would be only six syllables, and the second seven or eight (according as to whether -*dia*- is taken as one or two). What type of englyn could that be? If it is a *penfyr*, it would be necessary to have a word coming after *adiam***r*, and rhyming with *auctor*. But the state of the text being such as it is, it is hardly worth speculating.

1 a. **omnipotens auctor,** as a greeting 'Almighty Creator'. With this Latin tag cf. Meilyr Brydydd's opening *Rex regum*, H pp. 7, 23 (= MA p. 142 a, HGCr. p. 21, l. 30).

**ti dicones,** 'thou hast made'. On *digoni* 'make' see HGCr. p. 62, l. 30, Duw a *digones* lles a llyseuau; and glossary p. 284. [Cf. GMW. §133 (2); 164.] There is here no relative pron. before the verb, as in the above examples, but for further instances of the same construction cf. BBC 19, 7, Onit imwaredit or druc *digonit* 'unless thou savest thyself from the evil thou committest' (= HGCr. 6, 13, see n.); BT 40, 25, Maur *duw digones*, heul haf ae rywres. Ac *ef digones* bud coet a maes 'God has created much; summer's sun and its great heat, and he has created the produce of wood and field'. So also in 5 a below, *gur dicones*. For another example of the vb. in the 3rd pers. sing. after 2nd pers. sing. *ti*, cf. RBP col. 1182, 39, ys ti a *wrthyt* a wrthotter 'thou who refusest will be refused'.

1 b. **adiamor.** Thus Stokes, Skene, and Bradshaw. I am not certain of the *o*, it is possible that it is an *a*. There is no evidence on which to decide the value of medial *d* in the text, it could be for *dd* or *th*. And there is the same ambiguity with regard to the *m*: it could stand for either *m* or *f*. Since the letters *dia* are perfectly clear and indisputable, it is not possible to read either *tir a mor* or *a dair* (= daear) *a mor*. One could, however, read *in* instead of *m*, if this gave a suitable meaning. But cf. 3 a, 4 a, b, 5 a: in each instance the object of *dicones* is some word meaning a wonder or a miracle. In 3 a *ha* comes before the object, in 4 b *a* precedes it: both of them

[8] For an account of the variants in structure of the early three-line englyn, see K. Jackson, 'Incremental Repetition in the Early Welsh Englyn', *Speculum* XVI (1941), 304 ff.

represent the preposition *o*. (For a similar construction, cf. PKM p. 36, l. 9, a oed o *of* yn Iwerdon, lit. 'what there were of smiths in Ireland'. Further examples of this construction are cited in B I, 104–6: these include RM p. 140, l. 21, ac a oed *o vilwyr*, which shows that a pl. noun—such as *guirdou* in the present instance—can be used as well as a singular one.)

Perhaps one may compare Ir. *diamair*, *diamir*; a word which means 'hidden, secluded, remote, lonely', as subst. 'a hidden thing, a lonely or remote place, a mystery' [*Contribb.* degra-dodelbtha (1959) 60–1] *Wör.* pp. 477–8, CIL p. 630. But because of the fondness of the early poets for repeating an idea throughout a series of stanzas, giving equivalent meanings, I would prefer to find a word here which would also mean some kind of wonder or miracle, something like *marth* in Welsh; as in CA 19–20, *marth* ym pa vro / llad vn mab marro (see n., and B IV, 141–5); or, even better, like Ir. *amra* 'a wonder', *Wör.* p. 363. The whole poem follows closely the thought of a psalm such as lxxvii. 11–14, 'Thou art the God that doest wonders'.

2a. **nit arcup betid.** For *arcup* see n. on 3c. *betid* is 'baptism', but in the sense of all baptised people, i.e. Christendom, the Christian world, the whole world [G p. 53, PT p. 30].

**hi couid,** 'in a song'. *hi* is the preposition *i* 'in'; cf. VVB p. 154, Ox. I *in* sextario .i. *hi* hestaur mel. One can ignore the initial *h*; cf. *ha* = *a*, VVB p. 149, in Ox. I. For *couid*, if it is *cywydd* 'song', see Loth, RC XXI, 232; where it is compared with Ir. *cubhaidh*, and further in RC XXXII, 195; CIL p. 545, *cubaid* 'harmonious, fitting, meet, proper, legitimate' [cf. GPC pp. 836–7 on *cywydd*; cf. Arwyn Watkins B XVII, 137.]. Consider also the following instances:

Nifer a uu ac a uyd
vch nef is nef meint yssyd.
Ar meint a gredwys *yg kywyd*.
A gredis trwy ewyllis dofyd.—BT p. 7, ll. 2–4.

('The host that has been and will be, as many as are above and below heaven, and as many as have believed *yg kywyd*, have believed through the will of the Lord.')

neus duc yn geluyd
*kyureu argywyd*.—BT p. 19, ll. 5–6.

('He brought skilfully *kyureu argywyd*.')

Mydwyf Merweryd. Molawt duw dofyd.
llwrw kyfranc *kywyd*. kyfreu dyfynwedyd.—BT p. 31, ll. 21–2.

('I am Merweryd. Praise the Lord God, in the manner of a *kyfranc kywyd*, the song of a prophet.')

The first quotation alludes to belief *yng nghywydd*. Is this a mistake for *yn gywydd*, i.e. 'harmoniously, correctly', and hence 'truly'? In the second example, in conjunction with *cyfreu* 'song' *argywydd* could mean 'harmonious'. [For the rhyme here in *-ydd*, see PT p. 113, where IW notes that both *cywyd* and *cywydd* occur among the examples in early poetry; GPC also notes both forms.] In the third example, *cywydd* is once more combined with *cyfreu*, but the preceding word is *cyfranc*, and unfortunately this has more than one meaning (cf. PKM pp. lii, 109, 224; CLl.a Ll. 9). [GPC: (i) meeting, encounter, battle; (ii) adventure, story.] Leaving undecided the precise meaning of the word in the above examples, and without trying to decide whether *cywydd* in these is a noun or an adj., I believe that *couid* in the poem must certainly mean 'song' or 'skilful composition', because of its association with *canlou*. (If it be objected that *ci-* would be the O.W. spelling for *cy-*, and that the *co-* here would therefore suggest a Breton or Cornish form, one may point out that *co-* represents later *cy-* in 9 b, *couer*, and probably also in 7 c *comoid*, if this stands for later *cyfoeth*. One may also compare the vacillation in later Welsh between the forms *bywyd*/*bowyd*; *rhywiog*/*rhowiog*; *rhy hwyr*/*rhowyr*, etc.

**canlou.** Previous editors have read *canlon*, but I have no doubt about the *-u*. The components of the word are *can* 'song', and *lleu* 'bright, clear', cf. BT p. 33, l. 6, keint rac vd *clotleu* yn *doleu* hafren 'I sang before a lord of shining fame in the meadows of the Severn'; RBP col. 577, ll. 25–6, *clotlew* llallawc; but col. 578, ll. 26–7, *clotleu* goreu dyn dayar; l. 30, *clotleu* llellawc; (also col. 579, ll. 30, 40; 580, 2, 6, 12; 581, 23, 27, etc.). Compare also *clot ovri* vrawt RBP col. 578, l. 41; 580, 28, for a similar compound of noun and adjective; and *kerd oleu oreudyn* in RBP col. 578, l. 41, for a phrase which is equivalent in both form and meaning. *Cerdd-olau* would be a perfect synonym for *canl-ou*. For *lleu* as an adj. cf. PKM p. 274; BT p. 77, l. 5, katwaladyr *clot lathyr leu*. MA p. 182 a, Reen *reithleu* rieu; p. 231 a, Duw douyt rec ouyt *reithleu*. For the combination of *couid* with *canlou* there is a parallel in BT p. 34, l. 15, *Areith awdyl eglur*. *Areith* corresponds to *couid*, and *awdyl-eglur* to *can-lou*.

2 b. **cet treidin.** 'though they should sing'. For *cet* 'though' cf. *cet iben* in the previous poem, p. 96 above.

**treidin.** *d* sometimes stands for *th* in these englynion, e.g. 8 c *gueid*, *guoled*. For the *ae* in *traethu* affected to *ei* before *i*, cf. Ll.A. p. 105, yma y *treithir*; RBP col. 1179, l. 28, pan *dreithir* traethawt; BBC p. 86, l. 7, Nid ower *traethaud* imi ara*tretheis* (= treithais); p. 7, l. 5, *ritreithir*. In O.W. *-in*(*t*) occurs as a verbal ending of the pres. indic. 3rd pers. pl., cf. VVB p. 175, *limnint* [DGVB p. 242]; p. 214, *scamnhegint* [GMW § 130 b, i], but in Ml.W. *-ynt* is the ending of the imperfect 3rd pers. pl., as it is here.

*Traethu* is employed in a similar context to this in BBC p. 18, where it is said that if all the creatures that are in the sea and all the birds which God has created possessed three times three hundred tongues: Ny ellynt ve *traethaud* kywoethev y trindaud 'they would not be able to express the powers of the Trinity'. Thus at the end of the poem BBC p. 27, ll. 5–6, Nis ry*draeth* ryuetev (kyvoeth) ruyteu douit 'he cannot express the wealth of God's bounty'; p. 88, ll. 1–2, Kyuoethev Ri nisr*draeth* 'he cannot express God's wealth'; MA p. 190 a, 5, Cyfarchaf i Dduw...

Ceinfolawd ar *draethawd* i ti a *draethaf*; RBP col. 1156, ll. 9–11, Ny chyfrif nebavt, nar holl uydyssyavt byth nys traetha, a wnaeth yn ri o anryuedodeu hyt tra uu yma 'No one can count, nor can the whole world ever declare, what our King performed of wonders while he was here'.

Note that a pl. vb. comes before a pl. subject in OW [GMW § 199 n.; CA p. lxx, n.] as it does here. The subject of *treidin* is *guel ha guid*.

**guel haguid,** 'grass and trees', cf. MA p. 190a Duw ry ddigawn, A wnaeth *gwellt a gwydd*. In old poetry, the two words are often combined.

**guel** = *gwellt*. With *l* for *ll* in the text, cf. 9a *puil* = *pwyll*. For *ll* where today we have *llt*, see B 1, 229 (on earlier *gwyll* where we now have *gwyllt*). Also cf. LL p. 120, ll. 18–19, *dufyr ha guell* 'water and grass'.

2c. The next line is mutilated by a hole in the parchment. Before the hole, I deciphered the letter *t* with some uncertainty, and parts of three letters, of which the last is an *e*; after it there comes *rd*, then an obscure *u* or *o*, then *tou*. Next comes a gap, and *ti* or *di*, then *guir*, and the bottom part of *dou-* (most probably from the word *douid* 'Lord'). The line may therefore have read *t**erdutou ti guir douid*: my suggestion for the letters which have been lost is *ib*, hence *tiberdutou*, reading *d* as *th* in the second word (cf. n. on *treidin*, 2b). I read the whole line as 'Thy glories (riches), O true Lord'.

**berdutou.** Cf. BBC p. 81, ll. 7–8: Creaudir y creadurev *perthidev* muyhaw (a scribal error for *berthideu*, according to the editor, p. 133; so also Loth, ACL 1, 428). Loth (*loc. cit.*) translates 'merveilles' and compares MA p. 230a, l. 12, Duu dogyn *berthodeu*. The reference is again to God in BT p. 37, Mawr y *verthideu* y gwr ae goreu (referring to the marvels performed by the Wind); cf. also MA p. 195b, l. 39, Ruteur a dillad uad *uerthideu* (= HGCr. p. 50, l. 212; the glossary translates 'wealth') [GPC p. 274, *berthid* 'wonder, power, wealth'; *berthedd* 'splendour, beauty', *berthog* 'wealthy, rich, fair']. If *berthutou* is the word, it is the pl. of *berthud*, *berthid*; cf. other nouns in *-ud*, such as *meddud*, *molud*, and especially Breton *berzud*, *burzud*, and the variant *berhud* (E. Ernault, *Glossaire moyen-breton* (Paris, 1885), pp. 88–9). There is also O.B. *berth* (*Chr. Br.* pp. 109, 190, *Berth-uuor*, *Berth*ret, Ernault, *op. cit.* p. 59), also as an element in a personal name, *Berthutis*, LL XLIII, 267.

A similar variation to that between the terminations *-ud(ou)* and *-id(ou)* in this word appears in the pair *gofud*, *gofid* in Ml.W., PKM p. 157; also forms in the glosses like *crummanhuo*, *damcirchineat*, *damcirchinnou*, *enmeituou*, and the mixture in *dificiuou* (VVB pp. 90, 94, 101, 120). [Cf. DGVB s.v. *damcirhinn* p. 128, *enmetiam* p. 160.] Evidently there is a tendency for the termination *-ou* to affect *i* to *u*, so that *berthid* is also possible as the singular.

The meaning of the englyn, briefly, is that no created being can express God's wonders in song, however refined and skilful it may be—even though the grass of the field and the trees of the forest should give themselves up to singing; cf. the above quotation from BBC 'they would not be able to express the powers of the

Trinity'. My difficulty, however, is to determine whether *berdutou* is the object of *arcup* or of *treidin*.

**guir douid,** the Lord; cf. *gwir Dduw*.

3a. **pater,** cf. BT p. 38, l. 9, an *tat* an *pater*.

**harimed,** 'of wonders'. For *ha, a* with the meaning 'of' (later *o*) see B v, 231 (Ox. I), is *xxx ha* guorennieu; also PKM pp. 115, 216 [GMW § 39c]. See note on *adiamor*, 1b above, and B I, 104–6. Here we have a synonym, since *rimed* is a noun here, and if one were to say 'of wonders', cf. BBC p. 27, ll. 4–6 (quoted in n. to *cet treidin* 2b above), where *kyvoeth* is parallel to *ryueteu* and may have originated as a gloss upon it (as is argued in B I, 29). Cf. also BT p. 69, l. 10, Bedyd rwyd *rifedeu* eidolyd [see *Tal.* pp. 209, 212 for a discussion of the meaning of this line]; MA p. 230a, l. 2, Rex rysgollychuyf ruyf *ryvedeu*; BBC p. 88, l. 8, a thrydit *ryuet*.

Note that *harimed* rhymes internally with *pater*, and again with *cinimer* in line 2; i.e. it is 'Irish' rhyme between *-edd* and *-er* [On 'Irish' rhyme see below, pp. 126, 176].

**presen,** the world; cf. 8a below; MA p. 229a, ll. 42–3, Plant Adaf...yn y *pressen* y presswylyassant 'The children of Adam dwelled in the world'. The form *pressent* also occurs, e.g. BT 28, l. 17, yssit a pryderer or *bressent* haed.

3b. **is abruid** 'it is difficult'. *is* is pres. indic. 3rd sing. of the vb. 'to be', and *abruid* is *afrwydd* 'difficult'; cf. *nid abruid* in the Computus, B III, 262. Since the line is a syllable too long the *is* should be contracted to *'s*, as in *is discirr mi coueidid* in 3b of the former poem (pp. 97–8 above).

**icinimer,** lit. 'its equal number'. The reading *icunmer*, proposed by Bradshaw and Skene, cannot be correct: *cini* is perfectly clear with the second *i* long, almost like a *j*.

3c. **nis acup.** The *-s* in *nis* is the object of the vb. *acup*, and I take it as a pronoun referring back to *cinimer rimed pressen*. I understand *acup* as *achub*, but used in a special sense (see below). For *c* = *ch*, see 9b, *uuc* for *uch*, *uuch* 'above'.

**nis arcup.** I have not seen this verb anywhere except here and in 2a above. Because of the internal rhyme which adorns these englynion, I understand *-up* here as *-ub*, rhyming with *achub*. If it were not for the rhyme, one could read *-wb*, or *-uph*, *wph*, owing to the ambiguity of *u* and *p*; cf. LL XLIII (*Book of St Chad*) *Gripiud* = Griffudd, Gruffudd. But I cannot tell whether *argub* or *archub* is intended (see above on *acup*, for *c* = *ch*).

One must look for a suitable meaning for *arcup* by considering its context. In the second englyn we have *nit arcup betid*, where *betid* 'the inhabitants of the world', is the subject of the verb. It is not certain whether *berdutou* is the object of *arcup* or of *treidin*. In the third line, *leder* is the subject, and the *-s* in *nis* is the object, a pronoun referring to *rimed presen* 'the wonders of the world', or perhaps to *icinimer* 'their number'. To understand the whole sentence, it is necessary first of all to decide on the meaning of *leder*.

**leder.** Since there are so many instances of medial *-d-* for *-th-* in this text (cf. 2b on *treidin*), *l* for *ll* (cf. 2b on *guel*), and *e* for both *e* and *y* (cf. *remedau*[*t*] = *rhyfeddawd* in 5a, *celmed* = *celfydd* in 7a), I conclude that this word is *llythyr*, an early and regular development from Lat. *littera-e* [cf. H. Lewis, *Yr Elfen Ladin yn yr Iaith Gymraeg* (Cardiff, 1943), p. 41], cf. BBC p. 36, ll. 1–4, Athuendiguste... llevreu a *llythyr* 'May books and letters bless thee' (rhyming with *ether*, *hydiruer*); RBP col. 1170, l. 5, Ou*er* diuun*er* llyth*er* leawr; HGCr. p. 81, l. 29, where *llythyr* should certainly be emended to *llyther*, as it belongs to a sequence of 55 words all rhyming in *-er*. *Llyther* became *llythyr* in later Welsh, just as *broder* (the old pl. of *brawd*) became *brodyr*, on the analogy of a number of other plurals, in which *e* became affected to *y* (BT p. 23, l. 12, provides another example in which *llythyr* should be emended to *llyther* for the sake of the rhyme). In BBC p. 38, l. 11 the spelling *llythir* shows the later form to be established. The meaning varies from 'letters' (of the alphabet), 'letter' (epistle), to 'letters' (literature), i.e. everything written. In MA 477a (Brut Gr. ab Arthur) [= BD 6, 7] the phrase *y llythyr hwnnw* is sing. [but cf. BD p. 5, l. 20, *llythyr*...yn yr ymadrawd *hwn*, where the corresponding passage in MA has the pl., llythyr...ar ymadraud hwn *yndunt*]. Further instances of the pl. are SG p. 3, l. 12, *rei or llythyr*; p. 123, ll. 15–16, yd oed *llythyr* yn ysgriuennedic, rei o eur, ereill o aryant. In the present instant, *leder* means 'letters' in the fullest and most general sense.

**acup.** *achub* 'seize, save' < Lat. *occŭpo* [EL, p. 32], but the derivation is irregular, see WG pp. 86, 96; a compound of *capio* 'take'. Its chief meanings were 'to take possession of, to take up, fill with anything, to be beforehand with, to anticipate'. [See also GPC for the additional meanings 'contain, occupy, defend', etc.] We still use *achub* in the last sense in *achub y blaen* 'to anticipate, forestall', although 'to save' is the most common meaning now. But cf. PKM p. 75, *achub* y llall a wnaeth yn gyflym, kyt mynhei dianc nys gallei 'he caught him up quickly, before he could escape'; Wade-Evans, *Welsh Medieval Law*, p. 17, tra *achuppo* yr adar 'while he picks up the birds'; B II, 9, A *ymachuppo* or blaen o bell, agos y keiff y les 'who takes precautions in advance from afar, will receive the profit near by'; TW *praeoccupo*, rhagfeddiannu...*ymachub*. In O.B. *acupet* gl. on *occupat* [sic GPC p. 9, but DGVB p. 53 reads *acupot* 'il occupe'] *gwrec ac'hub* 'femme enceinte', Ernault, *Glossaire Moyen Breton*, p. 16. I therefore interpret *nis acup leder* to mean 'letters do not hold it, are not in possession of it', that is, of the innumerable wonders of the Creator. They are not to be found in a book, not in many books, nor in the whole of literature itself.

**arcup.** In the previous example, 2a, it is the whole of Christendom and of created things (the grass and the trees) which fails to express (*arcup*) the multitude of God's wonders. In this instance, books fail to express (*arcup*) God's wonders, or to 'contain' them (*acup*). In the first example, the verb *arcup* is paralleled by *treidin* (*traethu*) in its old meaning of declaring in song; in the second, the parallel word is *achub*. I therefore suggest as possible meanings for *arcup* 'to declare fully', or 'to contain, express'—remembering as I do the force of the vb. *capio* in the last verse of St John's Gospel (see below on 4c, nec ipsum arbitror mundum *capere posse* eos, qui scribendi sunt, libros 'I suppose that even the world itself could not contain the books that should be written'). Since the -*cup* in *achub* is derived from *capio*, it may be that *argub* in the text is a verb which has been formed on the analogy of *achub*.

4a. **dielimlu.** On *elyflu* 'host' see PKM p. 242 [CLlH p. 91]; *elyf* is a form of *alaf* 'herd, host'; together with *llu* it constitutes a compound of synonyms. [*Di* < **dē* is the preposition 'from' (not 'to'); see GMW §223, n. 1; B XIII, 1–10.]

**pbetid.** according to Bradshaw, *pro betid.* The *p*, however, looks to me like a scribal error; *presen* was the word at the end of the corresponding line in the previous englyn (the *gair cyrch*), and I believe that the scribe began to write this word again here, since the meaning was evidently suitable, and it was a frequent habit with the early poets to repeat the *gair cyrch* throughout a series of englynion; cf. *henoid* in the previous poem (p. 94 above). But on perceiving that *betid* was the word in the original, he wrote it in after having already written down the *p*. Under the *p* there is a mark which looks like a *t*. Is this a mark of deletion? (Or is the *t* intended to belong to *remedau* in 5a, so as to alter it to *remedaut*, in accordance with the requirements of the metre? It comes straight after the *u* in that instance, and one wonders why it was not added after the *u*, where there is sufficient space for it.) On *betid*, see above on 2a. *Di elimlu betid* means 'to the hosts of Christendom'. There is another word which means 'world' in the *gair cyrch* of 5a, that is *elbid*.

4b. **aguirdou** 'of miracles'; cf. MA p. 231a, l. 9, Duw dewin gwertheuin gwyrtheu. For *a* 'of', see above n. on *harimed*, 3a. For *d* = *th*, see n. on *treidin*, 2b.

**pan dibu** 'when he came'. On *dyfu*, perf. 3rd sing. of *dyfod*, see WG pp. 363, 368 [GMW §143, p. 134].

4c. **guotiapaur.** The *r* at the end of the word is not clear, except for the downward stroke, so that in this orthography one could read either *s* or *r*. Also in the narrow gap between *i* and *a* it is just possible to read the sign : (see p. 91 above, *n.* on 1c of the previous poem), as if it were a sign that one or more letters had been omitted. Above *tia* is a mark like a bridge, pointing towards the right, like the mark of a quill pen above a vowel, denoting the abbreviation for an *n* or *m*. And there are some indistinct letters written even more faintly above -*iapaur* and the space which follows it: I read hesitantly *otraban*. The *r* is like a *z*, or the *r* that follows rounded letters in early manuscripts [i.e. like the *r* which follows an *o* in BBC and BT]. But the *b* could also be read as *li*, and the *n* as *r*—so there is plenty of choice! I thought once that these letters were in the hand of Edward Lhwyd, and that he was trying to find a recognisable Welsh equivalent to -*otiapau*-. In any case, it is right to mention them here, since the mark above the *i* misled Bradshaw to read *guotc* instead of *guoti*: and the last stroke of the *n* in *otraban* forms the upper end of the *d* in Bradshaw's *dimer*, or at least they run into each other.

To me, the remaining part of the line is undecipherable. Above the space following *guotiapaur*, I can see perfectly clearly the *-an* which constitutes the final letters of *-traban-*. The last stroke in the *-n* runs into a letter beneath it, making this look like a *d*. Without this stroke, it would seem to be an *o*, but the bottom of the letter is not clear. After this doubtful *o*, there come marks which could be read either as *mi* or *nn* or *im*, then a tall thin *e* (uncertain), followed by a clear *r*. Afterwards a space, and marks which could one imagine to be *da* or *di* (with the *i* bent); then *du* quite clear. The readings *oimer* or *dimer* agree as well as anything with what I am able to decipher. What I should like to find would be the letters forming *nimer* (*nifer* 'number'), but so far I am not able to read it. Perhaps further light may come from a fresh examination of the manuscript. If *didu* is right, it would stand for *iddu*, the old form of *iddynt* 'to them'; cf. CLlH I, 39, where *elyflu* rhymes with *udu* (= *iddynt*).

It is possible that *guotiapaur*, with the *t* written above, could stand for *guotit a paur*, or *guoti atpaur*. With the last, cf. HGCr. I, 12, Ath uendicco de *attpaur* a dien (I understand *dien* here to be the noun 'grass', cf. BT p. 33, l. 7, y gwaet ar *dien*; CLlH XI, 52, ar wyneb *y gwellt* y gwaet—not the adj. 'new' as it is interpreted by the editor p. 283). [With *attpaur* cf. AP[2] line 12, *Atporyon uyd Brython pan dyorfyn*, and n. *Attpaur* 'that which springs up again' may be compared with *adladd* 'aftermath, aftergrass'.] If one reads *guotit*, what about *tit-* as in BT p. 37, l. 7, *tytwet*, CA l. 1235, a chin i olo atan *tit*guet daiar. (?) For *odit* 'a rarity' cf. BT p. 12, l. 26; p. 13, l. 1; CLlH I, 35b; III, 47b. On *tydwedd, tudwedd* 'earth' see HGCr. pp. 129–30. The idea, therefore, would be that the miracles which Jesus performed are, like the grass of the field in number.

The inspiration of this englyn, like the preceding one, I believe, is to be found in the concluding words of St John's Gospel (see above under *arcup*, 3c). But it will be seen that the *t* standing above the line, as if it were part of a longish word, renders all this merely a matter of speculation.

5a. **gur dicones.** *Gwr* is used for God, where now one would say *yr un a* 'He who'. Cf. BT p. 40, l. 4, Golychaf wledic pendeuic pob wa. *Gwr* a gynheil y nef. arglwyd pob tra. *Gwr* a wnaeth y dwfyr y bawb yn da. *Gwr* a wnaeth pob llat. For the absence of the rel. pron. cf. 1a, ti *dicones*, and n.

**remedau(t)** *rhyfeddawd* 'a wonder'. In the manuscript, the word may have been written first as *remedou*, and then the *o* changed later to *a*. For the *t* superscript, see above on *pbetid*, 4a. One must read *-aut* to get the rhyme.

**elbid,** *elfydd* 'the world'. [On *elfydd* < *Albio*, see IW's note, B VI, 134; PT II, 10; III, 2.]

5b. **anguorit,** *a'n gweryd* 'will save us'; cf. MA p. 195a, A Dewi an *gweryd*; MA p. 183a, Can *gueryt* creaudyr ae crettuy. Kan *guaraut* guerinwalch nevuy.

**anguoraut,** *a'n gwaredodd* 'who saved us'; cf. BBC p. 39, ll. 7–9, Duu an amuc. Duu an goruc. Duu an *guaraud*. [For this and other suffixless preterites see GMW § 133 (*c*) (i).]

5c. **ni guor gnim.** The construction in 9c, *nit guor gnim*, is more in accordance with later usage, by which *nit* is the neg. with nouns. *gnim*, later *gnif* 'work, hardship, battle'; Ir. *gním* 'labour'. [Cf. CLlH p. 59, *NLWJournal* II, 73.] The meaning is 'it is not too great toil' [the meiosis is a common feature of the early poetry].

**molim** > *molif* > *moli.* [For the loss of *-m*, *-f* in the final of the vn. after *i-*, see GMW §10, §178(*d*); CA pp. 11–12, Gwell gwneif a thi / ar wawt dy *uoli* (= dy uol*im*, as is attested by the rhyme; see CA p. lxiii and B XIV, 216).]

6a. **it cluis.** The *i* has been added beneath *clus*, cf. 7a, *it cluis it humil.* It is difficult to explain the *it.* As a preverb, *it*, (*yd*) is common in early poetry [GMW §190]; it remains in *yd-wyf*, *ydoedd*, etc. But in 7a it appears before the adj. *humil* < Lat. *humilis* 'humble'. It can hardly be *it* 'to thee', since one would expect *dit* from the preposition *di* at this early date. There are two examples of *it* in the glosses, *Martianus Capella* (ed. Stokes, *Arch. Cam.* 1873), p. 5, no. 14, *it dagatte ail*, gl. on *coniuere* (that is *con(n)ivere* 'to shut the eye') and Juv. *it darnesti*, gl. on *agitare*, VVB p. 168; Loth takes the *it* in these exx. as the verbal particle. [For full treatment and further refs. see now DGVB p. 234, where the relation between *it*, *ed*, *id*, Ml.W. *ydd*, Ml.Br. *ez* is discussed.] This gives no help towards understanding *it* with an adj. like *humil*; and if *humil* is an adj. it is difficult to take *cluis* as anything else. With an adj., *it* can mean the same thing as the adverbial particle *yn* in MW, or it can be synonymous with *ys* 'it is'. *It...it* can hardly correspond with Lat. *et...et*, since *ha...ha* occurs for that in 9a. If it is the adverbial particle, why should this appear as *int* in 9b? There is no sign for *n* over the *i* here, or in 7a either. Yet this would give a suitable meaning. If one tries to explain *it* as a verb, with the sense of *ys*, cf. the *t* in *nid*, *neud* before an adj. or noun. If it were the neg. here, *ni-t cluis* would be a perfectly natural construction.

**cluis** remains quite uncertain. It is not possible that the correct reading should be *duis*, since though confusion between *cl* and *d* sometimes occurs, there is plenty of difference between their representation in this text. The word here is combined with *ceinmicun* to describe the praise that is given to the Trinity; so also 7a, *cluis* and *humil* is the praise which is due to the Trinity. It could have arisen through provection or hardening (after *it*) of *gluis* 'fair, shining, holy'. (See Loth, RC XLII, 365, Irish *glése* 'bright'.) Or it could be an adj. from the root *clywed*, *clust* (see Boisacq, *Dictionnaire étymologique de la langue latine* (4th edn. Paris, 1959) on κλέος, κλέω with the meaning 'praiseworthy' or 'audible').

**diban.** This is what I read in the photographic reproduction; when I saw the manuscript I thought it might be possible to read *inbān* with a tall *i.* Above the *a* there is a broad horizontal line; is this an abbreviation for a second *n*, giving *-bann*? If *dibann* is the word, cf. RBP col. 1247, l. 1, Ieuan *diuan* deuawt; col. 1373, l. 38, A *glan* a *divan* ywr pendeuic; MA p. 287a, l. 40, Trugar gerennyd Dovyd *divan*; p. 339b, l. 13, Lluniais wawd ddefawd *ddifan*. D. gives *difann* = *immaculatus*, understanding it as *di* and *mann* 'spot, blemish', and therefore as the equivalent of *difefl* [GPC *difan* 'immaculate, faultless, perfect', etc.; *difefl* 'without reproach'].

The *b* in *dibān* does not exclude this, since from very early times both *b* and *m* between vowels were pronounced *f*, but the *f* that came from *m* was nasal. Parallel instances are *amcibret* in Ox. I, *trem* for *treb* (*tref*) in LL p. 43, l. 124; cf. also the variation between merthir *cimliuer* LL p. 32, merthir *cibliuer* LL. p. 44. *Difann* would go perfectly with *cluis*, if this is understood as an adj. to describe the praise of God.

To read *inbān* as two words; *in bann*, again gives good sense, since *ban* is used for a noise (as in *banllef*), cf. CLlH VI, 16b, *Bann llef* cwn yndiffeith G. 'uchel, soniarus, llafar'; CLlH XI, 34a, Eryr Eli, *ban* y lef heno.

If this is accepted, we must take *in* to be the adverbial particle, even though this occurs below in the form *int* in 9b, *int couer*. Both *int* and *in* (and perhaps also *it*) occur as variants of the adverbial particle. The form *int* is found in the glosses, VVB p. 86, l. 164 *in*(*t*) *coucant* 'certainly, completely' [DGVB p. 120]; see GC[2] pp. 615–16, where *en*, *enn*, *ent* are given as the Breton forms. [See now DGVB pp. 225–6 for full discussion of W. *in*, *int*, Ml.Br. *ent*, and further refs., including B VII, 96 ff., XIX, 295–304.] On *bann* see Stokes, RC IV, 345 [DGVB p. 78]. In consideration of Breton *bann* and Ir. *bind* 'melodious' [GOI p. 130], I would have translated *in bann* as 'tunefully, melodiously', were it not that *ban* in Welsh means 'high, loud' when it is used for a noise, so that one must translate *in bann* as 'high, loud'.

Though I see no way of reading *it bann* in the text, yet since there are only nine syllables in the line, it seems legitimate to supply *it* before the adj. to balance 7a. This will give a rhyme between the fifth syllable and the end-rhyme, as in 2a, 3a, 4a, 8a.

**iciman.** *i* is the preposition 'yn'; cf. 2a, *hi couid. Ciman* can represent the adj. *cyfan* or the noun *cyman* (as in *cyman-fa*) 'host, company'; cf. CA p. 882, where the B text reads Erdiledaf canu *ciman* cafa = A text 774 Ardyledawc canu *kyman* caffat ('A fitting song of a worthy company'). In CA 341–2 we get the two words together, ys deupo kynnwys yg *kyman* can drindawt en vndawt *gyuan* 'May he have a welcome among the host (of Heaven) in perfect union with the Trinity'. These two words were completely confused by Davies: *cymman* vid. an idem quod *cyfan*. For examples see BT p. 43, l. 11 [= *Etmic Dinbych* l. 27, p. 164 below], where *kyman* is used of an assembly feasting together in a fortress; AL II, 406, Tri chyffredin gwlad yssyd *kyman* dadleu a(c) eglwys 'Three universal things of a *gwlad*: an assembly, court, and church'; MA p. 201a, yg *kyman* yg kymelri; 241a, a *gyman* llu; cf. Ir. *comann* = community, company; *cummann* = companionship, CIL pp. 448, 564. SE also gives some examples of *cyman* used as an adj. [GPC p. 754 'complete, full, entire']. But here I believe it to be a noun, 'assembly'; cf. Psalm xxii. 25 'Thou dost inspire my praise in the full assembly'.

**guorsed,** *gorsedd* 'assembly, mound'; see PKM p. 120 for some of the meanings. Both *cyman* and *guorsed* seem to me to denote an assembly, but whether in heaven (as in CA p. 341, above) or on earth (in the church?) I do not know, until it becomes possible to establish the mood and tense of *ceinmicun* in the next line. But cf. BBC p. 34, ll. 4–6, Seith seint a seith ugeint a seithcant / a want *in un orsset*. Y gid a Crist guin. ny forthint ve vygilet...Crist ni buve trist *yth orsset* ('Seven saints and seven score and seven hundred went together in one assembly with holy Christ, they felt no fear...Christ, let me not be sad in Thy assembly').

6b. **ceinmicun**; *ceinmygu* means 'to praise'; D. quotes the proverb *Ceinmygir pob newydd* 'Every new thing is praised'; so also RBP col. 1033, l. 4, *keinmygir* pob kywreint; CLlH II, 2, *Keinmyg(i)r* uy eres 'My wonderful deeds are praised(?)'; II. 17b, Gwedy gwely *keinmic* 'After an honoured bed'; RBP col. 1055, l. 16, Golut byt eyt dydaw. ket *ymgeinmycker* o honaw 'the wealth of the world goes and comes, although one exults in it'. In RC XVI, 316, Ernault refers to *ceinmicun* here, and expresses uncertainty as to whether the mood is subj. or imperative ('nous honorons' or 'honorons'), but he compares its form with the O.B. personal name *Kenmicet* in Cart. Red. 75. As regards its form, *ceinmicun* could be pres. indic. 1st pers. pl., or imperf. 1st pers. sing. I prefer the first, since in 5b the poet is speaking in the pl. The difficulty is to decide whether we have here a statement or an exhortation or a command; i.e. to decide on the mood of the verb. I tend to take it as an imperative, 'It is not a hard task to praise the Trinity. Therefore let us praise, high and clear, in the great assembly.' Most unfortunately, the rest of the line is hard to read, and the whole of the last line is obscure.

**ucnou.** The *u* is certain; then one can read either *c* or *e*, then *n*, except that the second stroke is long and resembles a *j*, then comes *ou*, with a dot high up above the *u* which deceives the eye into wanting to read *ois*, but this would make the *i* quite different to every other *i* in the poem. Skene made out this dot to be the remains of a *t*, and read *ucmout*. The manuscript is blotched below the *c* (or *e*), and there is room for an *i* or for the first stroke of an *m*, if this were short. That is the reason for Bradshaw's reading *ucmou*. (The metrical length of the line would be against his alternative reading *ucinou*.)

**ran,** for *rhan* 'part, share'? But it should be remembered that in Irish there are two words *rann* 'share, part', and *rann* 'verse'.

I have nothing definite to offer with respect to *ucnou ran*. I would like merely to refer to *ygno* in BT p. 35, l. 14; p. 78, l. 13; as regards form this could come from *wc-no(u)*. Could there be a compound of *uch* + *gnou* 'famous'; cf. *Uchtrit*, LL p. 421. [On *-gno*, *-gnou* 'famous' as an element in personal names, see CLlH p. 138; TYP p. 397.] For *gnou* in Breton see *Chr. Br.* p. 133; for Ir. *gno(e)*, *Wör.* p. 599, *Contribb.* 'G' (1955), p. 125, 'illustrious, noteworthy' etc. Cf. the Irish names *Beogna* (*Beuno*), *Clothgna* (*Clydno*), *Midgna* (*Myddno*) cited by Meyer, *Betha Colman maic Luachain* (Dublin 1911), and pairs like *Gwyddneu*, *Gwyddno*.

6c. **ueatiutaut.** The *u* is clear; then, according to the editors, there comes a *c*, but what I saw was a high-topped *e*, with the curve of its top stretching down so as to look like a broad black line joining the *a*—very much like the *e* in *couer*, 9c.

After that *-at* is clear, followed by two uncertain letters—either *iu*, with *u* similar to that in *guorgnim* in 9c, with its base-stroke turning towards the right in an unusual manner, or else *ia*, with an open-topped *a* such as appears in *raut* in 8a. Bradshaw's *ri* seems more unlikely, for it would be a very unusual form of an *i*. The ending *-taut* is quite clear. It is possible that there is some mark or letter above the *ea*.

In **beantrident** the letters are clear, except for the slender line which joins the bend of the *r* to its vertical stroke. That is why it has been misread as *-tiu-*, but the *i* (in *tri-*) turns towards the left in a perfectly normal way. Afterwards there comes *o* or *d*. If it is *d*, there is not much that is visible of the long stroke, but cf. the *d* in *hamed*, 9a. In attempting to decide between them, note that in 7c two of the earlier editors read coni*d*id, where the third read the ending as *-oid*. Only on grounds of meaning can one decide here between the two letters. I can see no letter, nor any trace of one, after *-ent*. There is no rhyme: one would have to add a final *-ann* to give one (and this would give a line of nine syllables in place of rhe regular seven), or else alter the *-ent* to *-ann*; or else, since there is already an *an* in the line, and a mark like a comma above the *-ent* (which is possibly a sign for transposing words), one could move *bean* to the end of the line, and read *trident bean*. There is a tiny space after *bean* in the manuscript, but it is not as great as the usual gap between letters.

I do not understand the line at all.

7a. **it cluis it humil.** See n. on 6a. For *humil* (*ufyl*) < Lat. *humilis* 'humble' see Loth, RC XXXVI, 394. *Humil* does not afford the customary rhyme between the fifth syllable and the end-rhyme (see n. on *diban*, 6a) but it makes 'Irish' rhyme (*l: dd*) with the *gair cyrch* (*celmed*); for a similar rhyme cf. BT p. 46, l. 25, Gwr y *cussyl* y pop *ufyd*.

**in hared.** *in* is the preposition *yn* 'in'; *hared* = *areith* 'discourse' (*e* = *ei*, *d* = *th*), the scribe's mistake for *araut*, a word of similar meaning (see below on 8a), which must obviously be restored here, as it is required by the rhyme. He made a slip by anticipating the *-ed* that came at the end of the next word (the common scribal error of *homoeoteleuton*). Apart from that, the substitution of *araith* for *arawd* makes no alteration to the meaning; cf. BT p. 34, l. 15, *Areith* awdyl eglur; BBC p. 9, l. 8, Amhad anav *areith* awyrllav; RBP col. 1143, l. 17, rwyd *areith* o brifyeith brydu. Sometimes *araith* means 'language' [GPC p. 176] as in BBC p. 22, ll. 9–10, a dodute ar di *areith*; BT p. 75, l. 6, kymry pedeir ieith / symudant eu *hareith*. With the meaning cf. 2a above, *hi couid canlou* 'in song bright and melodious'.

**celmed,** *celfydd* 'skilful'. Other instances in the poem of *e* for *y* occur in the first syllable of *leder* in 3a, and of *remedau* in 5a. In VVB p. 67 [DGVB p. 100] *celmed* is found as a gloss on *efficax*.

7b. **rit,** the particle *ry*, and a *t* which is the end of the verbal particle *it*; cf. 8a, *rit* ercis; B V, 240, *immit* cel. It cannot be translated, as in the case of the *t* in *nit arcup*, 2a. To the bare eye, the *r* looks uncompleted and therefore like an *n*, but a magnifying glass brings to light a trace of the quill pen making the long down-stroke of the *r*, as well as completing the second stroke with a turn towards the right.

**pucsaun mi.** *Mi* is a suffixed pronoun which reinforces the verbal ending; it does not count in the metre. It proves that the form is pluperfect 1st pers. sing. (cf. *gwelswn*, *dybygswn*, etc.). According to WG p. 335, the only possible explanation of *-wn* in the imperf. 1st pers. sing. is that it is derived from *-wyn*, but here in a parallel form we have the termination *-aun*. Cf. the forms *petawn* and *petwn* in MW.

*Pucsawn* (with *c* = *ch*) comes from the vb. *puchaw*; cf. D *puch* = *voluntas*, *desiderium*; *pucho* = *desiderare*, *velle*, *optare*. It occurs more frequently in the compound form *rhybucho*; in this context the *ry-* precedes, but does not form a close compound. The meanings are 'to desire, to choose, to like', cf. RBP col. 1180, ll. 30–2, *puchysswn* arwyd croc. ymdwyn croes yr Crist ar vysgwyd. Agheu yr eneit avreit afvrwyd. Adaw y *buchaw* am bechrwyd; col. 1434, l. 22, Dywallaw dyr corn kann ym *puchant*; *Llan.* MS. 2, p. 276, nyt *puchau* heb vam; SG p. 198, l. 4, A unben, heb y gwalchmei, nyt yttoedut ti yn *puchaw* ymi dim o da; ibid. ll. 10, 30, nyt oes yma neb heb y wassanaethu o bop kyfryw vwydeu...or a *rybuchei* e hun; p. 43, ll. 20–1, Efo yr hynny a *rybuchei* y dywedut pei as llavassei; RBP col. 1402, l. 33, am *ry buch* oe wenllaw; YCM p. 220, *rybuchet* = 'goodwill, gift'; BBC p. 76, ll. 9–10, wy *rybuchwy*, wy *rypuched*; AL II, 356, ae yghyuarws ae yn *rybuchet* arall; RBB p. 246, l. 32, karedigyon gussaneu a geireu *rybuchedic* (= *osculis et familiaribus verbis*). I am unable to accept the translation of the line suggested by Loth, RC XXIX, 8, 'Je t'avais désiré moi, toi, ô Trinité'.

**ditrintaut,** *di*, the preposition 'to'. It is similarly combined with *pucho* in BT p. 75, l. 18, Nyt oed udu (= iddynt) y *puchysswn* anaw, etc., and cf. the quotation above from SG p. 198; also MA p. 228b, l. 39, Devaut dibechaut *ym* a *bucho*. These examples prove that the recipient of the wish follows *di* in the englyn. Bradshaw read *trimaut*, but the manuscript certainly has *trintaut*, although the *nt* is a bit obscure. But the underlying idea of the passage reinforces this reading, see below.

Note that there is no instance of the def. art. *ir* (= *yr*) in the nine englynion: a sure sign that they belong to the oldest poetry.

7c. **gurd,** *wrth* 'according to'; cf. PKM p. 99, *vrth* val y bo dy anryded; BBC p. 76, ll. 8–10, Caffaud hyuel urth y hoeweit wy ry*buchvy*.

**meint icomoid,** 'according to his wealth', or 'power'. Here *d* again stands for *th*, and *com-* for *cyf-*; cf. 2a *couid*; 9b, *couer*. The last stroke of the *m* is sufficiently far away from the rest of the letter to make it possible to read *conioid*—if there were such a word.

**imolaut,** 'his praise'; the possessive pron. *i* refers to *trintaut* in 7b.

8a. **rit ercis.** See 7b on *rit*. *ercis* 'he has asked', pret. 3rd pers. sing. of *erchi*. But Loth takes it to be 1st pers. sing. 'j'ai demandé' or 'je t'ai demandé'.

**d**raut.** The reading could equally well be *d*, *a* or *o*, since the lower part of the letter is lost. Then comes a space, and it is difficult to say if it once had letters in it—there would be room for two. The scribe may have written *anaraut* by mistake, or started with *ad* (from *adaut*), and then scratched the letters out. One thing however is certain, the metre would not allow for more than one syllable before *raut*, in order for the rhyme to be on the fifth syllable (see above on 6a).

If the word is *araut*, cf. the subscription *araut dinuadu* which is found at the end of the Juv. text: the meaning is clearly 'a prayer for Nuadu' [see GPC p. 177]. It comes from Lat. *oratio*, but since prayers were chanted, it came to mean also a song; perhaps to start with a religious song, but later praise in general; cf. RBP col. 1180, ll. 18–19, Na chysgwn, canwn canon *arawt*, kanyt o gysgu y daw gwas-gawt; col. 1183, ll. 28–30, Gwae ef draethadur...ny thraetho ohonawt *arawt* areith; col. 1227, l. 19, Archaf y grist naf araf *arawt*...ellwng ym vy ri; col. 1281, l. 24, Tauawt vn *arawt* Aneirin gwawtglaer; MA p. 185a, l. 13, Auch rotaf *arawd*; cf. D = *oratio, oratio encomiastica, encomiasticon poema*, G = *araith, traethiad, cyfarchiad*; GPC 'language, speech, utterance', etc. See above on *hared* (= *araith*) 7a.

On seeing how similar the initial letter is to the *d* that is found in *beantrident* 6c, and to that in *hamed* in 9c, and in view of the fact that the preposition *i* is employed after the vb. *erchi* in BT p. 3, l. 25, *Archaf* wedi *yr* trindawt; RBP col. 1179, l. 5, *Archaf* arch *y* duw; and that this preposition appears as *di* in two earlier instances in the poem (see above on 4a, 7b), I feel obliged to read *di rawt*, and to understand *rawt* as 'host'. In B I, 22 I have already cited examples of the word used in this sense (*rawd* o beleidr, *raud* o Saesson, *rawt* wenyc, *rhawd* ymlyniaid, *rhawd* o geirw); cf. RBP col. 1180, l. 22, where God is called 'rwyf naw *rawt*' or 'Lord of nine hosts'—that is, the nine orders of Heaven (BT p. 4, l. 4 *naw rad nef*). Although two instances in RBP (*archaf arawt* col. 1227, ll. 18–19, and *archaf arch* col. 1179, l. 5) favour reading *arawt* here, I have not found any instance of the preposition *di* (*y*) following this word, and I can see no sense in reading *ercis arawt* 'he has made a request', since this would leave *ercis* without an indirect object, and *piouboi* would be left in the air. One can understand the article to be implied before *rawt*, so that the meaning would be 'He has required of the host'.

**inadaut,** 'in the home' or 'dwelling'; G: *lleoliad, trigfan, adnau* ('site, place, dwelling'); see also HGCr. p. 277, RC XXIX, 16; D = *repositorium* [and cf. PKM p. 226 on *yspadawt*]; BT p. 54, ll. 8–9, Molaf inheu *presswyl* toruoed adef menwyt. Molaf inheu *adawt* goreu; RBP col. 1175, l. 3, per *adawt* paradwys; col. 1284, ll. 7–8, presswylawd gyntaf adaf *adawt*, *presswyl* glwys baradwys barawt 'Adam first settled his dwelling in the shining dwelling of Paradise prepared', B v, 130, poyd ef i *haddawd* yn nhref y drindawd a poyd i *gorffowys* yngwlat Baradwys.

**presen,** [*presen(t)* < Lat. *praesentem* or *praesentia* (H. Lewis, *Elfen Ladin* p. 45)] 'the world'; cf. 3a. With *adaut* cf. BT p. 11, l. 20; 12, 25, for the parallel phrase *gwlat pressent*.

8b. **piouboi.** With Stokes I read *o* for the last letter but one; it cannot be *u*, as Skene and Bradshaw supposed. For *boi* see B III, 266–7 [GMW § 144, p. 137], pres. subj. 3rd pers. sing. *bod* (MW *bo*). In the text it is combined with *piou* (the old form of *pieu* 'to whom is' ('belongs, owns')) [GMW § 88] and is therefore the equivalent of 3rd pers. sing. subj. *pieufo* [GMW § 89]. WG cites *pyefo* (where *f* = *ff*, it is claimed) from AL I, 196 (see GML p. 255 for instances of the forms *bieufo*, *byefo*, etc. from the *Black Book of Chirk*). The meaning here is 'those who may own property in (the dwelling-place of) this world'; or else 'those whom God possesses in this world'. I prefer the second of the two alternatives.

**int groisauc.** For *int*, see n. to 9b. *groisauc* is obscure to me. In the manuscript there is a mark of punctuation after *piouboi*, since it is to be taken as going with the following line. But the meaning is doubtful. In spite of its similarity to the root of *groesaw* (*graesaw*, *croeso*, PKM p. 129) I do not see how they can be equated. One might suppose it to mean 'warmly, fervently', cf. Ernault, *Glossaire du moyen Breton*, p. 295 on *grues*, *groesus* in Breton, also RC XXVIII, 193; but cf. Loth on *gris* in RC XXXVIII, 310. In Irish there is *grésach* 'lasting, perpetual, constant, habitual', *do grés* 'always, perpetually, continually' [*Contribb.* 'G', col. 156]. According to VKG I, 86, 136; II, 549, it comes from the root **ghrendh-*, and on the analogy of *glwys* < **ghlendh* (RC XLII, 365), that is, from **ghlendtio-*, I would suppose it possible that from **ghrendhtio-* we should get *grwys* (= *grois*? cf. Juv. *ceroenhou* = *cerwynau* 'vats'; Ox. I, *moi* = *mwy*; *troi* = *trwy*). If this can be accepted, the meaning of *int groisauc* would be 'continually, without ceasing'. [In a note in the *Journal of Celtic Studies* I (1949), 71, K. Jackson doubts the relationship with the Ir. words here proposed, but does not suggest any alternative meaning for *int groisauc*.]

It will be seen that *groisauc* rhymes with *inadaut* and *trintaut*—a further instance of 'Irish' rhyme. (Cf. two instances of *awc*/*awt* rhyming in the *Cyvoesi Myrddin*, RBP col. 579, ll. 6–8; col. 581, ll. 28–30.)

8c. **inungueid.** I understand this as three separate words, *in un gueid*—taking the last to be the word *gweith* (*gwaith*), in its meaning of 'time'—not that of 'labour' or 'battle' (though these also are both of frequent occurrence). *Gwaith* meaning 'time' is fem., but the orthography of Juv. does not indicate this by showing the initial mutation. Cf. the same phrase in RBP col. 1053, l. 8, Dydwyn dyn att duw *yn vn weith*, and the parallel Irish phrase *ind fhecht so* 'on this occasion, now'; *in oenfhecht* 'all at one time, together', 'on one occasion' [*Contribb. f-fochraic*, cols. 54–5], PH p. 696, *Wör.* p. 538, GOI p. 161.

*un* can mean 'one' or 'same', and the *in* before it is the preposition *yn* 'in' (cf. *ar* un waith)—rather than an old form of the article. Zeuss argued in GC² pp. 608, 615 [cf. GOI pp. 238–9] that the adverbial particle *yn* which precedes adjectives is the dative of the article: if this is so, *yn* fawr, *yn* fach etc. corresponds to the Ir. *in* már, *in* biucc. (But contrast WG p. 436, which claims that this *yn* < **endo* governing the dative.) Since *int* is the form of the adverbial particle before adjs. in these englynion (cf. 9b below, *int* couer, and possibly *int groissauc* in 8b), I have no hesitation in taking *in* before *ungueid* to be the preposition.

It is interesting to compare expressions such as *yn un swydd* ('on purpose'); cf.

CA l. 1175, *yn un gwaret* (= 'at a gulp'; see n.), BBC p. 42, ll. 2–3, *in vn llv* ir *vn lle* teccaw; p. 34, ll. 5–6, a want *in un orsset.* But it is perfectly safe to accept the meaning of the Irish phrase as expressing exactly the meaning of its Welsh cognate *yn un waith* 'at one time', i.e. 'together', as in MA p. 224b, l. 40, *yn unawr.*

**guoled.** If *-gueid* represents *gweith*, then one must read this as *goleith* to preserve the internal rhyme, as in 2a *betid hicouid*, 3a *pater harimed* (Irish rhyme), 4a *Ihesu dielimlu*, 6a *diban iciman*, 8a *raut inadaut*; similarly in the third line, 3c *acup nis arcup*, 5c, 9c *gnim molim.*

In opposition to earlier lexicographers [who took *goleith* as a compound of *lleith* 'death'] I explained its meaning in *Cy.* XXVIII, 185 as 'to avoid, evade, elude'. In RC XXIX, 30, Loth gave the meaning of *yd oleithid gwr* in MA p. 160b as 'On flattait un homme', and in RC XXXVIII, 311 he suggested that the meaning of *goleith* as a noun is 'souplesse, échappatoire, fléchissement, attendrissement', and with the neg. 'inévitable, sans pitié'. These translations came much nearer to the meaning which is found in the old examples. [The example Loth quotes from RC XXXIX, 65 may be discounted: it comes from a text redacted by Iolo Morganwg.] But Loth also claims for *golaith* the meanings of 'flatterie, tentative d'attendrissement', RC XXXVIII, 312. He compares Ir. *fo-llega* [*Contribb.* fochratae-futhu, col. 271 'spreads, blots'], VKG II, 562; I, 123, **leg-* 'melt, dissolve' from the root *llaith* 'wet'. Perhaps it would be best to give some examples, from which it will be seen that *osgoi* 'evade' is the principal meaning:

Yssit ym argluyd...
Ny *oleith* lleith yr llyvyrder. MA p. 176a

'I have a lord...who does not try to avoid death by cowardice.'

Gwell *goleith* meuyl noe diala. *Cy.* VII, 141

'It is better to shun shame than to avenge it.'

Dywal dir fydd ei *olaith.*
(Proverbs at end of D.'s dictionary.)

'A fierce warrior, one must avoid him (give way to him).'

*Goleith* dy yscarant amgant dy vro
Mal tan twym tarth yn yt vo. BT p. 38, l. 18

'Thy enemies shun the border of thy land, like fire, etc.'

Gwr a wnaei ar lloegyr llwyr anreith
A dwyn y dynyon yn geith
A chwytaw racdaw rif seith—riallu
Ny ellid y *oleith.* H p. 48, ll. 11–14

'One who plundered England, and enslaved its people; seven champions fell before him. There was no escape from him.'

ir nep *goleith* lleith dyppo. BBC p. 90, ll. 9–10

'Death will come, in spite of all attempts to dodge.'

*Lleith anoleith*, BT p. 15, l. 13 'unavoidable, inevitable death'; *tri trin dioleith*, MA p. 281b, 'three who never shirked a battle'; *gwell goleith no govit*, RBP p. 1055, l. 41 'Better is flight than suffering.'

Duw am gwnel *gochel* ffrawt oeruel ffreu
Duw am gwnel om gweith *goleith* gwelieu
Duw am gwnel *goglyt* selwyt sulyeu.

RBP p. 1177, ll. 31–5

In this last example we have three synonyms, *gochel*, *goleith*, *goglyt* (from *gogel-af*). The meaning is attested again in AL I, 614, where it is said that a judge must be:

Mut a bydar. Drut a llavar.
Vfuyd ac ofnawc. *Ac oleithawc* (= A goleithawc).

'Mute and deaf, bold and eloquent, humble and fearful, and...'

Although the editor, Aneirin Owen, has translated the last word as 'religious' it is obvious that 'watchful, cautious' is the meaning. In *Cy.* VII, 136, people are advised to '*ymoleithio* a glew'—that is, to avoid, retreat from, or not to cross the path of a champion. Further examples of the word are MA p. 192b 47, Dos was...na *oleith* dy lwrw 'Go, boy, and swerve not from thy path', MA p. 145a 16, 155b 39, 158a 2, 160a 32, 179b 31, 205b 14, RBP col. 1222, l. 18, BT p. 39, l. 6.

The above examples prove that *golaith* is both a verb-noun and also a verb pres. indic, 3rd pers. sing., and that 'retreat, evade, turn from the path of, avoid, beware' are its meanings [cf. G 552]. In praising his warriors, Owain Cyfeiliog says,

Mawr a weith yd oleithir
gwyr ny oleith lleith ony llochir.

RBP p. 1435, ll. 19–20

That is, they did not evade death, nor fear it, so that in battle it was found repeatedly that men who were less brave would flee before their faces. Those who did not fear death were feared themselves. In the englyn, I understand *goleith Trindawd* to mean the fear of God, the fear that retreats before Him, as it were. It is the object of *ercis* in 8a. To me, the meaning is therefore 'He demanded of the host that belong to Him in the world, that they should unceasingly and all together fear the Trinity'.

[In a note on *piouboi*, B XIII, 205, Henry Lewis advocated a different syntax and a slightly different meaning for this englyn. He took the relative clause introduced by *piouboi* to be the subject of *ercis*, its antecedent being left unexpressed: a not uncommon construction. He understood the subjunctive to be used here in a future sense, and accepting IW's proposal for *int groisauc* he would therefore translate the englyn, 'He who will own the host in this world for ever has asked of it (or 'them', i.e. the dwellers on the earth) that they should all together fear (or 'honour') the Trinity.']

9a. **un ha med,** 'one who possesses'. This is the old rel. pron. *ha*, the form which occurs also in the Computus, together with its variant *hai*; cf. B III, 25b, line 9, *habid* 'which will be', line 8, *haibid*; and in Ox. I at the beginning of the ninth century *ha beinn*, B V, 238. On *meddu* 'to have the right to, to be able', see B I, 28; BT p. 67, l. 9, *Un duw* uchaf dewin doethaf mwyhaf *a ued*; BBC p. 29, l. 12, *Duu vet*.

**Hapuil haper,** 'both wisdom and dominion'. The meaning of *a...a* is 'both...and', cf. RBP col. 1048, l. 9, As clywo *a* duw *a* dyn; MA p. 195b, l. 48, Collant *ar* llygeid *ar* eneidyeu; p. 208b, l. 10, *ath* hendref *ath* hauod; RBP col. 1032, ll. 26–7, *A* mwyalch ar y nyth, *A* chelwydawc ny theu vyth, 'A blackbird on its nest, and a liar are never silent'.

**puil,** *pwyll* 'wisdom'. It developed the meaning of 'discretion, careful deliberation'.

**per.** The rhyme with *meir* shows that it is necessary to understand the *e* as representing *ei* (cf. 8c on *guoled*); therefore *peir*. It is interesting to find an example of the same word in O.W. orthography in BBC p. 41, l. 7 (Duw), Yssi *per* gad*eir* gadarnaw. / Yssi *hael* di*wael* diweirhaw. / Yssi *haul uraul* gurhaw. For the meaning cf. MA p. 250a, l. 38, Ytra uo ef yny wengan gadeir. / Yn *ben* ban lleueir yn beir eiryan. See the collection of examples of the word in HGCr. p. 171; Lewis suggests here that the meaning of *peir* in these is '*arglwydd* lord, ruler' (the word *pair* 'cauldron' as in AL II, 822 and PKM p. 34, l. 18 is obviously unsuited to the context). In the englyn, however, 'lord' does not give good sense in conjunction with *pwyll*. Christ is said here to possess both *pwyll* and *peir*, above and below Heaven. In HGCr. p. 80, ll. 13–14, we have an example in which there is a play upon the similarity in the root of the two words *pair* and *peri*:

> Iolaf-y *beir* o bured arwar
> A *beris* amad ac adar.

'I praise the Lord...who has created plants and animals.' Compare with this the way in which *pennaeth* can be used for both 'lord' and also 'dominion' BT p. 18, l. 6 (= AP line 175) p. 72, line 16 etc. I believe that *peir* can also mean both 'lord' and 'lordship', i.e. 'dominion' (cf. Ir. *flaith* which can mean both 'country' and 'ruler' [*Contribb.* F-fochraic, p. 160]).

I owe the reading *hapuil* instead of *napuil* to Sir John Morris-Jones. It is difficult to see the upward stroke of the *h* in the manuscript, but I do not doubt that this is correct.

9b. **uuc nem isnem,** 'above heaven, below heaven'; cf. BT p. 7, l. 2 *vch nef is nef nyt gwledic namyn ef. Vch mor is mor. ef an crewys.*

**intcouer,** 'completely'. For *e* = *ei*, see above on 9a, *per*. For *int* as the adverbial particle (= *yn*), see above on 8b, 8c (and on *it, in* 6a, 7a). The gloss *int coucant* 'completely, certainly' attests *int* as the form of the adverbial particle in early Breton [DGVB pp. 225–6, 234]. In GC[2] 615–16, Zeuss gives the Cornish form as *yn*, Breton *en* (*en mat* = *yn fad* 'good, lucky') and also *ent* (before both vowels and consonants), *ent abil, ent certen, ent seder*, etc. in Ml. Breton. The text here shows that the form in Welsh was the same, whatever derivation may be assigned to it.

For *couer* 'complete, perfect' see B III, 55, and cf. Ir. *cóir* 'true, right, fitting', PKM 107, 124, 269. The meaning of *yn gywair* is 'all in order, complete' [GPC pp. 828–9].

9c. **guorgnim**. See above on 5c.

## *Chapter VIII*

# THE POEMS OF LLYWARCH HEN

BEFORE attempting to deal with the poems of Llywarch, I must first say a few words on the problem of the Cynfeirdd, or Early Bards, in general.

According to the *Historia Brittonum* of Nennius, if we may trust the Harley 3859 text of that much-debated work, poems were composed in the Welsh language as early as the second half of the sixth century of our era. This manuscript was written about the year 1100: the *Historia* itself is ascribed to various dates ranging from the close of the eighth century to the middle of the ninth. There is no need for me to discuss the Nennian problem in any detail.[1] All I ask is permission to cite Nennius as witness to a tradition, current in Wales about the year 800, to the effect that Talhaearn Tad Awen (*Father of the Muse*) sang in Welsh when the Britons of the North were fighting against Ida of Northumbria and his sons; and that four other Welsh bards flourished during the same period, namely, Aneirin, Taliesin, Blwchfardd, and Cian. That is our starting-point—the tradition, as early as A.D. 800, that Welsh poetry was composed between 550 and 600.

Not a line of Talhaearn's poetry has survived: this is true also of Blwchfardd and Cian. No forger even has troubled us with spurious poems in their names. Tradition has preserved—or if you like, invented—their names and their poetic renown. And that is all. It is different with Aneirin and Taliesin. In manuscripts of the late twelfth, thirteenth, and fourteenth centuries (the *Black Book of Carmarthen,* the *Book of Aneirin*, the *Book of Taliesin*, the *White Book of Rhydderch*, and the *Red Book of Hergest*) some thousands of lines are preserved, which are attributed without hesitation by the scribes to these two. Aneirin has over 1,400 lines: Taliesin, not far short of 4,000.

In the same manuscripts, however, we find many other poems, which are said to be by Myrddin Wyllt (*the Wild*) and Llywarch Hen (*the Old*), the latter having some 1,500 lines to his credit—at any rate in modern printed editions. These two poets also are placed by tradition

[1] On Nennius and Harleian MS. 3859 see above pp. 42–3; 51–2; 72–3; notes 5 and 7 to chapter IV, notes 8 and 9 to chapter VI; where the conclusions which IW here summarizes briefly are set forth in greater detail.

in the sixth century. Myrddin Wyllt corresponds to the Suibhne Geilt of Irish literature.[2] He became *gwyllt*, or a madman of the woods, through fear of Rhydderch Hael, the British king of Dumbarton, one of the allies against Ida and his sons mentioned by Nennius. Myrddin's lord and patron was the Gwenddoleu who lost the battle of Arfderydd (Arthuret, near Carlisle) in 575.[3] Llywarch also belonged to the north: he was cousin[4] to Urien Rheged, the leader of the confederation against Ida. (One other reference to the early Llywarch might be quoted. I found his name in the twelfth-century pedigree of the royal dynasty of Gwynedd. Rhodri the Great, king of North Wales and parts of South Wales in the ninth century, is shown as a direct descendant of Llywarch Hen. A royal pedigree should be above suspicion, and may be taken as sound evidence in a loyal court. So we can accept Llywarch as a historic person without more ado. Reckoning thirty years to a generation, Llywarch Hen fits into the sixth century very comfortably.)[5]

We have thus four candidates for sixth-century honours, and each must be examined separately. Aneirin and Taliesin have the advantage, for what it is worth, of the Nennian testimony: the absence of the other two from that early list, though not decisive against them, is certainly not a point in their favour. My favourite is Aneirin, the poet of the Gododdin, who sang to the heroes who rode forth with the dawn to the Battle of Catraeth.[6] Editor after editor has attempted to prove that this battle was one of the known historic battles of the North, fought in the late sixth or early seventh century, but every attempt has so far failed, definitely failed. What we do get in the Aneirin poems is the story of a

2 See J. G. O'Keefe, *Buile Shuibhne: The Story of Suibhne Geilt*, ITS XII; and on the word *geilt* (W. *gwyllt*, *gwyllon*) see IW in B I, 228–34. [See further A. O. H. Jarman, 'The Welsh Myrddin Poems', ALMA pp. 20 ff. and TYP pp. 469–74 for a summary of work on Myrddin published subsequently to the date of this lecture.]

3 HW pp. 166, 167 n. 22; [TYP pp. 208–10, 379–80].

4 Urien was the son of Cynfarch, son of Meirchiawn; Llywarch was the son of Elidyr Lydanwyn, son of Meirchiawn, according to *Bonedd Gwŷr y Gogledd* [EWGT pp. 72–4, TYP pp. 238–9]. In the tract *De Situ Brecheniauc* in Vesp. XIV, 11a, Nyuein daughter of Brychan is said to be Urien's mother, and Gwawr, daughter of Brychan, Llywarch Hen's mother; see *Cy.* XIX, 26, 33, 34 [EWGT pp. 14–16].

[5] Cf. p. 151 below; EWGT p. 36, etc. This passage and the two subsequent passages in the text on pp. 126–7; 151–2 which are enclosed between brackets have been interpolated from a broadcast talk 'The Llywarch Hen Poems' delivered by IW on 22 November 1952. See the introduction to this volume.

[6] See chapter V above. It may be recalled that the substance of chapter V had not yet appeared in print in English at the time when IW gave this lecture to the British Academy.

desperate, foolhardy, glorious raid into Yorkshire, by the war-band of a chieftain called Mynyddawg Mwynfawr, who had his court in the Edinburgh district, or Manaw Gododdin.[7] He collected a retinue of 300 youthful warriors, and feasted them royally for a full year in his hall at Caer Eidyn (Caredin, or Dunedin). Mead was the warrior's pay; these were paid in advance. During the year-long feast they had wine and mead without stint. The mead was sweet, and they paid for it with their lives.

Gwerth eu gwledd o fedd fu eu henaid.

At the end of the year, Mynyddawg sent them on an expedition or raid to Catraeth, a town in the midst of the enemy. I have no hesitation in identifying the place as Catterick in Yorkshire. He set them an impossible task. But they had drunk his mead, and they proved that they deserved it, *Talasant eu medd.* The heroes rode forth gaily, with laughter, to their doom. 'Three hundred fought a hundred thousand' says the bard. They reached Catraeth, and fell, all except one man who cut his way through the ranks of the enemy, and returned safely. This is the central theme of the Gododdin poems, the faithful war-band, obeying their lord, even when he sent them to certain death.

I do not know if there are many people in England who take an interest in the detailed history of the Crimean War, as set forth by Kinglake. Everybody knows 'The Charge of the Light Brigade'. The raid on Catraeth and the Charge of the noble six hundred have much in common. To the English historian the Charge was a blunder: Nennius did not deem the raid on Catraeth worth mentioning. The poets thought otherwise.

Taliesin comes next, especially in his songs to Urien and his son Owain. The Elphin poems are in a different category, as are the religious odes in the Book of Taliesin, the Alexander poems, etc.[8] But as Sir John Morris-Jones has dealt at length with this Cynfardd

[7] More properly we should say 'Manaw of Gododdin', since as Jackson has pointed out in OSPG pp. 69–75, 'Gododdin' in this name is not the second part of a compound, but an attributive genitive 'Manaw *of* (i.e. *in*) Gododdin' being distinguished in this way from the other Manaw, which was the Isle of Man.

[8] For IW's summary of the contents of the *Book of Taliesin* see LEWP pp. 51 ff., PT pp. xiv ff., and p. 172 below. He describes the 'Taliesin saga' as 'a folk-tale in North Wales with Taliesin as its hero' and 'probably composed in the ninth century at earliest'. It was this folk-tale which associated the poet with Maelgwn and Elphin. A version of it was translated by Lady Guest and appears in her *Mabinogion* (1849). Its contents have been fully discussed and analysed by IW in his *Chwedl Taliesin* (Caerdydd, 1957).

in his excellent monograph in the *Cymmrodor*,[9] I will say nothing more.

Myrddin and his vaticinations are certainly late, even post-Norman for the most part. There may be earlier material in the Black Book *Hoianeu* and *Afalleneu*—perhaps I ought to say there *must* be, as every forger imitates an original, so that even a faked antique poem may give useful hints on the type of metre, diction, grammatical forms, etc., to be expected in genuine early verse.[10] For the moment, we will just fail Myrddin, and pass on.

Now, what of Llywarch Hen? Dr Lloyd thinks 'that Myrddin has a suspiciously mythical air, and that Llywarch Hen was a chieftain of whose devotion to bardism there is no satisfactory evidence'.[11] I agree. I cannot prove, and I do not wish to prove that the sixth-century chieftain of that name was a poet. Yet the author of the Llywarch Hen englynion was indeed and very truth a great poet, and he was no forger or maker of false antiques. He belonged to a totally different class from Myrddin, the pseudo-Myrddin. A bard composing a *darogan*, or vaticination, to foretell the victory of the Cymry in the war against the Saxons, had no more scruples about lying than the propaganda department of a modern State at war. The *daroganau* were essentially propaganda, and had tremendous influence on the course of history, because men believed in them, and acted on them.[12] The Llywarch Hen poems, however, were not propaganda.

The first point to be noted about them is their metrical form: they are all *englynion* of the earliest known types. The Aneirin and Taliesin metres are much more elaborate, *odleu* and *gorchaneu* of various patterns.

9 *Cy.* XXVIII (1918) [= *Tal.*].

[10] See the references cited in notes 2 and 3 above. The suggestion which IW here makes concerning the probability of older elements in the Myrddin poems invites the comment that there is some evidence to justify the belief that Myrddin was indeed one of the authentic and genuine Cynfeirdd, and he has been accepted as such by some scholars; see Idris Foster in *Ysgrifau Beirniadol* (ed. J. E. Caerwyn Williams, Gwasg Gee, 1970) V, 20, and in *Arch. Cam.* CXVIII (1969), 12–13; Glanmor Williams, *Taliesin* XVI (1968), 31. For the evidence see my remarks on 'Y Cynfeirdd â'r Traddodiad Cymraeg', B XXI, 30–7, and cf. TYP pp. 471–2, 380. It would seem that this may indeed have been IW's own later view; see his note on the reference to *Mirdyn* in CA line 466, p. 188.

11 HW p. 170.

[12] On the genre of prophetic poetry in Welsh see M. E. Griffiths, *Early Vaticination in Welsh* (Cardiff, 1926); R. Wallis Evans, 'Trem ar y Cywydd Brud', *Harlech Studies* (1938), pp. 149 ff.; W. Garmon-Jones, 'Welsh Nationalism and Henry Tudor', *Cymm. Trans.* (1917–18), pp. 1–59; Glanmor Williams, 'Proffwydoliaeth, Prydyddiaeth a Pholitics yn yr Oesoedd Canol', *Taliesin* XVI (1968), 31–9.

Llywarch has only the *englyn*, either *englyn milwr,*[13] three-line stanzas, or triplets, of seven syllables, rhyming; or *englyn penfyr,*[13] triplets of 10, 6, 7 syllables—with the variants 11, 7, 6; 9, 6, 7; or with 8 in the last line; a few having 5 in the second—the last two lines rhyme together, and in most cases also with the seventh or eighth syllable of the first line. Occasionally the fifth syllable in the first line rhymes with the seventh. There is also assonance or alliteration, and internal rhyme, but these are not essential. The proportion of *englynion milwr* to the *penfyr* types is roughly 10:7. A few variants occur, e.g. 7, 6, 6, 6: 7, 5, 5, 7: 7, 8, 8; but they are exceptional. There are three kinds of rhyme: (1) the regular full rhyme, this is the usual form; (2) half rhyme, or *proest,*[14] the final consonant is the same, but the vowel or diphthong varies; and (3), a kind of rhyme which I have called *Irish rhyme,*[15] where the vowel or diphthong is the same in each rhyming syllable, but the final consonant varies, though it must be of the same class. Hard mutes rhyme together, e.g. *-awc, -awt*; so also the spirants *dd, f* (*v*), *l, r, n*; e.g. *-wyn, -wyf*; *-el, -er.*

Englynion of the above types, both triplets and quatrains, were regularly employed in early Welsh sagas, either as pure ornament to adorn the tale, or else as a convention in dramatic dialogue or monologue.

And this brings me to my chief thesis, namely, that the Llywarch Hen englynion, in my opinion, are the verse elements in a cycle of stories, tales, sagas, told in pre-Norman times in north-east Wales, in the eastern part of Powys bordering on England, opposite to, and perhaps including portions of Shropshire and Herefordshire. (The Northern tradition has not utterly perished, but the story there is a record of absolute defeat for the Welsh; and for the most part the Llywarch Hen poems centre round the courts and camps of what is today north-east Wales, Shrewsbury and the border country. The Saxons have advanced far from the eastern shores of Britain, the

13 J. Morris-Jones, *Cerdd Dafod* (Oxford, 1925), pp. 316, 320. [See also K. Jackson, 'Incremental Repetition in the Early Welsh Englyn', *Speculum* XVI, 308 ff.]

14 *Cerdd Dafod*, p. 254.

15 *Y Beirniad* VI (1916), 203–5, Kuno Meyer, *A Primer of Irish Metrics*, p. 7. [The term 'Irish rhyme' is now in general currency for the type of rhyme which IW here describes, and which he was the first to identify in early Welsh poetry, pointing out its similarity to the system of rhyme used in early Irish poetry. He described these archaic rhymes as 'Irish rhyme' for the first time in his review of J. Gwenogvryn Evans's 'amended text' of the *Book of Taliesin* in *Y Beirniad* for 1916. On the corresponding conventions in Irish poetry see now G. Murphy, *Early Irish Metrics* (Dublin, 1961), pp. 32–3 and refs. cited.]

midlands are in the hands of the enemies, and the fighting is almost on the boundaries of modern Wales. So it is clear that we cannot ascribe to the actual composition of the Llywarch Hen poems any earlier date than the middle of the ninth century.)[16] The prose setting has disappeared: the verse has survived in twelfth-century and fourteenth-century manuscripts, a few stanzas, even, in eighteenth-century copies of earlier manuscripts now lost.

The classics of Welsh story-telling are the *Four Branches of the Mabinogi*, an artistic fusion of the sagas of Gwynedd, Dyfed, and Gwent. Why was Powys omitted? We have been told that the prose tale was not popular in Powys; or that the prose sagas hail from the Goidelic districts of Wales, while the Brittonic Powys was the home of the englyn.[17] A study of these englynion has compelled me to reject these views, and to hold that Powys also at one time had its saga, complete with prose and verse; the prose has gone, but we can still enjoy the beautiful englynion that once adorned the tale. Only now we have to make more or less wild guesses at the context.

What was the relation of the englynion to the prose? What were the functions of verse and prose in the early tales? The Mabinogi helps us here a little, though not so much as one would like. In the Oxford edition,[18] the Four Branches fill 81 pages: there are five englynion only, while all the rest is prose. Three stanzas are addressed by Gwydion to the Eagle on the lonely oak-tree in the glen of Baladeulyn, and these three begin with the same words *Dar a dyf* 'An oak grows'.[19] This

[16] See n. 5 above and cf. LEWP p. 48, 'These sad tales and sad songs belong to Powys on the borders of Wales, facing Mercia: the period is somewhere round 850, that is the most likely dating I can make. Cyngen ruled over Powys from 808 to 854, he died at Rome, the last of his dynasty, in the latter year. During his reign the realm of Powys was reduced to sore straits, for in 822 it was overrun by the English. Offa's Dyke in the previous century had already cut off a big portion of the old Powys, leaving little to the Welsh save moor and mountain. The new frontier ran close to Llangollen, and it is worth noting that the graves of three of Llywarch Hen's sons are close by. All the places mentioned in the Heledd poems are on or just beyond Offa's Dyke, in Montgomeryshire, Denbighshire and Shropshire. The mood of the poet or author of these two sagas tallies very well with what one would expect in such a period of national calamity and humiliation.'

[17] For this suggestion see W. J. Gruffydd, 'The Mabinogion', *Cymm. Trans.* (1912–13), pp. 27–8; and cf. E. Anwyl, 'The Four Branches of the Mabinogi', ZfcPh. 1 (1897), 279.

[18] RM pp. 1–81.

19 RM pp. 78–9, PKM p. 90. For the other two englynion see RM pp. 38, 67, PKM pp. 43, 76; the one being spoken by Efnyssyen, the other by Math. In *Culhwch and Olwen*, RM p. 133, and again in the *Trioedd*, RM p. 308 [TYP no. 18], Arthur is credited with an englyn.

artifice of linking englynion together by repeating the same phrase at the beginning of each is characteristic also of the Llywarch poems:[20] and these 'chains' are useful guides to a critic who is trying to distinguish the various episodes in the long columns of the Red Book text.

These Gwydion englynion help in another way: it is admitted by all students of the Mabinogi that they are centuries earlier in date than the prose setting. They have preserved the old form of Lleu's name, where the prose has gone hopelessly astray (with its *Llew*, and *Llef*); and, what is of greater importance to us, the word *maes*, which had contracted into a monosyllable long before the twelfth century, is still a disyllable in them. It was disyllabic in 817 and 902, if the *Annales Cambriae* are evidence: so in *Armes Prydein*, a vaticination which must fall between 850 and 900.[21] It is a monosyllable in 1140, as attested by the *Book of Llan Dâv*, and also by the poems of Cynddelw. If that pedantic poet condescended to make a monosyllable of it in his odes (*circa* 1150), we are justified in assuming that the later pronunciation had at any rate a century's authority behind it, if not more. I found *maes* in a Llywarch englyn[22] where the rhyme and metre prove it a disyllable—a very useful indication of date. If it be objected that *ma-es* in this englyn is an attempt at archaism, the answer is obvious, englynion in sagas are not the work of Court poets, like Cynddelw and the other Gogynfeirdd, with their excessive fondness for the obsolete and archaic in form and construction. Those experts in antiquarian lore cared little whether they were understood or not by the common herd. The englynion-makers, on the other hand, were the champion story-tellers of Wales; and they knew, none better, that simplicity and directness are of the very essence of successful tale-telling. To tell a story well, your words must be simple, intelligible; your meaning must be grasped immediately, or else you will not grip your audience. When Cynddelw chanted his eulogies

20 For some Irish parallels see E. Windisch, *Táin Bó Cualnge* (Leipzig, 1905), 4146, 4150, 4155; 4164–86 [= C. O'Rahilly, *The Táin Bó Cualnge from the Book of Leinster* (ITS and Dublin Institute, 1967), 3539, 3543, 3547, 3556, 3564, 3569, 3574, 3579] Standish Hayes O'Grady, *Silva Gadelica* I, 143, 204, 230.

[21] AP l. 87, Yg koet *ymaes* ym bro ym bryn. In his edition of *Armes Prydein* (1955), IW subsequently dated the poem to *circa* 930, associating it with the events which preceded the Battle of Brunanburh in 937. The date suggested here is that which he proposed in his first published discussion of the poem in *Y Beirniad* VI (1916), 207–12. For dissyllabic *ma-es* in early poetry cf. PT II, 8, ny nodes na *maes* na choedyd; and on the corroborative evidence which this provides for the antiquity of the Four Branches see PKM pp. xviii–xx, 293.

22 [CLlH v, i]; MA p. 96a, i (from Panton MS. pp. 14, 133b; BM Add. MS. 14867, fo. 147b).

or war-odes, it did not matter very much if his lord and patron had only a vague idea of what they meant.[23] The rolling lines of alliterative verse did the business. But when the *Cyfarwydd*, as they called the story-teller in medieval Wales, recited his romances before the Queen and her maidens, or to the warriors in the hall, he had to make himself understood. That is why his prose is so beautifully simple and direct: that is why he uses only the simplest form of early verse, the englyn, to adorn his tale: that is why in this simple metre his language is so very unelaborate and unadorned that a twentieth-century Welsh peasant can understand without any difficulty much of his work. And that is the reason why many scholars find it so hard to believe that these simple lines are more than a thousand years old. Yet this simplicity is deceptive. When these englynion are carefully examined, they are found to contain archaic forms beyond the ken of the Cynddelw school.

The story of *Trystan and Esyllt*[24] is much more helpful than the Mabinogi, as an example of early Welsh romance partly modernised. All the copies known are later than 1550. Here the prose has been cut down to a bare minimum but there are twenty-eight englynion. The prose passages are late: not so the englynion. In two manuscripts there is first of all a short prose preface, telling how Trystan eloped with Esyllt to the Forest of Celyddon: her husband, March ap Meirchion, appeals to Arthur for justice, and Arthur with his warriors surrounds the wood. Esyllt hears the din of armed men, and trembles in Trystan's arms. All this takes fourteen lines of prose. Trystan tells her in an englyn to be of good cheer: then, sword in hand, he passes safely through the host. Cai, Arthur's steward, being in love with Esyllt's handmaiden, Golwg Hafddydd, tells Esyllt in an englyn that Trystan has escaped. She answers in another englyn. There are four englynion in this short colloquy, two each. Eight lines of prose follow, leading up to a longer interchange of stanzas (fifteen) between Gwalchmai, as peace-maker, and Trystan. Then he conducts the lover to Arthur's presence, and introduces him in an englyn to his lord. Arthur welcomes Trystan in three englynion, without getting a reply. A fourth englyn, stressing their

23 Cf. RM p. 160, 'Behold certain bards came to sing a song to Arthur: and no man but Kadrieith knew what that song was, except that it was a song in praise of Arthur' [Gwyn Jones and Thomas Jones, *The Mabinogion* (Everyman, 1949), p. 151; Melville Richards, *Breudwyt Ronabwy* (Caerdydd, 1948), p. 20, ll. 15–16].

24 Ed. by IW in B v, 115–29. [Translated by T. P. Cross, 'A Welsh Tristan Episode', *Studies in Philology* XVII, 93 ff. See also B XIII, 25 ff.; LEWP pp. 18–19; TYP pp. 332, 383–4.]

blood-relationship, is more successful. Trystan replies in an englyn, and submits. In a short prose passage, we are told that Arthur makes peace between the husband and lover; his decision is fair enough, one is to have Esyllt while there are leaves on the trees, the other when the trees are bare, and the husband is to have the first choice. March promptly chooses the season when there are no leaves, and Esyllt exultantly cries out the last englyn of all:

> Three trees, the holly, the ivy, and the yew,
> Put forth leaves all the year round.
> So Trystan will have me as long as he lives.

In the other two manuscripts, the only prose is a short and hopelessly unsuitable prologue of half a dozen lines, which could only have been invented by one who had never heard or seen the full version. This text begins with the sixth englyn, the colloquy between Gwalchmai and Trystan: it evidently derives from an incomplete copy which lacked not only the prose introduction, and the first five stanzas, but also all the other prose passages. We thus have for comparison two forms of a Trystan story, one consisting of englynion, and the other of prose and englynion.

Taking the complete version, I find that the function of the prose passages is to tell the story, and explain the circumstances, while the englynion in every case are used to express personal emotion, or for dramatic dialogue. The speakers are addressed by name, or else they name themselves, so that it is easy to identify the speaker of any particular englyn. The first line is a greeting, the second a description, the third carries on the conversation: or else, the two first lines contain gnomic poetry, or tags of nature poetry, and as before the sting comes in the tail. Occasionally, even as in modern verse, the whole stanza makes sense; this is somewhat rare. If the poet is in difficulties he just falls back on a proverb, or a word about the weather, anything that will rhyme with the remark his hero has to make at the moment. Very often this padding has no relevance whatsoever to the story.[25] Chains of en-

[25] Cf. LEWP pp. 21–2, 'In these dramatic tales, dialogue was regularly put into verse form, and their authors found considerable difficulty in fitting question and answer, the thrust and parry of lively talk, into a metric frame. Brevity is the soul of wit. Even a three-line stanza is too long for a neat reply; one line is ample in most cases. So they framed their dialogues in nature poetry and proverbs, which provided them with just the material required to fill up what was left of the line or *englyn* or poem. There was no chance of their listeners mistaking the frame for the picture, for this padding had no relevance whatsoever to the dialogue.'

glynion are linked together by the repetition of the initial phrase, as in the Mabinogi. Seven begin with *Trystan gynheddfeu*, three with *Gwalchmai gynheddfeu*.

All this is pertinent to the study of the Llywarch poems. Every feature mentioned above has its counterpart in them, except, of course, the prose framework. That is gone, completely. In the early stages of the tradition the minstrel knew the story by heart, at any rate the main lines of it. There was no necessity for him to be able to repeat it word for word, provided that he followed the original faithfully enough to bring in the englynion at the right moment. These, however, had to be committed carefully to memory; metre, alliteration, rhyme helped the *cyfarwydd* to store them in his mind exactly as he heard them. If he distrusted his memory, he could then write them on vellum, and by so doing would make it still more certain that these verse elements of the story would be preserved intact for centuries, practically in their earliest, and most primitive form. The prose, on the other hand, remained fluid: it could be modernised freely from generation to generation, in construction, in vocabulary, even in substance. At last the oral tradition comes to an end, the story is forgotten. The vellum remains, and the scribes take up the task; they have only the englynion, and they proceed to mishandle them in the various and devious ways of their kind, changing the orthography, disturbing the order of stanzas, inserting glosses, and interpolating generally. Even the metre suffers. I assume that the Llywarch poems have passed through these tribulations.

The *Black Book of Carmarthen*[26] is the earliest manuscript written wholly in Welsh; perhaps it would be more correct to call it the earliest collection of Welsh manuscripts, for there can be no doubt of its composite character, or of its being the product of the same scriptorium. Its date is probably the last quarter of the twelfth century.[27] Part II begins on p. 81, and breaks off in an incomplete state on p. 96. As it contains (pp. 85–7) a section of Cynddelw's Deathbed Song,

26 Ed. J. G. Evans (Pwllheli, 1906). [On the saga-poems contained in this manuscript, see further LEWP pp. 22–3.]

27 Part I, pp. 78–9, ends with an ode to the Lord Rhys; the author is Cynddelw, =RBP 173 b. col. 1436) Rhys died in 1197; HW p. 582. Cynddelw's Deathbed Song is in part II, pp. 85–7. Part III begins on p. 97, and contains on p. 103 Cynddelw's ode to the war-band of Madog ap Maredudd, lord of Powys: p. 104 his elegy to Madog, who died 1160. So that each part contains a poem by Cynddelw the great poet of Powys, who lived to see the rise of Llywelyn Fawr, and the victories of Aberconwy, Porthaethwy and Coed Aneu in 1194; probably also the capture of Mold, 6 January 1199; see HW p. 590; MA p. 189 b. Did the scribe come from Powys?

one cannot place it much before 1200. The sixth poem (pp. 89–93 [= CLlH no. VII]) begins with nature and gnomic poetry, with traces of dialogue here and there; soon the dialogue becomes unmistakable—a certain Pelis, who claims to have been nurtured by Owain Rheged, is one of the speakers. Then we hear an appeal to a war-band to stand firm, and not to incur shame 'after mead', followed by a reference to the death of Mechydd, son of Llywarch, at the hands of Mwngc's spearmen. The whole is in the englyn metre, and bears signs of considerable antiquity, but is too scrappy in character to make it possible for me to reconstruct the story lying behind it.[28]

Part III consists of pp. 97–108. At the very end comes a bunch of englynion under the title 'The names of Llywarch Hen's sons' [CLlH no. VIII]. There are twelve stanzas in all, and of these, four have already occurred in the Part II poem already mentioned. For this twelfth-century testimony to the Llywarch saga, in spite of its meagreness, one cannot be too grateful.[29]

The bulk of the poems with which I must deal are to be found in the *Red Book of Hergest* (*circa* 1400).[30] The scribe has evidently attempted to rewrite them in the orthography of his school. Fortunately he sometimes forgot to be consistent, and by copying mechanically a word here and there, he left unmistakable traces of a twelfth-century original—by that I mean a manuscript of the Black Book school of orthography. Occasionally this scribe in his zeal for modernizing, or in sheer thoughtlessness, spoils the metre by introducing fourteenth-century forms in defiance of rhyme and reason. How far this kind of substitution has taken place, initially and medially, where the rhyme scheme

[28] IW discusses this poem further in LEWP pp. 14–16. For a complete translation see now Clancy, EWP pp. 95–8, and for translations of the earlier part, which consists almost entirely of nature-gnomic and nature-descriptive englynion, see Conran, *Penguin Book of Welsh Verse*, pp. 96–7, and K. Jackson, *Early Celtic Nature Poetry* (Cambridge, 1935), pp. 50–3. The text of the earlier part is edited by Jackson, EWGP no. 1.

[29] Cf. LEWP p. 22, 'From page 81 to page 108 it (the BBC) contains for the most part what I take to be a collection of songs from our earliest sagas; amongst them are priceless fragments of the earliest Arthurian romances, pre-Norman, pre-Geoffrey of Monmouth.' IW's views concerning the nature of these early saga-poems are quoted and further developed by Thomas Jones in 'The Early Evolution of the Story of Arthur', *Nottingham Medieval Studies* VIII (1964), 15–18 (= B XVII (1958), 235–52).

30 RBP cols. 1036–49. Later manuscripts containing copies are Peniarth 111, pp. 125–67, a copy made in 1607 of a copy made in 1573 of the missing portion of the *White Book of Rhydderch* (cf. Peniarth 12, p. 132; *Cy.* VII, 123–54), therefore an earlier text than the Red Book (I believe the Red Book is a direct copy of this part of the White Book); Panton 14, p. 133 (1758) refers to other copies of the 1573 text made by Roger Maurice and Thomas Williams, Add. MS. 14867, fols. 147b–167a (1759).

provides no means of detecting such changes, one cannot say. Sometimes stanzas are run together: words are omitted, or half-lines, or even full lines. The order is palpably wrong in one part,[31] and at the end of one poem we find a jumble of stanzas which seemingly have no connexion with one another or with what precedes, except some kind of relation to the Llywarch Hen family.[32]

The material falls into three classes. I. Gnomic poetry, mostly, interspersed with nature poetry. II. Poems about Llywarch and his sons. III. The Cynddylan poems.

I cannot discuss Class I today. Stanzas of this type are hard to date, hard to localise. A reference to Gwynedd in the *Gnawd* series is too complimentary to have come from anyone but a poet of Gwynedd.[33] And an englyn may be chock-full of archaic forms, though composed at a late date, simply because it contains genuine early proverbs. That the bards kept on producing *Eiry Mynydd* englynion down to the fifteenth century, if not later, seems incontestable, if late forms in the rhyming syllable are a criterion.

Class II, the Llywarch englynion. There is no title in the Red Book, but I should like to call the first twenty-one stanzas in the *Kynn bum kein vaglawc* series 'The Song of the Old Man'.[34] I have translated some of these, as literally and faithfully as I could.

Before my back was bent, ready of speech was I.
What is wonderful is praised.
The men of Argoed[35] have always fed me.

[31] RBP col. 1036 presents Llywarch's 'Lament for his old age' as the first poem in the series, followed immediately (col. 1037) by the dialogue between Llywarch and Gwên, and Llywarch's elegies for Gwên and Pyll and (more briefly) for others of his sons. In his edition IW transposed the order of these poems (CLlH nos. I and II), arguing that the dialogue and the elegies would have come from an earlier stage in the story than the old man's lament.

[32] RBP cols. 1038, l. 35–1039, l. 8 (= CLlH I, 40–8).

33 RBP col. 1031, ll. 7–8, *gnawt gwr tec yggwyned.* Class I (gnomic and nature englynion) were ascribed to Llywarch because they immediately preceded the poems about Llywarch and his sons in RBH (cols. 1028–34). I can think of no other reason. [These poems have been edited by K. Jackson in his *Early Welsh Gnomic Poems* (Cardiff, 1935) and translated in his *Early Celtic Nature Poetry* (Cambridge, 1935).]

[34] CLlH II; translated LEWP pp. 41–3; Conran, *Penguin Book of Welsh Verse*, pp. 87–9; Clancy, EWP pp. 76–8. Both these last translations follow the text as edited subsequently by IW in CLlH II, and include four stanzas whose doubtful interpretation caused IW to omit them in his own translation.

35 Not the northern locality, but Powys, or a part of Powys; cf. the parallel references in the next stanza, and RBP col. 1046, l. 10 (= CLlH XI, 45c). Cynddelw also uses *Argoedwys* as equivalent to 'men of Powys', RBP col. 1396, ll. 30–1; 1398, 27 (where

Before my back was bent, bold was I.
I was made welcome in the ale-house
Of Powys, the paradise of Wales.

Before my back was bent, comely was I.
My spear led the attack.
Now my back is bowed. I am heavy. I am sad.

The last line is very effective, in its full alliterative form,

*Wyf kefngrwm. Wyf trwm. Wyf truan.*

The old man then addresses his stick:

Little staff of wood, it is now autumn.
Brown is the bracken. The stubble is yellow.
I have given up what I love.

Little staff of wood, it is now winter.
Men talk much over their drink.
No one comes near my bedside.

Little staff of wood, it is now springtime.
Brown[36] are the cuckoos. Bright is the foam.
No maiden loves me.

Little staff of wood, it is now May.
Red is the furrow. Curly is the young corn.
It grieves me to look at thy beak.

Little staff of wood, O kind branch!
Support thou a sorrowful old man,
Llywarch the babbler!

Little staff of wood, be kind
And support me still more.
I am Llywarch, long babbling.

*argoetwys* is paralleled by *powys* in the succeeding stanzas); 1399, 34, *argoedwys bowys*. Further, cf. RBP 1421, 15–16; 1391, 12; 1399, 4; 1400, 36. There are several places called Argoed near Kerry, and round Clun Forest.

[36] Conran's translation (*loc. cit.*) reads 'Cuckoos *hid*, clear their grieving'. This follows an emendation of the text proposed by Thomas Jones, B XIII, 14–17, who argues that the original is likely to have read *Kud(d)* ('hidden') rather than *Rud(d)* ('brown'). This seems likely on orthographical grounds, as well as giving much better sense in the context. For the second half of the line, IW later rejected the MS. reading *ewyn* 'foam' (CLlH p. 103 n.) in favour of *cwyn*, which can mean either 'feasting' or 'lament'. Hence his translation in LEWP 'There is light at a feast'. In the note referred to, Thomas Jones gives good reason for preferring the second alternative, and his suggestion has been followed by Conran in his translation of this line quoted above.

This leaf here, the wind is chasing it.
Alas for its fate!
Old already, born this year!

What I loved in my youth, now I hate,
A woman, a stranger, a young horse.
In truth I am not suited for them.

The four things I have always hated most
Have come upon me at one and the same time,
Coughing, old age, sickness, sorrow.

I am old, I am lonely, I am unshapely, and cold,
After an honoured bed,
I am wretched, I am bent double.

I am bent double, old, peevish, perverse,
I am foolish, I am irritable.
They that loved me, love me not.

Maidens love me not. No one visits me.
I cannot move about.
O Death! why does it not come to me?

Neither sleep nor joy comes to me
After the death of Llawr and Gwên.
I am irritable and withered.[37] I am old.

Sad was the fate ordained for Llywarch.
From the night he was born,
Long toiling, weariness without relief.

These well-known stanzas are linked by meaning, by form, by repetitions; and have become the classic monologue of the old man in our literature.

Then without any break whatsoever in the manuscript comes a chain of thirteen englynion, which are obviously out of place here, if the old man's song is to precede them, for in these, Gwên, one of the two sons, whose death is mourned by the old man, is still alive.[38] Their place, in

37 Or 'a withered (irritable) carcass' (*wyf anwar abar*). *Abar* means 'body, carcass, skeleton'. [Cf. LEWP p. 43, 'The difficulty lies in combining *anwar* "irritable" and *abar*, a contemptuous word for a dead body, just like *carcass*. The suggestion is that his withered enfeebled body is as good as dead, except that there is still in it enough life to complain and grouse.']

[38] RBP col. 1037, ll. 1–36 (= CLlH I, 1–13). See note 31 above.

my opinion, is at the end of a long tale giving the youthful exploits of this Gwên ap Llywarch—a Powys Mabinogi to balance the Mabinogi of Lleu in Gwynedd, that of Pryderi in Dyfed, and that of Gwri in Gwent—and then should come the death-tale of Gwên, ending in its turn with the death-song of the hero.

The first englyn begins with two lines of gnomic and nature tags in the usual way:

> Arm not after the evening meal. Be not sad of heart.
> Keen is the wind. Bitter is poison.

Then comes the significant third line:

> Accuse me not, Mother.[39] I am thy son.

She answers:

> The thrill in my heart tells me
> That we are of the same blood.[40]
> Long hast thou delayed thy coming, O Gwên!

Then, in alternate stanzas we have the colloquy of Gwên and his mother,[41] a fine dramatic dialogue, which the translators have utterly spoilt by a rendering which is often meaningless and absurd.[42] The boy has evidently been away from home for a considerable period, and has just returned; his mother barely recognises him. A surge of feeling—here called *Awen*—tells her who the youthful warrior is, who calls her Mother. There is room here for a long prose passage: we ought to be told at the outset the reason for the absence, and why the mother is likely to blame her son on his return. As I read these verses, I cannot help feeling that she is taunting him with cowardice,[43] and his absence

[39] The line reads *Amgyhud vy mam mab yt wyf*. In LEWP p. 38 IW gives the amended translation 'My mother declares that I am thy son'; after explaining in detail his reasons for concluding that the opening dialogue is between Gwên and his father Llywarch—rather than between Gwên and his mother. The change depends upon the interpretation of *amgyhud*, which IW subsequently concluded has the meaning of 'declares' rather than 'accuses' in the present context (see LEWP pp. 73–4; CLlH 2nd impression (1953) p. 56; the change from 'Mam' to 'Tad' as Gwên's interlocutor in the opening dialogue is followed in this impression).

40 I read *o un achen* for the MS. *cun achen*. This gives sense and metre.

[41] I leave the following passage in its original form without alteration, since the necessary change from 'Mother' to 'Father' (see note 39 above) as the speaker does not involve any significant change in the argument.

42 See W. O. Pughe, *The Heroic Elegies of Llywarch Hen* (London, 1792), pp. 127–9; FAB I, 329–31.

43 Cf. the poem about Mechydd ap Llywarch, BBC pp. 89–93 [= CLlH VII; for translations see refs. given in note 28 above. An important discussion of the theme of

is the occasion for the charge. Perhaps—remember this is pure conjecture—Gwên had left home to avoid going to the war. A prince of Powys in the seventh century, Tysilio by name, is said to have fled from his father's court to the church at Meifod, later to an island in the Menai Straits, and finally to Brittany, as he preferred the life of a saint to that of a warrior prince. Gwên may have acted similarly from similar motives. Even the great Maelgwn Gwynedd spent some time in a hermit's cell. If Maelgwn and Tysilio, why not Gwên? And if something of the sort was the reason for his long absence, one can understand the tone of the whole colloquy. While he was away his brothers, twenty-three in number, all fell in the incessant fighting, and at last there is no champion left to guard the ford of Morlas on the river Llawen. The news reaches Gwên; the call is irresistible, and he hurries home. When he enters, his mother fails to recognise him, or at any rate welcomes him very coldly, and he appeals to her, 'Don't blame me, Mother, I am thy son'. There is reproach, to say the least, in her answer, 'Long hast thou delayed thy coming, O Gwên!' He replies:

Keen is my spear, flashing in the fight.
I am making ready to guard the ford.
Though I may not return, God be with thee![44]

She answers like a Spartan mother, or like the Lady of Gogerddan in Ceiriog's song:[45]

If thou survive, I shall see thee again.
If thou art slain, I shall weep for thee.
*Lose not the honour of a warrior.*

To that stern exhortation, Gwên replies:

I shall not lose the honour of a warrior.
When the brave puts on his armour for battle.
I shall endure hardship, ere I budge from my post.

cowardice in early Welsh poetry, and of the significant difference in the attitude expressed and implied towards it between the period of the Cynfeirdd (Aneirin and Taliesin) and that of the Llywarch Hen poet—corroborating IW's argument that this poetry is later in date than the Heroic Age of the Cynfeirdd—is given by A. O. H. Jarman in HI. This discussion is also published in Welsh as 'Y Delfryd Arwrol yn yr Hen Ganu', *Llên Cymru* VIII (1965), 125–49].

44 The phrase is *Duw gennyt*. Cf. MA p. 185a, l. 8; WM col. 130, l. 6, *bendith duw genhyt*.

[45] 'I Blas Gogerddan'; *Ceiriog: Detholiad o'i Weithiau* ed. T. Gwynn-Jones, p. 51.

Omitting proverbs and padding, and giving only the significant lines, I give the rest in brief, beginning with the mother's scornful retort: *Gnawt ffo ar ffraeth*! 'Too ready to talk, too ready to flee.'

*Gwên.* I can say this, spears will be shattered where I am.
  I do *not* say that I shall not *flee.*
*Mother.* A promise not kept, is no promise at all.
*Gwên.* My shield will be pierced, before I retreat.

Then the mother relents:

The horn that Urien gave thee
With its golden chain about its neck,
Sound it if hard pressed.

The answer is spirited enough now:

However hard pressed I may be before the warriors of England,
I shall not shame my honour.
I shall not waken the maidens!

Then another voice breaks in, the voice of an old man. Evidently Llywarch Hen has been listening, probably in the fireside corner!

When I was of the age of that boy yonder,
Who is putting on his spurs of gold,
I used to rush swiftly against (hostile) spears.

The boy turns on him, almost savagely:

Of a truth faithful is thy warranty!
Thou art alive. Thy witness is slain.
A feeble old man has never been a boy!

Then without any break in the manuscript comes a chain of mournful englynion, the Elegy of Gwên:[46]

Gwên by the Llawen kept watch last night.
In the fight he fled not,
Sad is the tale, on Gorlas[47] Dyke.

Gwên by the Llawen kept watch last night,
With shield on shoulder.
Since he was a son of mine, bold was he.

[46] CLlH I, 14–28; RBP cols. 1037–8.
47 *Gorlas* may be an adjective 'green', or a scribal error for *Morlas*.

Gwên by the Llawen kept watch last night
With shield and armour.
Since he was a son of mine, he escaped not.

Gwên, I knew thy nature.
Thy rush was like the swoop of a sea-eagle.
Had I been favoured of fortune, thou wouldst have escaped.

When warriors set out to battle,
Gwên, woe to the old old man who grieves for thee.

When warriors go forth on a raid,
Gwên, woe to the old old man who has lost thee.

My son was a man, stubborn in conflict.
He was Urien's nephew.
At the Ford of Morlas, Gwên fell.

Four and twenty sons had I.
With golden torque, leader of a host,
Gwên was the best of them all.

The chain ends with an englyn, which in my opinion is the end of the poem. These brave lads have fallen, and their fate is told in two words, two passive forms, long obsolete, *lledesseint*, 'they have been slain'; *colledeint* 'they have been lost'. I think the poem should end on that note, *colledeint*. In the manuscript, however, we get a jumble of englynion to the other sons of Llywarch, and Grave Stanzas (*Englynion Beddau*),[48] some of which are to be found also in the *Black Book of Carmarthen*.

I must go back now to the end of the Colloquy summarized above, and the abrupt transition to the death-song of Gwên. There must have been a prose interlude here also in the original version; and its nature is easily inferred. No minstrel worth his salt (and mead) would have missed the chance of inserting here a description of Gwên, as he rode forth to battle at the fatal ford. We know that he went on horseback—his golden spurs are sufficient proof. His weapons are named, they are the early ones, *gwaew* 'long lance', *pâr* 'javelin', *ysgwyd* 'the great shield' (not the later *tarian*); the golden torque round his neck, and the battle horn, Urien's gift, suspended by its gold baldric. His horse is

[48] CLlH I, 40–8. [For text, translation, and discussion of the Grave Stanzas, see now Thomas Jones, 'The Black Book of Carmarthen "Stanzas of the Graves"', PBA (1967), pp. 97–137.]

mentioned elsewhere in a stray englyn [= CLlH no. x]. How a *cyfarwydd* would handle this theme we know from the classic description of Culhwch setting forth to Arthur's court.[49] After this there ought to be an account of the fight at the ford, as in the Irish *Táin*, and of the hero's death; and then the messenger bringing the bad news in the morning to the mother who had sent him forth so sternly the previous day, and to the old man who had taunted him with his lack of eagerness for the fray. Now is the time and place for the old man to raise his voice and chant the death-song of the last and best of his warrior sons, who had fallen in the course of the night or at dawn, when the enemy attacked. 'Gwên by the Llawen kept watch *last night*.' And most certainly this is *not* the place for the englyn to Gwên's grave, which has slipped into the text here (between the two last stanzas of my translation).[50] That is antiquarian stuff, written in the margin, and as usual, incorporated in the text by a later copyist.

And what of Gwên's gibe at the old man before setting out? This recalls another fragment consisting of eight englynion in the Red Book,[51] the *Song of Maenwyn*, one of Llywarch's many sons. In this also Llywarch, as the old warrior, 'babbles' of his prowess in the days of long ago. The first englyn begins with the very words which roused Gwên to sudden anger, *viz.* 'when I was of thy age'. That provocative opening remark has always caused trouble between the old and the young; and always will.

Maenwyn, *when I was of thy age*,
No one trod on my mantle.
No one without bloodshed ploughed land that was mine.

And so on, 'Maenwyn, when I was young, no enemy crossed my borders, no enemy cared to incur my wrath'.

Maenwyn, when I was in my prime,
I was fierce in the fray.
I played the man, while yet a boy.

Maenwyn, act discreetly,
Let Maelgwn seek another steward.

49 WM cols. 454–5; RM p. 102; [Gwyn Jones and Thomas Jones, *The Mabinogion* 97].

[50] CLlH I, 23; XII, 3 (= BBC p. 64, ll. 13–14). Translated by Thomas Jones, *op. cit.* p. 121, 'Whose is the grave of good repute, who would lead a compact host against Lloegr? The grave of Gwen son of Llywarch Hen is this.'

51 RBP cols. 1041–2 [= CLlH IV. On the poem see LEWP p. 44; translated by Clancy, EWP pp. 72–3].

The next stanzas are not Llywarch's but Maenwyn's, though there is no sign in the manuscript.

Choicest of boons to me with its sheath about it
(A blade) with keen point like a thorn,
It is not a vain task for me to whet a stone.[52]

A gift has been stolen from me, from the valley of Mafwrn[53]
Blessings upon that stranger hag,
Who said from the door of her cell,
'Maenwyn, leave not thy dagger behind.'

Here again the verse does not tell the story, it only hints at it. We want to know what Maenwyn was doing at Maelgwn's court—rather an anachronism,[54] by the way. What was the knife he was whetting, who gave it, and who stole it? In particular, who was the hag that warned him so opportunely, and how did the story end? It is most irritating! But, at any rate, this fragment proves the existence of other tales, adorned with englynion, and having as their theme the adventures of another son of Llywarch. And further, it shows that in these also his character has become a convention, a type. Llywarch (was he not called *Hen*?) had always to play the part of the old man who stayed at home and sent his sons to war, 'babbling' meanwhile of the wonderful prodigies of valuor he had performed in the days of his youth. Perhaps Gwên may be forgiven for his fit of temper. He had heard all this so often, and now, when he has nerved himself to face death at the ford, like his brothers before him, he hears the familiar opening phrase, 'When I was of thy age', and can stand it no longer. He blurts out, 'All this is very well, but where are the witnesses, besides thyself, to all this valour? All dead. An old man does not realise what it is to be a boy (fighting his first battle).'

There is a somewhat similar development in the Charlemagne and

[52] *Nyt ouer gnif ym hogi Maen*. IW quotes this line as a striking example of the fondness of the early poets for punning. '*Maen* in Welsh means a stone, just like Peter in Greek, and the temptation to play on the name is not to be resisted. So here—"It was not a vain task for me to try to sharpen *Maen*". The verb *hogi* means to sharpen a weapon by rubbing it on or with a *stone*, whetting. In this case, it was the *stone* that was sharpened, the boy Maen, and the whetstone was his father's rough tongue.' LEWP p. 44.

53 *Dyffryn mewyrnyawn* in the manuscript. The line is a syllable too long; the rhyme in lines 2 and 3 is *-wrn*. *Mefyrn* might be the genitive of *Mafwrn*, or an error for *Mafwrn*, a place on the river Dore, Herefordshire; cf. LL pp. 162, 163, 171, 173.

54 Maelgwn died *circa* 547 (HW p. 131): it is unlikely that a son of Llywarch could have served under him. [For traditions of Maelgwn Gwynedd see TYP pp. 437–41.]

Arthurian cycles.[55] In *Culhwch*, for instance, Arthur, with great oaths, is always threatening to do something really heroic. When the time comes, if there is danger, he meekly allows his knights to take his place. The only feat performed by him in his own person during the long hunt of the Twrch Trwyth was the killing of one old woman. This I must say, he did rather neatly, bisecting her at one blow, by throwing his dagger at her—from a safe distance.[56] Emperors must not risk their skins.

Yet there is a difference. Arthur did not start his career in legend as a killer of old women, and a great warrior by proxy. He was gradually pushed into the background by the popularity of his knights. He became old. Llywarch Hen from the beginning was the typical old warrior: he is always old.[57] And if a minstrel occasionally ridiculed in his person the characteristic failings of old age, he could always count on the applause of the young.

One thing is becoming clearer and clearer. Llywarch Hen himself cannot be the author of these poems: he would never have made a laughing-stock of himself in this manner. It is inconceivable that he should be the author of the colloquy between Gwên, his mother, and himself, or that with Maenwyn; any more than Arthur can be the author of the colloquy between himself and the eagle.[58] Llywarch is a character in a drama, a character study, cleverly and realistically drawn. He is not the author; he is not the artist. Hamlet did not write *Hamlet*. That fact does not prevent us from enjoying the play, and we never dream of calling it a forgery. So with these englynion. They are the finest creations of the Early Welsh *cyfarwydd* (story-teller), and in their way, masterpieces of dramatic art. It is tragic that only fragments have survived.[59]

55 Cf. YCM p. 50; T. Powel, *Ystorya de Carolo Magno* (London, 1883), pp. 32–3 (Otuel's gibes at Charles).

56 RM p. 142; [Jones and Jones, *Mabinogion*, p. 136].

[57] For speculation as to the original significance of the epithet *hen* 'the Old' see TYP p. 432. Cf. the additional instances of this epithet in early sources cited by Bartrum, EWGT p. 226, and the discussion by P. Ford, *Speculum* xlv (1970), 442 ff.

58 B II, 269–86. [Cf. TYP p. 521.]

[59] Cf. LEWP p. 48, '...they (the Llywarch Hen poems) are the nearest thing to great drama that Wales ever produced.' The potential comparison between these poems and classical Greek drama has been enlarged upon by Bobi Jones, *I'r Arch: Dau o bob Rhyw* (Llandybie, 1959), pp. 38–46, who lays emphasis on such elements in the style, presentation, and underlying philosophy of the Llywarch Hen poems as suggest that they might have owed their inspiration directly to the tradition of Greek and Roman tragedy, which could conceivably have been handed down in Powys, even at a late remove—

Perhaps you will allow me a few minutes to discuss the Urien poem, *Dymkywarwydyat unhwch* [= CLlH III]. There is no dialogue, so far as I can see; it is all monologue. The text is not sound, and certain sections are difficult, e.g. the first five stanzas. Then comes a chain of twelve englynion, each beginning with *Penn a borthaf* 'I carry a head'. The head is that of Urien, the poet's lord. How he came to lose it we are not told! Dunawd is mentioned in the first two stanzas as an enemy, and also later on in the poem; if the prose had survived, perhaps we should have heard something of the internecine warfare in the North between the British chieftains. Nennius states that Urien was killed through the treachery of Morgan, one of his allies against Ida.[60] When Urien fell, his men cut off his head, and the poet bears it away, to save it from insult.[61]

I carry a head against my side,
He was a combatant between two hosts;
It once belonged to the son of proud Cynfarch.

I carry a head against my side,
The head of Urien the generous; he used to captain a host.

Then comes the contrast: his headless body has been left on the field,

*Ac ar i fron wen frân ddu.*
'And on his white breast a black crow.'

I carry a head in my belt,
The head of Urien the generous—he used to rule in a Court—
And on his white breast crows are feasting.

And so on, ending with a play upon the word *porthi*, which means 'to carry' (Latin *porto*) and also 'to feed', *Penn a borthaf a'm porthes*, 'I carry a head that once fed me'. A chain of eight stanzas follows, to *y gelein veinwen* 'the slender white corpse'. His body has been recovered, and is being buried today under the earth, under the stones; Woe to

whereas later European drama was re-born from the tradition of the ecclesiastical miracle plays. Like the Greek plays whose subjects were based on ancient myths, the Llywarch poems also dealt with well-known traditions: it must therefore have been the interpretation rather than the story itself which interested their original audiences.

60 HB chapter 63; Mommsen, *Mon. Ger. Hist.* p. 206 [TYP p. 517].

61 Cf. Bede, HE chapter xx. Edwin's head, after the Battle of Haethfelth, is carried off and buried at York, 'Adlatum est caput Aeduini regis Eburacum, et inlatum postea in ecclesiam beati apostoli Petri.' [On the significance of dismembered heads in pagan Celtic belief and ritual, see now Anne Ross, *Pagan Celtic Britain* (London, 1967), pp. 61–126, *et passim.*]

my hand! Owain's father is slain...*My cousin is slain*, The son of Cynfarch is slain, etc. The speaker is evidently Llywarch Hen, for the pedigrees show that he was in fact Urien's cousin. Urien's sister was called Efrddyl: so the pedigrees, and the poem.

Sad is Efrddyl tonight (*henoeth*)
And hosts of others also.
At Aber Lleu[62] Urien was slain.

Sad is Efrddyl because of her loss tonight (*heno*)
And because of the fate ordained to her.
At Aber Lleu her brother was slain.[63]

The orthography here calls for mention. The last word of the first line in both stanzas is *tonight*. In the first it is written *henoeth*—that is the Old Welsh form, copied mechanically.[64] In the second, the scribe remembered his job, and modernised it to *heno*, the medieval and modern form. But that is not all: in line 1 he wrote *trallot*, a late form of *trallawt*, even though it is his rule to preserve this final -*awt* unmodified, and even though -*ot* is metrically impossible here, for the word rhymes with *daerawt*, and *brawt*. This shows what our scribes were accustomed to do. When copying old texts, they rewrote them in the orthography of their own age and school, modernising ruthlessly in the process, even to the extent of ruining the metre. When genuine old forms happen to survive in spite of their efforts, I think that we have a right to make the most of them. Their value as evidence of early date is considerably increased.

In the remainder of the poem[65] I can distinguish three episodes or, it may be, stanzas from three different tales. The first group is in praise of a certain Rhun: the second shows two parties waging war on one another, Dunawd against Owain son of Urien, and his brother Pasgen; Gwallawg against Elphin; Brân and Morgan against the poet:

62 According to Nennius chapter 63, Urien besieged the Saxons for three days and nights *in insula Metcaud*, or Lindisfarne, and while he was campaigning (*dum erat in expeditione*) he was slain. [Cf. chapter v, p. 52 above and note 9; TYP p. 517.] This suggests that Ross *Low*, on the mainland, almost opposite Lindisfarne, may be the Aber *Lleu* of the text.

[63] CLlH iii, 30–1. For Efrddyl (and other instances of the same name) see TYP p. 340; EWGT p. 185.

[64] With *heno, henoeth* in this poem cf. *henoid* in the Juvencus englynion, chapter vii, pp. 90, 94–5 above.

[65] CLlH iii, 32–5, 37–46, 47–59; trans. Clancy, EWP pp. 65–70. For the characters mentioned, see TYP pp. 334, 375, 479, etc.

Morgan and his men planned to drive me into exile
And burn my lands.
*A mouse scratching against a cliff!*

Then in the third group, the cliff has been scratched to some purpose. Evidently this series comes from another tale, or it may be, from the very end of the Urien saga. In linked englynion the poet laments over the desolate ruin which once was the court of Urien and his sons. They, by this time, are all dead. The hearth of Rheged is overrun with thorns, brambles, and weeds—there is desolation where once a jovial band of warriors feasted and made merry.[66]

The exact position of Rheged has been a matter of controversy for a long time, and various localities have been suggested. The discovery of the place-name *Dun-rechet* in the *Martyrology of Oengus* (*circa* A.D. 800), and its identification as Dunragit, near Stranraer in Galloway, by McClure,[67] seems to me to have settled the question. Rheged was a district in the south-west of Scotland.

How did Llywarch leave the North for Powys? In two late manuscripts[68] eight englynion survive, which fill the gap in the story. Here again the verse forms a dramatic dialogue of the old type. An early date is suggested by the disyllable *ma-es*. The first line is ambiguous; it may mean 'Conspicuous is a rider over a plain', a proverb; or 'Thou noble rider over the plain', a greeting. The remainder is straightforward.

While God willed what was good for me,
I did not eat mast like swine.

A prince riding over the plain, or through the forest, has chanced upon Llywarch, half starved, subsisting on acorns, as a cowherd (*bugail lloi*), and recognises him. The old man as usual is ready with his tale of woe, and the stranger tries to cheer him:

Llywarch Hen, be not sorrowful,
Thou shalt have a kindly welcome,
Dry thine eyes, and weep not.

[66] CLlH III, 47–59. Trans. Conran, *op. cit.* pp. 93–5; Clancy, EWP pp. 68–70.

67 E. McClure, *British Place-Names in their Historical Setting* (London, 1910), p. 124 n.; cf. Hogan, *Onomasticon Goedelicum*, p. 388, *Dun reichet is na Rendaib*; the same tribal name is in *Mag rechet* (= Morett) near Great Heath of Maryborough, Leix; ibid. pp. 529, 579. [On Rheged see chapter VI, pp. 82–3 above, and note 57.]

68 Panton 14, part I, fol. 133b; BM Add. 14867, fol. 147b; MA p. 96a; W. Owen Pughe, *The Heroic Elegies of Llywarch Hen* pp. 144–6. They are copies of a late sixteenth-century manuscript. [The poem is translated by Clancy, EWP pp. 70–1.]

Llywarch answers:

I am old. I cannot overtake thee.
Where shall I ask a reward for counsel?
Urien is dead. Need is upon me.

The stranger tells him that all the sons of Urien are dead, and bids him make his way to Llanfawr (*Llanfawr llwyprawd*): and he retorts querulously:

There is a Llanfawr over seas,
Where waves roar all round it.
Friend, I do not know if that is the one.

There is a Llanfawr beyond Bannawg,[69]
Where the Clwyd joins the Clywedawg.
I do not know if that is the one, O friend!

The answer is explicit enough:

Make for the River Dee and along it
From the Meloch to the Tryweryn.
They also run to Llanfawr.

So this Llan-fawr, or 'great church', is not in Brittany or in Scotland. Meloch, Tryweryn, Dyfrdwy prove that this is the Llanfor near Bala, Merionethshire. And close by even to this day there is a circle of stones known as *Pabell Llywarch Hen* (the tent of Llywarch): while local legends associate Llywarch with Rhiwedog in the immediate vicinity.[70]

69 Cf. *Vita Sancti Cadoci*, chapter 36 [A. W. Wade-Evans, *Vitae Sanctorum Britanniae et Genealogiæ* (Cardiff, 1944), p. 100.] Jamdudum isdem venerande memorie patronus in *Albania, citra montem Bannauc, venustum* lapideo opere *monasterium* composuit. A giant tells Cadog also in *cap*. 26 (p. 82) that he had been king *ultra montem Bannauc*: his name is Caw of *Prydyn* (the old name for Scotland). Cf. also RM 121, 13 *mynyd bannawc*. The church built by Cadog was Cambuslang, 'and through the adjoining parish of Carmunnock runs a range of hills called the Cathkin Hills, which separates Strathclyde from Ayrshire', LBS II, 22, FAB I, 174. [On these references see now OSPG pp. 5–6, 78–9. Professor Jackson argues that *Bannog, mynydd bannawg* refers not to the Grampians, but to 'the hills in which the *Bannock* burn rises', i.e. between Stirling and Dumbarton. He quotes the opinion expressed earlier to this effect by W. J. Watson, *Celtic Place-Names of Scotland* (Edinburgh, 1926), pp. 195–6. Jackson makes the same point in *Antiquity* XXIX (1955), 81, where he describes *Bannawg* as a mountain range 'which must have constituted an uninhabitable no man's land dividing the Picts and Gaelic Scots from the Britons'.]

70 Siôn Dafydd Rhys, *Cambrobrytannicae Cymraecaeve Linguae, Institutiones et Rudimenta* (1595), p. 183; Peniarth 267, fol. 39 (1635–41); Pennant's *Tours in Wales* (ed. J. Rhŷs, Caernarvon, 1883), II, 303; BM Add. 31055, fol. 129 (1594–6).

Falling back upon conjecture, one assumes that the stranger was a prince of Powys, a chieftain living at Rhiwedog, and that he brought the old man to the neighbouring Llanfor to find sanctuary in the heart of Meirionnydd. I should like to transpose the *Song of the Old Man* from the beginning of the poems, where it stands in the Red Book text, and insert it here, at the very end.

The third class of poems, usually ascribed to Llywarch, are the Cynddylan series.[71] The best known is the chain of englynion to *Stafell Cynddylan*:

Stafell Gynddylan ys tywyll heno,
heb dân, heb wely.
*Wylaf wers, tawaf wedy.*

This is the most artistic line in the whole poem, with the *w* of the old lament throbbing in every word of it.

The hall of Cynddylan is dark tonight,
Without fire, without bed.
I shall weep a while, and then be silent.

The hall of Cynddylan is dark tonight,
Without fire, without candle.
Who but God keeps me sane?

The hall of Cynddylan is dark tonight,
Without fire, without song,
Tears wear away my cheeks.

Cynddylan has fallen, the screaming eagles are ready:

The Eagle of Eli was screaming tonight,
Wallowing in the blood of white-skinned warriors.
The Eagle of Eli, I hear him tonight,
Bloodstained is he, I dare not go near him.

Also the Eagle of Pengwern, 'with his loud cry, greedy for the flesh of Cynddylan'. And still more dreadful, the Eagle of Pengwern 'with its claw uplifted, greedy for the flesh of the one I love'. That upraised talon is unforgettable. But I must cease quoting.

Sixty to seventy years ago there raged a fierce controversy between Thomas Wright, Dr Guest, Thomas Stephens, and Harries Jones,

[71] CLlH XI; RBP cols. 1044–9; selections (trans.) in Conran, *op. cit.* pp. 90–3; Clancy, EWP pp. 79–86.

over these englynion and their date.[72] Wright asserted that they were propaganda disseminated by the bards during the rebellion of Owain Glyndŵr (*circa* 1400). The others on the whole favoured the traditional date, the sixth century: and saw in them an account of the fall of Uriconium or Wroxeter, the burning of Pengwern, on the site of Shrewsbury, etc. It was a merry fight while it lasted, and it lasted for years. If those doughty warriors were here this evening, they would join forces to annihilate me: for I hold that Wright was over 500 years too late in his dating, and the Welshmen two or three centuries too early. And of course I am compelled to reject very emphatically their translations. Sixty years of linguistic study have made a difference. And yet many lines, even complete stanzas, not to mention individual words by the dozen, remain painfully obscure. Progress has been made, much remains to be done.

The Cynddylan poem in the Red Book has 109 englynion, 5 must be added from later manuscripts,[73] a total of 114. Not a single englyn claims to be by Llywarch Hen. There is not a single reference to Llywarch Hen or his sons in the whole 114. What we do have is a series of dramatic monologues declaimed by Heledd (or *Hyledd*), sister of Cynddylan, lord of Pengwern. She stands on one of the neighbouring heights, and looks down on the blazing ruin of her home. In chain on chain of englynion she laments the destruction of Pengwern, of *Eglwysau Bassa* (or Baschurch), and the white homestead in the valley. She bewails the death of her eight sisters, and that of her seven valiant brothers. She bewails her own wretched fate, comparing her present lot with the happy luxurious days of old. Her couch is now of goatskins, rough and hard. Once she rode on trained steeds, and wore red raiment and yellow plumes.

*Hir hwyl haul: hwy fy nghofion.*
'Long is the course of the sun: longer are my memories.'

Farther on she witnesses a battle in which Caranfael, son of Cynddylan, takes part. There are bits of dialogue scattered about; and the inevitable bunch of grave stanzas, the same kind of medley that one finds added

[72] Edwin Guest, 'On the English Conquest of the Severn Valley', *Arch. Cam.* IX (1863), 134–56; Thomas Wright, 'On Llywarch Hen and the Destruction of Uriconium', ibid. pp. 249–54; Thomas Stephens, 'Llywarch Hen and Uriconium', *Arch. Cam.* X (1864), 62–74; further letters follow, ibid. pp. 152–76. Cf. LEWP p. 35.

73 BM Add. 14867, fol. 166b (quoting from Dr Davies); cf. MA p. 91b, l. 31–92a. 9; Panton 14, part I, fol. 107; see *Rep.* II, 822.

on to the Llywarch poems. And I find myself driven to a similar conclusion here also: the Cynddylan poems are not historical compositions, but the verse elements in a Powys saga, which at one time also contained prose. The latter has disappeared, as in the case of the Llywarch tales. I should like to mention in this context that Heledd in three different stanzas (= CLlH XI, 46b, 57c, 86b) cries out in agony that she herself is responsible for these disasters, for the burning of Eglwysau Bassa, for the death of her brothers, *fy nhafawd a'i gwnaeth, o anffawd fy nhafawd yd lesseint, fy anffawd a'i gorug*. Everything is due to her tongue, to the misfortune of her tongue. It is a curious remark, and I cannot conjecture what may be behind it. One can hardly believe that these misfortunes happened to Powys in sober fact because of a girl's unlucky tongue. In a saga all things are possible.

The place-names mentioned are significant. I can only refer to a few. *Maes Cogwy* (written *togwy* in the late manuscripts) refers to the Battle of Maserfield, near Oswestry, where Oswald was slain by Penda in 642.[74] Cynddylan is said here to have been present as an ally, *Cynddylan oedd cynhorthwy*. This settles definitely that Llywarch Hen, cousin of Urien (*circa* 550–60) cannot be the author. *Dwyriw* is the fork made by the two Rhiw rivers, not far from Manafon in south-east Montgomeryshire. To the south-east of Manafon is Bryn Cae *Meisyr*; this preserves to this day the name of one of Heledd's sisters. Farther south still, to the east of Newtown, and close to Kerry, is the river named *Meheli*, a formation from *ma* 'plain', and the *Eli*, whence one of the eagles got his epithet, cf. *Ma-thafarn*, *Ma-chynllaith*, *Ma-llaen*, and especially *Me-chein*, where the *Ma-* has been modified to *Me-* by the *i* in the following syllable. The river *Trenn*, so often mentioned by Heledd, is probably the Shropshire Tern. *Trebwll* may be so called from any one of the numerous pools in this border district, though Welsh-*pool* might have a prior claim, as *The* Pool. Its usual Welsh name, however, is *Trallwng*, another word for 'pool'. *Ergal* or *Ercal* looks like the name which has given High *Ercall*, Child's *Ercall* in Shropshire.[75] *Pengwern* I cannot trace. There are several places in Wales so called, but none known to me on the border, though Tref-*wern*, north of Welshpool, tempts one with its *Gwern*, and Long Mountain would make a fine platform for Heledd! Most people assume, and they

74 See B III, 59.

75 *Arch. Cam.* IX (third series), 253; E. J. Bowcock, *Shropshire Place-Names* (Shrewsbury, 1923), pp. 69, 98–9; *Montgomeryshire Collections* I, II, III.

may be right, that Pengwern is the site of Shrewsbury. Camden and Leland are of that opinion. The Welsh name, however, is *Amwythig*. *Eglwyseu Bassa* cannot very well be other than Baschurch. *Dinlle ureconn* has been connected with *Uriconium*, and The Wrekin, but the reading is doubtful. The syllable *-ure* should end the line, and rhyme with *werydre*, *vrodyrdde*. The second line of the *englyn* is a syllable short, and *conn* must be carried over to fill this gap. *Dinlleufre* is a possible form, cf. *Dinthill* Hall, 4 miles west of Shrewsbury.[76] The name of *Ffreuer*, one of the tragic sisters, occurs in *Nantffreuer*, near Llandderfel.

Most of these names, if correctly identified, belong to the border districts from Kerry, Berriew up to Oswestry. On the other hand, the Llywarch tales are staged at first in the Rheged district of south-west Scotland; then the scene shifts to Powys. Preesgweene (*Prys Gwen*) is said to be so named after *Gwên* ap Llywarch. *Rhyd Forlas* is a stream running into the River Ceiriog; here Gwên fell. *Sawyl*, a brother, was buried at Llangollen [CLlH I, 43 b]; *Gwell* at Rhiw Felen [CLlH I, 43 a] close by: while the old man finds sanctuary at Llanfor, near Bala [CLlH V]. Pyll, one of his sons, was killed on the banks of the River *Ffraw* [CLlH I, 29 c]: this is the Welsh form of the river name which survives as *Frome*[77] in England. So I am tempted to identify this *Ffraw* with the Herefordshire Frome. The Book of Llan Dâv gives us *Clawdd* ('dyke of') *Llywarch Hen*,[78] near Llyn Syfaddon, Brecknock, and this fits in with the Brychan pedigrees in the *De Situ Brecheniauc* where Gwawr, daughter of Brychan, is styled the mother of *Loarch hen* (with *hen* glossed by *veteris*!).[79] And of course, there is a *Bryn Llywarch* close to Kerry, but I can find no early record.

Both Sagas have thus left traces in the topography of Powys and the border. What of the date of composition? My guess for both is the middle of the ninth century. One must allow time for the sixth-century Llywarch to become legendary. If Cynddylan fought at Maserfield in 642, he too must be given a sufficient interval for the same reason. More important still, Wales must dwindle and shrink to something like its present size, for these tales deal with the present border mostly—a few miles to the east is the limit of interest. Powys produced them, but not in a period of triumph over the enemy; rather in a period of acute de-

76 Cf. Panton 30 (= Richard Thomas's translation of Llywarch Hen's songs), *Rep.* II, 839, '*Dintle* a small village not far from Shrewsbury', see W. Owen Pughe's *Heroic Elegies of Llywarch Hen*, VI.

77 McClure, *British Place-Names*, p. 251 n.

78 LL p. 146.

79 *Cy.* XIX, 26 [EWGT 11].

pression, gloom, and despair. Take the known facts: the victories of Mercia under Offa (died 796): Offa's Dyke, a sign of Mercian supremacy, cutting right through Powys to the sea, built before 796: in 822 the *Annales Cambriae* state that the Saxons then brought Powys under their sway (*in sua potestate*); the last of the old Powys dynasty, Cyngen, in 854 or 855, 'died a pilgrim at Rome'—I quote Dr Lloyd's words—'whither he had been driven *by old age and misfortune*'.[80] This old man, driven from his lands and dying in exile, reminds one inevitably of Llywarch Hen. The disastrous fortunes of Powys during the latter part of the eighth and the beginning of the ninth centuries would thus provide a suitable background. They created the poet who sang these sorrowful englynion: gave him his material, and a sympathetic audience. Assuming that Nennius compiled his *Historia* just before 800, on this supposition he could not have heard Llywarch's englynion to Urien. If he had, one would have expected him to put Llywarch on his list side by side with Taliesin, the bard who extolled Urien above all other kings. And Llywarch was Urien's cousin. A later date than 850 is not so suitable: for Mercia, and Wessex also, will soon be fighting for their lives against the Danes, while Rhodri Mawr, *a descendant of Llywarch Hen*,[81] is uniting Gwynedd, Powys, and certain districts in South Wales, into a single realm; and the bards will be inciting the Welsh to join the Danes and Irish, and form a confederation strong enough to drive the English into the sea.[82] There is no hope in these englynion even of winning back the Shropshire marches.

The language of the poems does not help much. (A poem may have been composed and sung or chanted in the halls of a Welsh prince for the first time in 850. The transmission at first would be by word of mouth only. The bard would give repeat performances, by request, from hall to hall. His pupils were expected to learn his masterpiece off by heart, and recite it in their turn. A generation later a minstrel whose memory was failing might write a copy for his own use on vellum before he forgot any more, and this again might be copied and re-copied from generation to generation, by bards, or monks, in royal palaces, or monasteries great and small. Errors due to faulty oral transmission or to careless writing, or to fading ink—all these are possible at every stage. And of course a living language is always changing. Old words become obsolete, and must be replaced by more modern forms if the

80 HW pp. 324–5.    81 HW p. 323. See p. 123 above.
82 In the poem *Armes Prydein* (= AP), BT pp. 13–18.

song is to be intelligible to its hearers. Sometimes we are lucky and discover copies ranging from an early period to the later ones, and we can then trace the development of the text step by step. But when, as in the case of the Llywarch poems, we have only one or two late copies, there is nothing we can do except take frantic leaps into the dark past, calling our guesses essays in the lower or higher criticism! Sometimes we land with a thump on the prostrate bodies of others who have jumped before us into the bog of the Dark Ages. It may not be long before we too feel the weight of new arrivals. Let us dare to hope that even our dead theories may be of some use as stepping-stones to reach the firm ground of historic truth.)[83] The orthography is *mainly* that of the fourteenth century, *partly* that of the twelfth, and certain forms prove definitely a pre-Norman date. That is as far as I will go now.[84]

What of the metric art? Was this possible in 850? To this question the answer is an emphatic *Yes!* Just about this very date, a Welshman wrote in a beautiful hand three englynion on the margin of a manuscript (the Juvencus Codex), which is now preserved in the University Library, Cambridge.[85] Bradshaw has decided that the handwriting belongs to the ninth century. Whitley Stokes suggested the eighth or ninth. These englynion might well be a part of the Llywarch saga. In them we have the same metre, the same type of alliteration and repetition, the same use of *tonight* at the end of the first line, the same mournful note, and the same artistic reticence and restraint. The language is no whit more archaic (except for orthography) than our poems. If the Juvencus poem goes back to *circa* 850, I see no reason why our englynion should not derive from the same period, and from the same school.

And further, granted a ninth-century date, we can understand what happened at a later stage. By the eleventh or twelfth centuries, a collection of triads was forming, based on the old sagas, to which it formed a kind of triadic index, heroes and incidents being grouped in threes.

83 See p. 123, n. [5] above.

84 Twelfth-century survivals are the use of *w* = *f* in the orthography; *i* = *y*, as in *argoetwis*, fol. 16a, l. 10; *regethwis* 13a, 21; *t* = *dd*, *bedit* 13a, 27. Pre-Norman are *e* = *ei*, in *atles* 15b, 44, = *atleis*; ? *henoeth* for *heno*, 13a, 22; *hynnydd* for *hynny*, proved by the rhyme, 13a, 31; *hi gyua* for *yn gyfa* 16b, 30; *karanmael* for *Caranfael* 17*a*, 18: imperfect 3rd sing. in *-i*; verb-nouns in *-if* 14*a*, 6; present indic. 1st pers. sing. in *-if*, occurring in 11*b*, 10; proved by rhyme in 11*b*, 7–8, though modernised in spite of the rhyme to *-wyf*; rare forms of the verb *to be* used freely, such as *bwyat*, *buei*, *bwyn*, *bydat* (? *bwyr*). Also the free use of Irish rhyme, e.g. 11*b*, 2, *-wyn*, *-wyf*: 11*a*, 37, 38, *-ar*, *-al*; *-awl*, *-awdd*; 13*b*, 31, *awr*, *-awl*. *Maes* too as a disyllable.

[85] See chapter VII above.

Amongst these triads there is one which has significance for us here:[86]

*Tri trwydedawc llys arthur. a thri anuodawc. llywarch hen. a llemennic. a heled.*

*Trwyddedawg* means 'one who has permission tostay indefinitely in a lord's court, and is maintained at the lord's expense': *anuodawc* may be read *anfodawg* or *anfoddawg*. The latter means 'dissatisfied, sulky'. My choice is the former, which I take to be 'wandering, home-less', in contrast to *preswyl-fodawg* 'having a fixed home'.[87] The triad would thus mean, 'The three guests at Arthur's court, and the three homeless wanderers, Llywarch Hen, Llemennig, and Heledd'. Whoever compiled that triad had before him three stories; one told of the homeless old man, who lamented over the desolate hearth of Rheged; another told how Heledd wailed above the desolate hearth of Cynddylan; and the other told of Llemennig. Of the latter I know nothing, except that he was buried at Llanelwy, according to the Black Book,[88] and that he is mentioned in two englynion tacked on at the end of a Cynddylan fragment in a late manuscript,[89] a fact suggestive in itself. These tales were old enough to merge in the more popular Arthurian cycle,[90] before the triad-forming period. Powys and Llanfor have been forgotten, as also the chronology,[91] and the three homeless ones are given shelter in the halls of Arthur, with other waifs and strays from sagas of all ages. But time is required for the substitution of Celliwig or Caerleon for the earlier Argoed, and Llanfor.

If those three tales were extant, we in Wales would have a trilogy comparable with the Irish *Three Sorrows of Story-Telling*.[92] As matters

86 RM p. 306 [= TYP no. 65; cf. also no. 8, and notes.]

87 Cf. B IV, 60, on *bodawg*.

88 BBC p. 68, l. 4 [= T. Jones, PBA (1967), p. 126 (no. 50); TYP pp. 419–20].

89 Panton 14, fol. 107; MA p. 92a, ll. 10–15 = CLlH XI, 112–13.

[90] *Llys Arthur* 'Arthur's Court' is in fact a formula whose growing popularity can be observed in *Trioedd Ynys Prydain*, where it progressively supersedes the older *ynys Prydein* formula in the heading of individual triads (TYP p.l xxxi)

91 According to AC, Camlan was fought in 537; Llywarch became a homeless wanderer after the death of Urien who fought Hussa *circa* 590 (HW p. 163). [On these dates see above p. 123.]

[92] In MSS. from the sixteenth century onwards, the three tales *The Fate of the Children of Uisneach, The Fate of the Children of Ler* and *The Fate of the Children of Tuirenn* are frequently found grouped together under the collective title *Tri Truaighe na Sgealaigheachta* 'The Three Sorrows of Storytelling'. See R. Flower, *Catalogue of Irish Manuscripts in the British Museum* (1926), II, 347 ff.; J. E. Caerwyn Williams, *Traddodiad Llenyddol Iwerddon* (Caerdydd, 1958), pp. 105–6.

stand, I can at any rate claim for Heledd a place side by side with the Irish Deirdre. Indeed much of what has been said tonight on the function of englynion in saga could have been illustrated equally well, if not better, from the oldest Irish tales, such as *Líadain and Curithir* (ninth century), and *The Voyage of Bran*. Meyer's note on the latter must be quoted in full:[93] he says that it 'was originally written down in the seventh century. From this original, some time in the tenth century, a copy was made, in which the language of the poetry, protected by the laws of metre and assonance, was left almost intact, while the prose was subjected to a process of partial modernisation, which most affected the verbal forms. From this tenth-century copy all our manuscripts are derived.' The dates of these manuscripts are: one fragment, *circa* 1100; the six others belong to the fourteenth, fifteenth, and sixteenth centuries. The proportion of verse to prose is 57 quatrains (228 lines) to 75 lines of prose. In the *Agallamh na Senórach* the prose is much more extensive than the verse, cf. our *Mabinogi* and the *Trystan*. Meyer's account of the transmission of the *Voyage of Bran* will serve almost word for word as a summary of the theory which I have attempted to put before you, to account for the poems of Llywarch and Heledd.

To return to the starting-point of this lecture, one method of tackling the problem of the sixth-century Cynfeirdd is by a process of elimination. I have tried to eliminate Llywarch Hen from that early group, by finding for him a comfortable home in the ninth century.

93 K. Meyer and A. Nutt, *The Voyage of Bran* (London, 1895), p. xvi. [More recently this tale has been assigned to the eighth century; G. Murphy, *Early Irish Lyrics* (Oxford, 1956), p. 216.] Cf. also Meyer's note on the tale *Líadain and Cuirithir* (London, 1902), pp. 8–9, 'The story has reached us in two late manuscript copies only...In spite of the late manuscript tradition I have no hesitation in claiming our tale, both prose and poetry, on linguistic grounds, for the ninth or early tenth century.' [On this comparison with Irish saga see LEWP pp. 35–6.]

# Chapter IX

# TWO POEMS FROM THE BOOK OF TALIESIN

## I. THE PRAISE OF TENBY

IN the *Book of Taliesin* (pages 42–4) there is a poem in praise of a fortress which is easily recognised as that of Tenby, Pembrokeshire—known as *Dinbych y Pysgod* ('of the Fishes') to distinguish it from the other *Dinbych* in the Vale of Clwyd in North Wales. The first of these became 'Tenby' and the second 'Denbigh' on the lips of strangers, but *Dinbych* is the original form of both. *Din* means 'fortress' and *-bych* 'small' (as in *bychan*). Since I have already discussed the name *Dinbych* fully in another place,[1] where I have given my reasons for maintaining that both elements in it are Welsh, there is no need for me to enlarge upon the matter further here. It is enough to say that there is no validity at all in the argument that it is a Scandinavian word: *Dinbych* 'little fort' corresponds with *Dinmawr*, *Dinmor* 'big fort' in Anglesey, the one being just as much a native Welsh name as the other. If it be asked why there is a 'T' in 'Tenby', compare 'Tintern' in Monmouthshire with its Old Welsh form *Dindyrn*.[2]

Unfortunately this poem has received an inept and rather amusing title—*Mic Dinbych*. This is how it came about. In the first place, the scribe wrote the title on the margin of the manuscript (as is the case with other poems in BT) to give an indication to the artist who was to come later to inscribe an ornamental title. Afterwards there came a fierce binder with a sharp knife, wanting to cut the edges of the pages of the manuscript so as to make them even: he was quite without pity in his desire for uniformity, and he was no less ready to cut off the initial letters of words than to cut into the blank parchment. In this way he has cruelly abbreviated some of the titles.[3] As a rule, two to four

1 *The Journal of the Welsh Bibliographical Society*, v, 256–60.

2 LL p. 141, l. 8, *Dindyrn*; p. 209, ll. 26, 27, *din dirn*; note the form *ryt tindyrn*, p. 141, l. 24, in which *D-* is hardened to *t* after the *-t* in *ryt* (similarly the initial of *Dinefwr* is hardened after *-th* in LL p. 78, l. 18, *gueithtineuur*; and the initial of *Dindaethwy* is hardened in speech in *cwmwd Tindaethwy*).

3 B vi, 131 (with a full list of instances).

letters have been lost from the beginning of a word: for instance, there remains only *ronwy* of the title *Daronwy*, and of *Plaeu yr eifft* there is only *u yr eifft. Mic Dinbych* is therefore merely a further example of a title which has been shorn of its head under this executioner's knife. I believe that the first word was originally *Etmic* (i.e. *edmyg* in modern orthography), a good old word meaning 'praise', and one which suits perfectly with the subject-matter of the poem. However, not one of the previous editors perceived that *mic* was a body without its head, so that in all seriousness they presented the poem to the history of Welsh literature as *Mic Dinbych*. Presumably they were only prevented from baptising the poem previously referred to as *U yr Eifft* by the fact that the illuminator had supplied the full title on the middle of the page, so that it was not only to be found in its truncated form in the margin. But there was no such means of avoiding error in the case of *-mic*, for this time the illuminator had carelessly omitted to put in the full title, so that only that part of it which had been spared by the knife was preserved for succeeding ages.

Now that we have got a fitting title for the poem, we can begin to study it seriously, and I believe that it richly repays the labour. The English translation by the Rev. Robert Williams, Rhydycroesau, in FAB I, 303, is the only one that I know of which was at the disposal of historians of the last century.[4] This was published in 1868: a little too soon for us to be justified in expecting accuracy in the meanings given to archaic constructions and to rare old words. After two generations of hard work, there are still some lines and some individual words which remain extremely obscure. What wonder, then, that the Rev. Robert Williams, the first translator, should fail so frequently? Nevertheless, without imputing any blame to him, one must state plainly that he failed lamentably in his task, and that his incorrect interpretation of the poem has robbed historians of the information to which they have a right.

Although the *Book of Taliesin* has been dated to *circa* 1275, we can see now that the text it gives of *Etmic Dinbych* is a copy of an older manuscript which belonged to the same school of orthography as the *Black Book of Carmarthen*, and which must therefore have been written about the beginning of the thirteenth century, or at the end of the twelfth. One of the archaisms characteristic of this school was the use of

[4] The poem was translated subsequently by J. G. Evans, *The Poems of Taliesin*, pp. 116–20. Two further translations have appeared recently (both of them based upon IW's interpretation as given here): A. Conran, *Penguin Book of Welsh Verse*, pp. 80–2; J. P. Clancy, EWP, pp. 89–91.

*i* for *y*: in line 14 of the poem (see below) the text has *llyn* where both the meaning and the internal rhyme with *erbin* require us to read *llin*. This suggests that the scribe had become so much accustomed to having to turn *i* in his exemplar into *y* that he had come to do so quite mechanically, even when there was no need to do so, and without any thought for the meaning. In the BBC *w* is used for *f*; cf. line 36, where *wleidud* stands for 'Fleiddudd' (the lenited form of the personal name *Bleiddudd*). The importance of this is that this is the name of the man who was lord of Tenby when the poem was composed, or a little earlier. He is named again in line 54, *bleidut*: this time the last letter of his name is *t*. In the BBC, -*t* is the letter used for the sign which is commonly written -*d* in BT (cf. line 36) and is written -*dd* today; cf. *Aduwyn* line 33, *Atuwyn* line 34; *gorllwyt* (= 'gorllwydd') line 54, and in particular *vynet* for (G)*wynedd*, lines 60, 65. Further evidence for copying from an older manuscript is to be found in the use of *u* for *w* in *deruin*, line 31; everywhere else in the poem *u* represents *u* or *f*. In line 29, *llyfyn* is an obvious mistake for *llewyn* in the original (pl. of *llawen*). Similar evidence is found also in *pwyllad* (-*d* for -*d*) line 55, and in *affein*, line 54 (see n.).

These indications do not stand by themselves. BBC p. 46 gives the whole of the last stanza (lines 58–67) by itself, written in the normal orthography of that manuscript. There are enough variations between the two to prove that this is not the source of the BT text, even for this single stanza, let alone for the rest of the poem. There must have been another copy in existence, contemporary with that of the BBC (which is our oldest Welsh manuscript), and it is this which must have been the source of the extant version in BT. Therefore without hesitation we can date the poem as having been composed before 1200.

On the evidence of a single significant mistake, we can date it even earlier than this. In line 17 *nac* occurs where the context demands *rac*. Nobody could be expected to mistake the kind of *r* that is found in the BBC, *circa* 1200, or that in LL, *circa* 1130, or even that in the Computus,[5] *circa* 920. But it would be very easy, as I know through bitter experience, to misread the *r* in the glosses of the previous century as *n*.[6] It would be stupid to over-emphasise so small a point, but it would also be stupid to ignore it.

[5] B III, 245–72.

6 See the clear discussion of this point by Sir John Morris-Jones, *Tal.* pp. 134–9 (with reproductions of the various early types of *r*).

A consideration of the linguistic evidence alone does not enable me to arrive at an exact date. The vocabulary and syntax is much simpler than that of Taliesin's poems to Urien Rheged, or that of Aneirin's elegies to the men of Catraeth. Its general character is more like the language of *Armes Prydein* (BT 13–18), a poem which by reason of its historical content cannot be dated earlier than about 900. Nor is the vocabulary unlike that of *Canu Llywarch Hen*, which I have ventured to date about 850.[7] That, in brief, is the impression made on me by the language of *Etmic Dinbych*: it is a poem which belongs to the latest period of the Cynfeirdd; that is, to the ninth or tenth century. It does not display any of the technical complexity which distinguishes the work of the Gogynfeirdd in the next generation; yet we find here the incipient beginnings of that complexity, in the metrical uniformity of the stanzas, the alliteration, the main rhymes and internal rhymes—but as yet the ornamentation does not tend to smother the meaning. A few lines are left entirely without embellishment.

Now for the subject-matter. The poem begins in the customary manner with a request for God's blessing and protection.[8] Then there are eight stanzas in praise of a certain lovely fortress, which is situated either on an island or on a peninsula (ll. 3, 11, 19, 33, 58). The wave surges against it (l. 7): it is a strong fortress surrounded by the sea. Its name is *Dinbych* (l. 35); its lord in former times was *Bleiddudd* (ll. 36, 54). The descendant of a certain *Owein* is feared (l. 57), and the heir of the line of a certain *Erbin* is praised (l. 14). There are several allusions to the roar of the sea about the fortress (ll. 5, 46), and to the spray descending on it (l. 51); to the sea-birds (ll. 28, 35)—which are on the top of the crag (l. 52). The slaves of Dyfed will get a better reception than the yeomen of Deudraeth (l. 24; see n.). Turning now to the *Inventory*[9] of Pembrokeshire, the map facing p. 395 shows the position of Tenby. We see that the castle is on a peninsula, with a slender neck of land joining the headland to the mainland, where the town is now situated. It would be impossible to find a more suitable place for the old fortress of Dinbych than the very spot where the 'keep' or Norman castle now stands. This height is the 'fair headland' of line 4, about which the roar of the waves is heard. The seabirds fly to the fortress upon it; so also

[7] See chapter VIII above.

8 Cf. BBC p. 29, *Moli duu in nechrev a diuet* 'The praise of God at the beginning and in the end'.

[9] *Royal Commission on Ancient and Historical Monuments in Wales and Monmouthshire*, VII (1925); *Inventory of the County of Pembroke*.

does the bard. When the noise of the tempest is loudest outside, the joyful revelry of the poets is at its height within (ll. 5, 6). The poet's description can relate to no other place but the *Dinbych* which is 'Tenby' in Dyfed.

A word in passing on a remark in the *Inventory* (p. 394). 'Tenby seems to have commenced its existence as a Viking settlement, under the early Norse form of Tembych. This may, of course, have been preceded by an earlier Celtic settlement, but there is no archaeological evidence in the nature of camps or megalithic remains for such a view.' I see nothing against the first observation, since it only means that when the Scandinavians first came there they called our *Dinbych* 'Tembych'. But there is a footnote to this passage which calls for protest, for it says 'The idea that the name Tenby is derived from the Welsh form Dinbych is erroneous, though the ancient Welsh poem "Mic Dinbych" may refer to Tenby.' The first statement is manifestly false: as for the second, if *Etmic Dinbych* is an 'ancient Welsh poem' in praise of the Pembrokeshire *Dinbych*, ought it not to be proved that though 'ancient' it is nevertheless later than the coming of the Scandinavians to Dyfed? As for the statement that no evidence for an earlier fortress has survived, may I refer to a remark made a little further on in the *Inventory* (p. 395): 'The earliest historical buildings of which definite indications exist at the present time in Tenby are the castle, built in the latter half of the thirteenth century... *Of a previous moundcastle not a trace is discoverable, though such a post unquestionably existed*, there being record of the burning of the wooden defences several times during the twelfth and early thirteenth centuries.' I have italicised some of the words: it is true to say that the absence of traces does not prove that there was not a 'moundcastle' there formerly, for in making the new castle the remains of the old one would have been destroyed. How much more, therefore, would not the building of two subsequent castles have obliterated all trace of the little stronghold which was there before either of them? One could not expect a primitive earthwork of rough stone and soil to have left any trace on the ground after the lapse of a thousand years, in a place where there had been such continual rebuilding. Even less would one expect to find traces of the perishable wooden buildings, such as the hall, comprised within the *llys*. The old stone would have gone into the new walls, and the rafters and side-walls of Bleiddudd's hall would have crumbled into fine dust, and vanished. According to Sir John Lloyd: 'Dinbych y Pysgod...was a stronghold of the lords of Dyfed ages before the English learned to call it Tenby.'[10] He refers to a passage in the Laws of Hywel Dda[11] where it is stated that there are four places in Dyfed where a *prepositus* ('steward') has a special privilege, and one of them is *Dynbyc* (the form in the Latin text of the Laws, with -*c* for -*ch*, is an obvious survival of Old Welsh spelling).

The name of the lord of Tenby, at the time when the poem was composed, was *Bleiddudd*, a compound of *blaidd* 'wolf', and -*iudd* 'lord'; in the second word the *i* was assimilated to the *u* which followed, giving -*udd* in Middle Welsh. Later on, after *u* and *y* had become confused in unaccented syllables, the name is found as *Bleiddydd* (as in Lewis Dwnn).[12] In the *Book of St Chad* (written before the time of Bishop Wynsi, 974–92) it is found as the name of a slave who bought his freedom: the form is *Bleidiud* in Old Welsh spelling.[13] In LL p. 204 *Bledud* occurs as the name of a layman. In the *Harl. Gens.* no. XVII the descent of a certain Cuhelyn son of *Bleydiud* is traced back to Cunedda[14] (cf. the same genealogy in Jesus Coll. MS. 20, no. 40, where the name is given as *Bleidut*,[15] just as it is in l. 54 of our poem). This *Bleiddudd* must have been a famous man, and since there were fourteen generations between him and Cunedda, he must have lived about the ninth century. Unfortunately I cannot tell whether or not he belonged to Dyfed.

The other genealogical references in the text are *ab Erbin* (l. 14), and *gorwyr Owein*, 'great grandson of Owein' (l. 57). In Jesus Gen. 20, no. X,[16] Morgan ab Owain king of Morgannwg (d. 974)[17] is traced back to Geraint *ab Erbin*; and in nos. XII and XIII to Gwrdeber m. *Erbin* m. Aircol lawhir m. Tryphun m. Ewein vreisc. According to LL p. 118 *Aircol lauhir* was a contemporary of St Teilo; p. 125, *Aircol lauhir*, son of *Tryfun* and king of *Dyfed*, was the owner of *liscastell*, a *llys* traditionally located at Lydstep,[18] five miles to the south-west of Tenby; cf. Harl. Gen. no. II, *Guortepir*[19] m. Aircol m. Triphun m. Clotri

10 HW p. 265.

11 AL II, 879. [See now H. D. Emmanuel, *The Latin Texts of the Welsh Laws* (Cardiff, 1967), p. 248.]

[12] Lewis Dwnn, *Heraldic Visitations of Wales* (ed. S. R. Meyrick, Llandovery, 1846), I, 310.

13 LL p. xlvi.

[14] EWGT p. 11.

15 [EWGT p. 48.] Cf. Hywel ap Caradog, Jesus Gen. XXXIX—if his father was the Caradoc who was killed in 798 (HW p. 237). He was thirteenth in descent from Cunedda.

[16] EWGT p. 45.

17 HW p. 338 n.

18 HW p. 262 n.; LBS IV, 236.

19 [EWGT p. 11.] Has *m. Erbin* been lost from the pedigree? There are a number of examples of one or more names becoming omitted from genealogies of the kind. [On Guortepir or Voteporius see chapter I, pp. 8–9 above, and n. 26.]

(*not* m. Ewein vreisc, as above). This Guortepir is believed to have been a contemporary of Gildas in the sixth century. If it was believed that the Bleiddudd of Tenby was a descendant of Erbin son of Aircol, he must have belonged to the most famous family in Dyfed—indeed to its royal line; and there was a close connexion between this line and a fortress or court near Tenby. The poet wishes that the line of *ab Erbin* may remain in possession of Tenby, but he gives no indication as to how far that line already stretched back at the time when he composed his poem! Nevertheless, the genealogy and the district correspond so well that there seems no need to trouble further with the other Morgannwg line which was descended from Geraint ab Erbin, and which originated from Devon.

As for the second point: if I understand lines 56–7 correctly, *gorwyr Owein* was an enemy, or at any rate he was someone whom the poet did not wish to get possession of Tenby. According to the second of the *Harl. Gens.*, the wife of Hywel Dda was Elen daughter of Llywarch m. Hyfaidd m. Tangwystl daughter of *Owein* mab *Margetiud* mab Teudos (cf. nos. XIII–XIV). In AC p. 811 the death of *Eugein m. margetiud* (Maredudd) is noted. If this is the Owein of *Etmic Dinbych*, it would put his great-grandson *circa* 900. He would belong to the same generation as Llywarch, the father-in-law of Hywel Dda, the *Loumarch filius hiemid* who died in 903, according to AC. Perhaps he himself was this Llywarch! If so, this would put the poem a little before 900, say 875, and this dating agrees perfectly with the impression given by its language and craftsmanship, which may be compared with that of *Armes Prydein*, *circa* 900, as was said earlier. This dating is also consistent with the poet's silence with respect to the Scandinavians: for him it is the *Ffichti* (the Picts) who rove the seas (l. 8). That is all that I can weave out of the threads of evidence which the poem provides.

The allusions to Gwynedd in the last stanza are obscure, and to the battle of Cefn Llech Faelwy. I prefer to turn to something which is of greater interest to me, the allusion in lines 45–7. This tells us that in the last half of the ninth century, within the boundary of the old fortress of Tenby, there was a *cell*: a room or building in which were to be found *ysgrifen Brydein* 'the writing(s) of Britain', and that there was someone who showed great *pryder* or concern for these writings; they were his chief care (*pryffwn*). To this place the poet would go when he had an opportunity; and there, in the sound of the waves, above one or more old Welsh manuscripts, he experienced such happiness that he could do no less than wish that this *cell* should last for ever!

Following on this, there is another point to which I would like to draw attention. The Mabinogi depicts the Welsh princes as men who lived in *llysoedd* or native strongholds. But a fortress such as Caer Dathal was not the same as a Norman residence or castle. Cynan *Dindaethwy*'s epithet was not derived from that of a Norman castle, but from the old stronghold which is still to be seen on the top of a crag near Menai Bridge. Looking at the desolation of such fortresses at the present time, it is easy enough to forget the wooden houses and halls and buildings of various kinds which used to be safeguarded by the encircling dyke of earth and rock. There were storehouses for food and drink, of course: we know that a *meddgell* or mead-cellar was essential. It is good to think that there was also a *llyfr-gell* or library, at least in the fortress at Tenby. I would give a great deal to see the catalogue, and even more to obtain a glimpse of its contents!

I give below the text of the poem, divided into lines and stanzas. I have italicised words which have no metrical value. Then I have attempted to translate the whole into English, as best I could, and almost literally. Afterwards, in order to justify the meanings I have offered for individual lines and words, or to show that my suggestion is merely one out of various possibilities, I have added some notes. I would not like anyone to suppose that my translation is final, and so it is right to point out the passages in which there is uncertainty as to the meaning.

*Etmic Dinbych*

Archaf *y* wen y duw plwyf escori.
perchen nef a llawr pwylluawr wofri.

Aduwyn gaer yssyd ar glawr gweilgi.
bit lawen ygkalan eiryan yri.
Ac amser pan wna mor mawr wrhydri.
ys gnawt gorun beird uch med lestri.
Dydybyd gwanec *ar vrys* dybrys idi.
Adawhwynt ywerlas o glas ffichti.
Ac am bwyf o dews dros vygwedi.
pan gattwyf amot kymot a thi.

Aduwyn gaer yssyd ar llydan llyn.
Dinas diachor mor oe chylchyn.
gogyfarch *ty* prydein kwd gygein hyn.
Blaen llyn ap erbin boet teu voyn.
Bu goscor a bu kerd yn eil mehyn.
Ac eryr uch wybyr a llwybyr granwyn.
Rac vd felyc nac escar gychwyn.
Clot wascar a gwanar yd ymdullyn.

Aduwyn gaer yssyd ar ton nawuet.
aduwyn eu gwerin yn ymwaret.
ny wnant eu dwynuyt trwy veuylhaet.
nyt ef eu defawt bot yn galet.

*The Praise of Tenby*

I ask God's favour, protector of the people,
Lord of heaven and earth, great in knowledge and wisdom.

There is a fine fortress standing in the sea.
Gay on each festive day (Calends) is that fair headland.
And when the sea rages with great fury,
Loud is the revelry of bards over the mead horns.
When the swift wave surges against it,
They will leave the grey-green ocean to the tribe of Picts.
And may I, O God! in answer to my prayer,
When I keep (my) pledge, make my peace with thee.

There is a fine fortress on the broad ocean,
A mighty stronghold, sea-girt.
Inquire, Britain, to whom does it rightfully belong?
Head of Ab Erbin's line, may it be thine!
There was a retinue in the court, and a host besides,
And the eagle flew high on the track of pale-faced (enemies).
Before the noble chief, before the router of enemies,
Prince of widespread fame, men stand ready for battle.

There is a fine fortress on the ninth wave,
Fine are its men when taking their ease.
They make merry without reviling.
It is not their custom to be niggardly,

Ny llafaraf eu ar vyn trwydet.
noc eillon deutraeth gwell kaeth dyfet.
kyweithyd o ryd wled waretret.
kynnwys rwg pop deu goreu kiwet.

Aduwyn gaer yssyd ae gwna kyman.
medut a molut ac adar bann.
llyfyn y cherdeu yn y chalan.
Am arglwyd hywyd hewr eiran.
kyn y vynet *yn y adwyt* yn deruin llan.
*ef* am rodes med a gwin o wydrin ban.

Aduwyn gaer yssyd yn yr eglan.
atuwyn y[t] rodir y pawb y ran.
Atwen yn dinbych gorwen gwylan.
kyweithyd wleidud ud erllyssan.
Oed ef vyn defawt i nos galan.
lledyfdawt y gan ri ryfel eiran.
A llen lliw ehoec a medu prein.
hyny uwyf tauawt ar veird prydein.

Aduwyn gaer yssyd ae kyffrwy kedeu.
oed meu y rydeu a dewisswn.
Ny lafaraf *i* deith, reith ryscatwn,
ny dyly kelenic ny wyppo hwn.
yscriuen brydein bryder briffwn.
yn yt wna tonneu eu hymgyffrwn.
pereit hyt pell y gell a treidwn.

Aduwyn gaer yssyd yn ardwyrein.
Gochawn y medut y molut gofrein.
Aduwyn ar eu hor escor gynfrein.
Godef gwrych dymbi hir y hadein.
dychyrch bar karrec crec mor ednein.
llit y mywn tyghet treidet trath[r]umein,
A bleidut gorllwyt goreu affein.
Dimpyner oduch llat pwyllad cofein.
Bendith culwyd nef gytlef a fein.
ar nyn gwnel yn vrowyr gorwyr owein.

No false charge shall I bring against their welcome.
Than the yeomen of Deudraeth better are the slaves of Dyfed.
A throng of (its) free men, keeping festival,
Will include, two by two, the best men in the world.

There is a fine fortress, where a multitude
Makes loud revelry, and so do the singing birds.
Joyous were its songs (? hosts) at the Calends (New Year's Eve)
About a generous lord, bold, and brave.
Before his passing into the oaken church,
He gave me mead and wine out of a crystal bowl.

There is a fine fortress on the promontory,
Graciously each one there receives his share.
I know at Dinbych—pure white is the sea-gull—
The companions of Bleiddudd, lord of its court.
My custom it was on New Year's Eve
To sleep beside my prince, the glorious in battle,
And wear a purple mantle, and enjoy (every) luxury,
So that I have become the tongue of Britain's bards.

There is a fine fortress, resounding with songs (?).
Mine were the privileges that I desired.
I shall not speak of rights, due order would I keep,
He merits no feast-gift who is ignorant of this.
The writings of Britain were the chief object of care,
Where the waves make their roaring.
Long may it remain, that cell I was wont to visit!

There is a fine fortress on a height,
Lavish its feasting, loud (?) its revelry.
Beautiful all round it, that fort of champions,
Is the flying spray: its wings are long!
Hoarse sea birds make for the top of the rock.
Let anger, under a ban, speed away over the hills,
And Bleiddudd enjoy the highest bliss.
At the ale-feast may this song to his memory be welcome!
The blessing of the Lord of harmonious heaven will prevail,
He who will not make us the cowherds of Owain's grandson.

Aduwyn gaer yssyd ar lan lliant.
aduwyn yt rodir y pawb y chwant.
Gogyfarch *ti* vynet boet teu uwyant.
Gwaywawr ryn rein a derllyssant.
Duw merchyr gweleis wyr ygkyfnofant.
Dyf ieu bu gwartheu a amugant.
Ac yd oed vriger coch ac och ar dant.
Oed lludued vynet dyd y doethant.
Ac am Gefyn llech vaelwy kylchwy vriwant.
Cwydyn y gan gefyn llu o garant.

*BBC 46*

[Adwin caer yssit ar lan llyant.
Adwin yd rotir y paup y chwant.
Gogywarch de gwinet boed tev wyant.
Gwaewaur rrin. Rei a darwant.
Dyv merchir. gueleisse guir yg cvinowant.
Dyv iev bv. ir. guarth. it adcorssant.
Ad oet bryger coch. ac och ar dant.
Oet llutedic guir guinet. Dit y deuthant.
Ac am kewin llech Vaelvy kylchuy wriwant.
Cuytin y can keiwin llv o carant]

There is a fine fortress on the shore of the sea.
Graciously there his desire is granted to everyone.
Ask Gwynedd,...
...May they be thine!
Spears, rough, unbending, they deserved...[1]
On Wednesday, I saw men contending together.
On Thursday, they suffered the shame (of defeat).
There was blood on men's hair, and wailing on (harp) strings.
Weary were the men of Gwynedd the day they came,
And on the ridge of Maelwy's rock they shatter shields.
With (my) nephew's son, a host of kinsmen fell.

1 The line is a syllable short.

## *Notes*

*Metre.* Lines of nine or ten syllables with end-rhyme; when affixed pronouns are discarded and glosses omitted the number of the latter is just over one-fifth of the whole. The glosses are *ar vrys* l. 7, *yn y adwyt* l. 31. In line 32, read *am rodes* for *ef am rodes*: l. 64, *At oed* for *ac yd oed* (cf. BBC text). Lines 41–2, instead of end-rhyme, have *odl-gyrch*; the two together form one long line of nineteen syllables, with *kedeu* rhyming with *rydeu*, and *dewisswn* having the end-rhyme of the stanza. The first two lines are a conventional invocation of God. The rest of the poem forms eight stanzas, each beginning with *Aduwyn gaer yssyd*, a customary method of linking stanzas (called *Cymeriad*): a similar artifice links lines, e.g. 19–20, 21–4, 25–6, 33–5, 58–9, 60–1, 62–3. Internal rhymes are fairly frequent, and there is a good deal of primitive alliteration or consonance, though some lines, *in their present form*, have neither, e.g. l. 1. If, however, the old form *dwyw* be read for *duw*, we get a good rhyme with *plwyf*, cf. BT p. 10, l. 10, where the same restoration is necessary.

To save space I shall not comment on words already dealt with by Lloyd-Jones in G or by me in CA, etc. Most of the notes will deal with textual points, new readings suggested, and corrections of orthography. Rare words of uncertain meaning will be specified. Numbers refer to lines.

3. **Aduwyn,** to be read *addwyn* throughout, a cpd. of *dwyn* 'fine, beautiful', as in the saint's name, *Dwyn-wen*; cf. BT 8, 10 and below l. 21.

4. **yri,** cf. *Er-yri* 'highland', B IV, 137–41.

7. **ar vrys** is a gloss incorporated in the text, explaining *dybrys*, cf. BT p. 66, ll. 20, 24. When these two words are omitted, the line is of correct length.

8. **ywerlas.** Obscure. Cf. *gwerlyn*, BT p. 40, l. 6; or the gloss *guird-glas*, Loth, VVB 140, a kenning for sea. If so, *o glas* must be changed to *e* glas, cf. BT p. 17, l. 11, and p. 17, l. 14. For *clas* 'people' cf. BBC p. 57, l. 4; BT p. 15, l. 21.

9. **dews,** 'God', Latin *deus*, cf. BT p. 10, ll. 4, 12. *am bwyf* does not construe: read *am bwy fi, am bwy*, for Old Welsh *am boe* 'may there be to me', usually modernised to *am bo*. For *tros* cf. MA 191a, 16; 466 a, 12, 17; if *trus* be read (cf. LL p. 140) we get an Old Welsh form, having the same meaning as *tros*, but rhyming with *de-ws*.

11. **llydan llyn,** a kenning for 'ocean', cf. BBC p. 58, margin.

14. **blaen llin** not *llyn*, because of the rhyme with *erbin*, cf. BT p. 24, l. 11. With *boyn*, cf. l. 60 *bwyant*; BBC p. 96, l. 2, Gueisson am *buyint*.

15. **goscor,** a variant of *gosgordd*, cf. BT p. 21, l. 26 (*g*)*oscord*, rhyming with *-or*. If there is internal rhyme, *kerd* must be changed to *cor* or *cord* 'cordd', i.e. 'tribe, *llwyth*'; see G p. 164.

**yn eil mehyn.** Obscure. Occurs also in BT p. 61, l. 15. *Mehyn* 'place' is fairly common, but *eil* is ambiguous in this context. But cf. *eil* and *adeil*; and the Irish *aile* 'fence'. Was the *caer* defended by a palisade? Cf. CLlH p. 169, alaf yn *eil*.

16. **gwybyr** 'clouds'. Correct *allwybyr* into *ar llwybr* 'in the track of'.

**gran(n)wyn,** cf. BT p. 14, l. 23; MA p. 159a, l. 40; 163a, l. 49; 165a, l. 38; 166a, l. 29; 207a, l. 32; *Cy.* VIII, 205; *Granwen* mab llyr, RM p. 159, WM p. 111a; cf. BT p. 39, l. 2. In Welsh *grann* meant 'cheek'; and 'white cheek' suggests a frightened pale-faced enemy, cf. CA p. 46, Kwydassei lafnavr ar *grannaur gwin* 'blades had fallen on white faces'. The faces, however, may be 'naturally' pale. As *gran(n)wyn(n)* (plural, *granwynyon*) in contexts where the sense is fairly obvious, always means 'enemy', I should like to suggest that it was at first a nickname (like *gwyr brychwyn,* BT p. 77, l. 25) given by dark-skinned Welshmen to their fair-skinned Saxon enemies, cf. the use of *Paleface* by the American Red Indians. With the text cf. RBP col. 1441, l. 6, *Brat bryneich branes ae canlyn,* 'entrapper of Bernicians (= English), a flock of ravens follows him'. [On *g(a)ranwynyon* see now AP p. 35, PT p. 36.]

17. **felyc.** Must be for *ffeleic* 'lord', 'noble'.

**nac,** for *rac* in copying an Old Welsh original, see above.

20. **eu.** Read *e* 'ei'. The same mistake occurs again, l. 50.

**yn ymwaret,** cf. CA l. 1178, nyt oed hyll yd ellyll*en emwaret*; and p. 333, on *yn vn gwaret*: also the peculiar use of the verb *gwaredu* in BBC p. 94, l. 4; PKM pp. 101, 128; AL II, 234; RBP col. 1148. 3; *Meddygon Myddveu,* p. 8; RBB pp. 200, 214, etc. The meaning 'deliver' is well attested: also 'remove, get rid of' (cf. *cael gwared o*). In the text, with *ym-,* it may mean 'to take one's ease'; the noble company, one and all, cast away care, and enjoy themselves.

21. **dwynuyt,** dwyn-fyd, cf. on l. 3, *addwyn.* The opposite to the text is the mocking of Peredur when he first visited Arthur's court. With the form *meflha-ed* cf. *sarha-ed,* later, *sarhad.*

24. **eillon Deudraeth.** The *eillon* 'yeomen' were the class between the *uchelwyr* and the *taeogion,* cf. BT p. 29, l. 6, *Eillon* a ui *kaeth,* a prophecy of bad days to come. The only Deudraeth known to me is that in Merionethshire. A jibe at Gwynedd (to extol Dyfed) seems reasonable, but why choose Deudraeth? For rhyme's sake? [On this line cf. further TYP p. 180.]

25. **gwaretred** has a variant *gwaratret*; and in BT p. 4, l. 21, the former is corrected to the latter by the scribe, cf. also MA pp. 163a, 259a, RBP col. 1150 l. 7 for *gwaradret,* and MA pp. 147b, 223b, 225a, 248b for *gwaredret.* A comparison of BT p. 4, l. 21, and p. 6, l. 15, shows that it is a synonym of *achles*; this suits BBC p. 16, l. 7, also.

26. **pop deu,** cf. BT p. 41, l. 9, in another reference to a feast. Giraldus Cambrensis in his *Description of Wales,* chapter X, says that guests in Wales in his time were arranged in threes, instead of couples as elsewhere; but cf. Wright's note, p. 493 (*The Historical Works of Giraldus Cambrensis,* trans. R. Colt Hoare, ed. Thomas Wright (London: Bohn, 1863)). The text shows that the men of Dyfed at the date of this poem messed two by two, whatever their custom might have been in Gerald's days.

29. **llyfyn,** a misreading of *llewyn* pl. of *llawen,* in the original.

**cerdeu,** may be pl. of *cerd* 'song', or a mistake for *cordeu* ('hosts') reading *-e-* for *-o-*, cf. on l. 8. Also cf. 41, *kedeu*.

30. **eiran,** also l. 38, cf. l. 4, *eiryan*. The omission of the consonantal *i* is fairly common in this MS.

31. **yny adwyt** 'in death', a gloss on *mynet yn deruin llan*.

**yn deruin llan,** cf. CLlH pp. 50–1, oni fwyf *i'm derwin* fedd : *im derwin* llednais; *i'm derwin taw*. The *deruin* refers to the oak coffin, or the material of the *llan*, 'church', or 'monastery'.

32. **gwydrin ban,** a cup or bowl of glass, cf. BT p. 32, l. 14, A chorwc gwytrin. On *pann*, see CA pp. 79–80.

34. **ytrodir,** cf. l. 59.

35. **gorwen gwylan,** a gnome used here to fill up, cf. BT p. 61, l. 4, *gwyn gwylein*. There is, however, a sense connexion: the picture of Dinbych in the poet's mind includes the white seagulls seen round the headland.

36. **ud erllyssan,** i.e. *ud(d)* 'lord', and *erllyssan*, probably a compound of the prefix *are-* and *llys-an*, a diminutive of *llys* 'court', cf. Ir. *airles* 'enclosure, precincts of a house'; *lesán, lisán* 'small earthwork'; and the Denbighshire township *Llyssan*. Similar formations are *Din, Dinan* (*Dinam*); *Tref, Trefan*. That Dinbych 'little fort' should also be called *Llysan* confirms the etymology given above.

38. **lledyfdawt y gan ri,** cf. BT p. 26, ll. 8–10, Kysceis yn porffor...yg kylchet ym perued rwg deulin teyrned.

40. **tauawtar.** His superiority as a bard makes every other bard mute, cf. BT p. 8, l. 18, Digonaf y veird llafar llesteir; MA p. 171 a Gosteg beirdd bardd a glywch. **hyny uwyf** 'oni fwyf, hyd oni fwyf', 'until I become, so that I am'.

41. **kedeu** 'gifts'. Read *kerdeu* 'songs' or *kordeu* 'hosts', cf. l. 29.

42. **rydeu,** cf. CA pp. 143–4, *ryd* 'cyfle', and *an-rhyd-edd* 'honour'.

43. **teith,** cf. CA p. 184; Ir. *téchte* 'right, law': also BT p. 4, l. 14, glan ieith glan *teith* dy *teithi*...hyt pan *rychatwyf* vyn *teithi*.

44. **dyly.** Read *dly*.

45. **priffwn,** old orthography for *pryffwn*, CA p. 367.

46. **ymgyffrwn.** Unknown to me; probably means 'tumult, noise', cf. l. 5; BT p. 76, l. 12, am *gyffwn*.

47. **pereit,** 'par-he-id', cf. CLlH p. 233. May be pres. indic. 3rd pers. or imperative.

49. **gochawn** is related to *gogoniant*, cf. CA p. 369.

**gofrein** is unknown to me; the context suggests an adj., 'loud', 'high', from the same root as *bre* 'hill', cf. *dwyre, dwyrein*.

50. **ar eu hor,** cf. on l. 20: read *ar e hor*. The noun *or* means 'border, edge, limit'.

51. **gwrych** means 'hedge' and also 'spray' and 'sparks'. Here the choice is between 'hedge' and 'spray'. The repeated reference to the waves in stanza after stanza favours the latter meaning. For *godef* cf. CLlH p. 165.

52. **crec,** for *cryc* 'hoarse', modern *cryg*.

53. **trath-mein.** After the *th* the MS has a letter partly erased which begins a new line. Dr Evans in his text printed *a*, but in his notes he says that *il* is a more likely reading. R. W. (F.A.B. i, 303–6) evidently read *traeth a mein* and translates 'sand and stones', but the first *a* is quite certain. In Old Welsh *treiddiaw* meant 'visit, go to and fro, cross', see CLlH p. 210 and cf. above l. 47. It is often followed by *tra* 'beyond, over' (variants, *trach, trac, trag*), cf. MA p. 249b *treitaw trac* eryri. In the text of the Gododdin (*c.* 1250), l. 641, we find *dra thrumein*, for older *tra drumein*, with *drumein* as plural of *drum* (later *trum*) 'ridge, bank, hill', cf. an appropriate example, MA p. 150a, *ar drumain mor* 'on the sea cliffs'. So I suggest that the correct reading here is *treidet tra thrumein*. What Evans read as *-il-* was obviously *-u-*, the digit surviving is too short for an *l*. There is scarcely room for *-ru-*; if the scribe wrote *trath/umein*, the erasure of most of the *-u-* was intended to make room for the correction *-ru-*. Where the *r* should be there is a nice blot on the margin, and in it (if you want to) you can read this *r*!

**llit** suggests that there had been some disagreement or other between the bard and Bleiddudd, before his death. The tone of the whole poem in fact is like that of the usual 'reconciliation' (or *dadolwch*) poems of the Gogynfeirdd (cf. ll. 21–2, 37, 57, etc.).

**ymywn tyghet,** cf. PKM p. 79, mi a *dynghaf dyghet* idaw. So does the bard with *llit*. He lays a taboo on it. All anger, disagreement, etc., must go over the hills and far away, never to return. This, I think, fits better than 'Let the anger within Fate pass over the hills'. Cf. (in an elegy) MA p. 236a, Chwedl mwyfwy garw *dramwy drumain.*

54. **gorllwyt,** old orthography for *gorllwydd* 'good luck, happiness, bliss'; cf BBC p. 106, l. 15, nim haut [bit] *gorlluit*; H p. 257, kerd *orllwyt* arglwyt (printed *ked* orllwyt, MA p. 199b); RC XXIV, p. 359; *dymgorllwyd*, MA p. 147a.

**affein.** Read *-ff-* as *-f-* (as often in BBC), and divide into *a fein*, cf. B v, 237–8, hou *bein* atar *ha beinn*, in a sentence written down in A.D. 820, where *ha beinn* may mean 'a fai'. The poet wishes Bleiddudd to have every bliss that there may be (in the other world).

55. **dimpyner.** Another difficult word. For *dim-* as prefix to verbs, cf. BBC p. 27, ll. 2, 3; CA p. 270, *dimcones, dimbi, dymbi, dymgofu*. The stem *-pyn-* may be for *-pynn-* (as in l. 44, *kelenic* for *kelennic*); so cf. *dibynnu* (L. de-*pend-*), *derbyn* (Welsh *penn*), *pwnn* (L. *pondus*). The choice lies between 'May he be admitted or received' ('to the heavenly feast') and 'Let the words (thought, purpose) of my elegy be weighed' or 'welcome' at the (funeral) ale-feast on earth. The second seems more suitable. One jibs at calling the heavenly feast an 'ale-feast', as if it were another Valhalla! On *od uch* 'above'; *llat* 'ale'; *pwyllat* 'meaning, purpose'; *cofein* 'memories, commemoration' see CA pp. 101, 104, 107; CLlH p. 170.

56. **afein.** Dr Davies, *Dict. Duplex* (1632), gives under *a fano* as a common phrase *Bendith Dduw a fano it!* guessing the verb to mean 'faustum esse, prosperare', Welsh *tycio*. The pres. indic. of this verb would be *manaf* with *main* as 3rd pers.

sing., cf. MA p. 236a, Bychan hudd (read *budd*) ei (? i) fedydd *a fain*, Oer gywasg gywisg pridd a main; 150a, Yn ail gerd i'm rwyf yn rwyd *yd fain*. So compare the root of *an-myn-edd* (modern *amynedd*), Latin *maneo*, and its cognates, 'remain, last, endure'. This also may be the root of the *menit* of CA p. 309; BT p. 40, l. 22 *menhyt* yn tragywyd, cf. the other instances quoted there. The sense is near enough to *tycio* 'avail, profit', in several cases. In the text, *a fein* goes with *Bendith culwyd nef* synonymous with *Bendith Dduw* in Dr Davies's phrase, for *culwyd* 'culwydd' means 'lord' in the old poetry.

57. **arnyn gwnel**, cf. BBC p. 7, ll. 6, 11, for *ar ny* 'the one who...not'. *vrowyr* looks like a mutation of *browyr*, translated 'brodorion' by Lloyd-Jones, G p. 77. If so, there is no internal rhyme with *gorwyr*, which I take to be 'great grandson', *gor-* and *ŵyr* 'grandson', as in BBC p. 75, l. 7, *goruir* Edwin. A good rhyme would be *Bro-Wyr* 'Gower', cf. L. Dwnn I, 237, but what of the sense? Neither 'brodorion' nor 'Gower' seems suitable in the context. And so I prefer to see here a cognate of the Irish *bruig-fher* 'a kind of cow-herd'. The sense would then be 'the blessing of God...who (we pray) will not make us the cowherds of Owain's great-grandson'. The Irish term is a compound of *bruig-* 'cultivated land, farm, farmhouse' (= Welsh *bro*) and *fer* (W. *gŵr*): thus *bro-wŷr*, the plural, could mean 'men working on the land, cultivators of the soil, herdsmen'. The poet prays that he and his friends may not, after Bleiddudd's death, become the vassals of this (unloved) descendant of Owain. The fact that such a use of *bro-wr*, *browyr*, is not known elsewhere in Wales may be discounted by referring to the important Irish settlement in Dyfed (*Cy.* XIV, 112). The tribe of the Deisi could have made *bruig-fher* the current term in the district under their control. When Irish ceased to be spoken there, their descendants would use the Welsh term most nearly resembling it.

60. **vynet**, in the BBC text *gwinet*: so *Gwynedd*, to match *Prydein* in l. 13 in the same rhetorical phrase. But no question follows (as one would expect after *gogy-farch*). There, *boet teu* is addressed to Erbin's dynasty: here, it looks as if Gwynedd were to have something or other (a plural noun, since *bwyant* is a plural form, matching *boyn* in the other passage). Then l. 61 has no connexion, forward or backward, and the two versions clash. It seems safe to assume that in the original of both, two half-lines at least had dropped out.

62. **kyfnofant** (cf. CA p. 125), a better reading than BBC *cvinowant* (read *ciunowant*).

64. **ac yd oed**, read *atoed*.

65. **lludued** read *lludd-wedd*, or *lluddedig* with BBC.

67. **cefyn**, read *ceifyn*, cf. G p. 123; *ceifn*, Richards *A Welsh-English Dictionary* (Bristol, 1753), 'a grandchild's grandson, a son in the fourth degree'; Davies, *adnepos*, which is explained by T. W. as 'nai fab nai, gorwyr'. Can we read *fy ngheifn*?

The poem, according to the convention of the Gogynfeirdd at least, ought to end with line 57. This last stanza seems to be a 'stray': it was the only one known to the BBC scribe, and BT stuck it on at the end, *after* the reference to God, which usually concludes such a poem. The text in both versions is unsatisfactory.

## II. AN EARLY ANGLESEY POEM

The manuscript known as the *Book of Taliesin*, or Peniarth MS. 2, now in the National Library at Aberystwyth, was written, according to Dr Gwenogvryn Evans, *circa* 1275.[1] It contains a curious medley of early Welsh poetry: historical poems in praise of Urien and his son Owain; vaticinations or prophetical poems foretelling the future glory of the Welsh people when Cynan and Cadwaladr shall lead them victoriously against the Saxons; riddle poems and nature poetry of various types; religious poetry; a poem on the achievements of Alexander the Great; and in addition a considerable body of mythological poetry or early saga which in my opinion at any rate once formed part of the *Tale of Taliesin* in its most primitive form.[2]

Amongst the various unclassified scraps of verse included in this remarkable collection I should like to mention two poems which have definite Anglesey associations. One is entitled *Daronwy* (p. 28), and you will remember that the Society two or three years ago visited the interesting dwelling-house which still bears that name. The other, however, is my immediate concern. There is no title in the manuscript (p. 68), but as the two stanzas of which it is composed begin with *Echrys ynys*, we can use these two words in lieu of a title. The second line begins with *Mon* and ends with a reference to *Menei*, so we need have no hesitation about the identity of the *ynys* mentioned by the poet: it is our Môn. As the poem was written down nearly seven hundred years ago, and may have been composed several centuries earlier, it deserves to be studied with the same thoroughness that archaeologists show when dealing with ancient monuments in wood and stone found in our island. It is one of our antiquities.

In the manuscript the whole is written as prose (to save space), but the end of each metrical line is marked by a full stop, as elsewhere throughout the volume. After *Echrys ynys gwawt hu-* in line 1 a space was left for the title, but by an oversight the rubricator left it unwritten.

[1] On the possibility of a slightly later date for BT see above chapter IV, n. 14. This possibility does not of course affect the linguistic arguments for the date of the contents, based upon traces of copying from earlier manuscripts.

[2] On the contents of BT see chapter VIII above n. [8], and refs. there cited.

Capitals mark the initial words of most of the lines; they are, however, not used to denote proper names. In my copy I shall print the lines in the modern way, and use capitals where necessary. Unaccented words joined on to the following word are separated in my version where possible.

Echrys ynys gwawt huynys gwrys gobetror,
Mon mat goge(i) gwrhyt eruei. Menei y dor.
Lleweis wirawt gwin a bragawt gan vrawt escor.
Teyrn wofrwy diwed pop rwyf rewinetor.
Tristlawn deon yr Archaedon kan rychior.
Nyt uu nyt vi yg kymelri y gyfeissor.
Pan doeth Aedon o wlat Wytyon Seon tewdor.
Gwenwyn pyr doeth pedeir pennoeth meinoeth tymhor.
Kwydynt kyfoet ny bu clyt coet gwynt ygohor.
Math ac Euuyd hutwyt geluyd ryd eluinor.
Ymyw Gwytyon ac Amaethon atoed kyghor.
Twll tal y rodawc ffyryf ffo diawc. ffyryf diachor.
Katarn gygres y varanres ny bu werthuor.
Kadarn gyfed ym pop gorsed gwnelit y vod.
Cu Kynaethwy hyt tra uwyf uyw kyrbwylletor.
Am bwyf i gan Grist. hyt na bwyf trist ran ebostol.
Hael Archaedon gan egylyon. cynwyssetor.

Echrys ynys gwawt huynys gwrys gochyma.
Y rac budwas. kymry dinas. aros ara.
Draganawl ben priodawr perchen ymretonia.
Difa gwledic or bendefic ae tu terra.
Pedeir morwyn wedy eu cwyn dygnawt eu tra.
Erdygnawt wir ar vor ar* tir hir eu trefra.
Oe wironyn na digonyn dim gofettra.
Kerydus wyf na chyrbwyllwyf am rywnel da.
Y lwrw Lywy pwy gwahardwy pwy attrefna.
Y lwrw Aedon pwy gynheil Mon mwyn gowala.
Am bwyf i gan Grist hyt na bwyf trist o drwc o da.
Ran trugared y wlat ried buched gyfa.

The orthography of the poem agrees for the most part with the date of the manuscript, i.e. about 1275: final *-p*, *-t*, *-c*, correspond to modern *-b*, *-d*, *-g*; final *-d* corresponds to modern *-dd*. Medial *-d-* may stand for

[*] In the MS *heb* has been written above *ar*, perhaps in the hand of the original scribe.

modern *-d-* or *-dd-*. It is unnecessary for me to go into details here, but perhaps I ought to remind my readers that it was the custom of the Welsh medieval scribe to change the orthography of his originals to that current in his day, or in the monastery where he worked. And so when we say that this poem is written in the orthography of 1275, that does not prove that the poem itself was composed in 1275. The scribe may have found it in a manuscript written centuries before, in a much more primitive orthography, and proceeded to 'modernise' the spelling according to the rules of his particular school and period. The only chance we have of discovering the date of his original is when he inadvertently forgets to 'modernise', and copies mechanically the exact spelling of the manuscript before him. These *slips* are often very interesting and helpful, and preserve valuable indications of date. Unfortunately the scribe of the Book of Taliesin was a very efficient fellow, and his slips are rare. All the more reason that we should emphasise them. For instance, take the first word in lines 13 and 14. On the first occasion he wrote *katarn* and on the second *kadarn*. Why? We know from scraps of Old Welsh preserved in Latin manuscripts written between A.D. 800 and A.D. 1100 that *-t-* was the symbol used during that period for the sound which we now write as *-d-*, and which the scribe of the Book of Taliesin usually wrote as *-d-*, e.g. *pedeir*, lines 8 and 22 (pedair); *priodawr*, l. 20; *gwledic*, *bendefic*, l. 21 (gwledig, bendefig). Is it not possible, even probable, that the *-t-* in *katarn* gives us a glimpse of the original from which he was copying? He corrected himself in the next line, and wrote *kadarn*. But he had already made the same mistake in lines 7 and 11, where he wrote *Gwytyon* though his orthography required him to write *Gwydyon* (as on page 33, line 24, of the manuscript).

Take *hutwyt* in l. 10. The modern *hudwyd* makes no sense. Have we caught him out again? Assuming that his original belonged to the Old Welsh period, or if you like, that it was pre-Norman, *hudwyd* would have been written in it as *hutuit*. Now, the most difficult letters to read in some early manuscripts are what he supposed to be *-ui-*, and modernised into *-wy-*, writing *w* for the old *u*, and *y* for the old *-i-*. The three strokes *ui* sometimes cannot be distinguished even by expert palaeographers from *iu*, *in*, *ni*, or *m*. The *i* was not dotted or distinguished in any way from the other digits, until the scribes discovered a useful dodge, namely, inserting later above the *i* a faint sloping line made with the edge of the pen. The modern dot is derived from this useful mark. If we read *hutint* where we saw *hutuit*, we get a plural verb, 'hudynt', to go with the two subjects *Math* and *Euuyd*. According to the Mabinogi *Math* was a powerful magician, even more powerful than Gwydion: the two joined forces, and created a woman, Blodeuwedd, out of certain flowers, to be the wife of Lleu Llawgyffes. They gave her beauty, but forgot to give her morals, as you will remember. On page 36 of this manuscript a poet refers to this old tale. *Gwydyon ap Don...a hudwys gwreic o vlodeu* 'Gwydion son of Don...made by magic a woman out of flowers'. The verb here too is *hudo*, as in the text. On p. 25, ll. 21–6, Taliesin of the Saga asserts that he was not born of mortal parentage, but created by Math from fruit and flowers, *Am swynwys i Vath* 'Math made me by enchantment'. The verb here is *swyno*, a synonym of *hudo*. So Math in the early tales was reputed to have fashioned by his spells not only a beautiful woman but a richly endowed poet. This helps to explain the reference in our poem: *Math* and *Euuyd* made, or rather used to make (in order to get the full force of the old imperfect tense) by magic a *celfydd*, a word used to describe a skilled craftsman, an artist, poet, magician, even Math himself (cf. BT 1–3, bum gan wyr *keluydon*, gan *Uath* hen, gan *Gouannon*, gan *Iewyd*): the poet boasts that he has been with men renowned for their skill or art, Math the Old, Gofannon, and Iewydd (who may be the *Euuyd* of our text). The *Amaethon* of line 11, like Gwydion and Gofannon, was a son of *Don*, who corresponds in Welsh mythology to the goddess *Danu* of the ancient Irish.[3]

Leaving the mythology for a moment, the point I want to make now is this: if we read *Math ac Euuyd hutint geluyd* we get sense, and also correct construction. After the personal form of the verb, *hutint*, the object *celfydd* would be mutated, but not after the impersonal form, *hutwyt*. So *hutwyt* is impossible for a second reason, that it does not account for the mutated form *geluyd*. If the case for an original *hutint* stands, we have three indications in the orthography which suggest an early date for the manuscript copied by our scribe: -*t*- was preserved medially; *u* was written for *w* (for he assumed *u* here) and *i* for modern *y*. The first takes us back to *circa* 1100 and earlier; the other two need not be earlier than *circa* 1200, as instances of both occur in the *Black Book of Carmarthen*. They are, however, the standard forms of *circa* 1100 and

[3] *Danu* was the mother of the Irish divine pantheon, the *Tuatha Dé Danann* or 'Peoples of the Goddess Danu'. It has long been recognised that her Welsh counterpart is the *Don* of the *Mabinogi*; see in particular G. Murphy, 'Donu and Tuatha Dé Donann', *Duanaire Finn* III (Dublin, ITS, 1953), 208–10; also W. J. Gruffydd, *Math vab Mathonwy* (Cardiff, 1928), p. 148 n.; TYP p. 327.

earlier. The manuscript copied by the scribe may of course have been a copy of a much earlier one.

In line 17 the scribe wrote *cwynwyssetor*, and placed a dot under the first *w* to delete it. In a pre-Norman manuscript the word would be written *cinuissetor*, and if that was the orthography of his original his mistake can easily be accounted for. Before him he saw *c* followed by three digits. He took the first two to be for *u*, and automatically changed it to *w* according to his custom, exactly as he treated the same digits in his *hutwyt* for *hutint*. Here, however, he saw his error immediately. It was too late to correct the *w*, so he underdotted it, and as he now read *cin-* he must in his orthography change the *i* to *y*, and this he proceeded to do.

In line 2, *goge* is an obvious error for *gogei*, as a rhyme is required with *eruei*. In this metre the fourth syllable of each line must rhyme with the eighth. This mistake may be sheer accident, yet it is worth noting that in Old Welsh manuscripts *-e-* was used for *-ei-*, as in the Juvencus englynion of the ninth century,[4] or the *Mene* in Nennius (ed. Mommsen, chapter 75) for *Menei*.

In 29 lines there is only one instance of the definite article (l. 5): on this, as a characteristic of early Welsh poetry, see CA p. lxvii.

In support of these indications of a fairly early dating, suggested chiefly by minor points of orthography, the occurrence of what I have called 'Irish rhyme'[5] in the first stanza deserves mention. The end rhyme in the first stanza is *-or*; in line 14, however, it is *-od* (modern *-odd*), and in line 16, *-ol*; so that *l*, *r*, *dd*, are rhyming consonants. This type of early rhyme passed out of use soon after 1100; at any rate I have failed so far to find instances in any poem later than that in the *Black Book of Carmarthen*, pp. 73–7, to Hywel ap Goronwy (died 1106).

The metre of *Echrys Ynys* is the *rhupunt*:[6] lines of twelve syllables with end rhyme. Each line is divided into sections of four syllables; the end of the first section rhymes with the last syllable of the second, and occasionally (cf. 1, 2, 3, 7, 8) also with the first or second syllable of the last section. In addition to these internal rhymes, alliteration is used here and there to link the sections together. As *rhupunt* occurs in the Urien poetry, the metre itself does not help one to settle the date of the poem, but its technical development, I think, does help. Compare the simple technique of *Anrheg Urien*[7] with the *rhupunt* used in the Eulogy to

[4] Chapter VII above.

[5] On 'Irish Rhyme' see chapter VIII, p. 126 above, and n. [15].

6 For details see J. Morris-Jones, *Cerdd Dafod*, pp. 312, 331.

7 RBP col. 1049.

Hywel ap Gronwy mentioned above, which, luckily, can be definitely dated between 1096 and 1106, and I think you will agree that the metre of the second poem belongs to a later stage of bardic craft: it is much more elaborate. I am inclined to ascribe *Echrys Ynys* to the same period of elaboration. Rhymes like *da*, *gowala*, *terra*, in my opinion cannot be very early, while Irish rhyme is unlikely to occur after 1100 (especially in the work of a craftsman with the metrical skill of this poet), and so my guess for the date, after considering orthography, vocabulary, and metre, is some time in the eleventh century. The absence of any reference to the Normans is in favour of the first half of that century. I doubt if it can be placed earlier. Nine hundred years is a respectable, even a patriarchal age for any poem!

Now for the subject of the poem. I can only give a tentative version, as some words are obscure to me, though most of them are intelligible enough, occurring as they do in many of the early songs. A few are only known from this poem, and their meaning must be guessed from the context or, failing that, by etymologising, both being risky methods. The diction as in other early poetry is condensed, curt, abrupt, and for that reason almost untranslatable, even when the meaning of the words is known. Take the first line. *Echrys* means 'hurt, injury, damage', and *ynys* 'island'; *gwawt* is the old word for 'poetry'; *huynys* is unknown; if it is an error for *huenys* it may be an adjective meaning 'glorious, splendid', from *huan* 'sun'; *gwrys* is 'strife, violence'; *gobetror* contains *petr-* 'four', and *-or* 'corner, side'. And so we infer that an island renowned for or in poetry has suffered a severe loss, and that strife rages throughout or about its four corners. I shall translate as literally as I can, and use points where a word has completely beaten me. Then each reader can amplify for himself, or fall back on the incredibly bad version given in Skene's *Four Ancient Books*, I, 299–300.

Harm (has befallen) an island splendid in song; strife on all sides.
Môn, fortunate..., famed for valour, (with) Menai for its defence (door).
I have drunk liquor, wine and bragget, with my true brother,
A joyous lord; he had been laid low, the end of every monarch.
Sorrowful are the nobles of the *archaeddon*, since he has fallen.
There has not been, there will not be his peer in battle.
When *Aeddon* came from Gwydion's land, the fortress of Seon,

Bitter (it is) that there came four bare-headed (women?), in the dead of night.
Warriors fell: forests gave no shelter: (furious?) was the wind.
Math and Eufydd (?) fashioned by magic a skilful (poet?), free...
When Gwydion and Amaethon lived, there was wisdom (counsel).
Pierced was the front of his shield: mighty, loth to flee, mighty, resolute.
Strong in the press of furious fighting: he was no pirate.
Strong at a carousal; in every assembly his will was done.
Beloved *Cynaethwy*, as long as I live he shall be praised.
May I receive from Christ an apostle's share, that I may not be sad.
Generous *archaeddon*, he shall be welcomed by angels.

Harm (has befallen) an island, splendid in song; strife all around.
In the presence of a victorious youth, refuge of Welshmen, it was delightful to dwell.
Dragonlike hero, rightful lord in Britain.
The prince has perished, most high chieftain, earth covers him.
Four maidens after their feasting, cruel their (arrogance?)
Cruel truth, on sea, on land, long their (shame?),
For his faithful henchman that they could do not a whit.
Blameworthy am I that I praise not the one who has been good to me.
After *Llywy* who will forbid, who will bring order?
After *Aeddon* who will guard Môn, (with its) plenteous wealth?
May I receive from Christ, that I may not be sad, in good or evil fortune,
A share of his mercy in the land of glory, life everlasting.

The whole poem is so confusing that I am tempted to paraphrase as well as translate! At first I took it to be one of the mythological group, because of the references to Math, Gwydion, and Amaethon (ll. 7, 10, 11). The verbs in lines 10, 11, however, refer to the past, and Eryri might be called Gwydion's land in any type of poem, as Dyfed is called the 'land of Pryderi', even by Dafydd ap Gwilym.[8] The real

[8] T. Parry, *Gwaith Dafydd ap Gwilym* (Caerdydd, 1952), no. 150, l. 32.

crux is the reference to the four maidens in line 23, and probably in line 8; this may be from a forgotten saga (cf. the mention of an unknown *Eufydd* with Math) or else a jibe at the four proud daughters of the bard's dead chief. Obviously he does not love them, and the reason is not far to seek; they have done nothing for their father's faithful henchman, his *gwirionyn*, line 24. He turns away from their niggardliness to recall Llywy and Aeddon, who have been good to him in the past. And may we not explain the reference to Math and Gwydion (line 10) in a similar way? The four 'bareheaded' ladies set no store on poets and skilful rhymesters. In the old days, when gods and demigods like Math and Gwydion lived in Arfon, did they not create by magic a master of words, a true poet, even Taliesin? In these degenerate days, the cruel truth must be declared, some women will not even feed a poet (ll. 23–4). There is real feeling in the conventional tag at the end of both stanzas. May the poet (and his old patron) have a share in the glories of heaven! If worldly wealth be denied him, may God be generous and enrich him to all eternity!

Perhaps the four maidens were not Aeddon's daughters, after all, but captives taken in an attack on Caer *Seon* in Eryri[9] (on Conway Mountain? Cf. *Black Book of Carmarthen*, 102, 2), who later on became the chieftain's favourites. Such things have happened. They were brought over in the dead of night (line 8), and *gwenwyn* 'poison, bitterness', is the fit word to describe their coming. If slave girls of yore were bareheaded, the *pedeir pennoeth* of line 8 would be very apt, and the *tra* (for *traha*?) in line 22[10] describes their drunken arrogance.

In the translation I have left *aeddon, archaeddon* in lines 5, 7, 17, 27, untranslated, because they look like proper names, and have been so taken. Further, the Brut refers to a certain *Aeddan* ap Blegywryd, slain by Llywelyn ap Seisyllt, probably in 1018,[11] so Sir John Lloyd tells me. The date is tempting: nothing more is known of this Aeddan, and so why not place him in Anglesey? May he not be the *Aeddon* of our

[9] For an account of the excavation of the hill-fort on Conway mountain known variously as *Castell Caer Seion* or *Caer Lleion* see W. E. Griffiths, *Arch. Cam.* CV (1957). IW's identification of the site with the *Caer Seon* of this poem and of BBC p. 102, l. 2, is here accepted. The name *Mynydh Kaer Lheion* is given in Gibson's *Camden* (1695), col. 670; this appears to be a corruption of *Caer Sion* or *Süon* given in Lewis Morris's *Celtic Remains* (ed. D. Silvan Evans, London, 1878), p. 393, and as *Sinnodune* by Leland (1536–9) (*Itinerary in Wales*, ed. L. Toulmin Smith, London, 1906, p. 84). *Caer Seon* is evidently the older form.

10 Cf. BT p. 80, l. 4; CLlH XI, 75b.

11 RBB p. 264, ll. 33–4.

poem? Unfortunately the form *aeddon* is proved by the rhyme in line 7, and line 27; it does not occur elsewhere as a man's name, and Professor Lloyd-Jones rightly takes it as a common noun meaning 'lord'.[12] If *aeddon* were a proper name, the *archaeddon* of lines 5, 17 would be inexplicable. Taking *aeddon* as a common noun, 'lord', we can either explain *archaeddon*, on the analogy of *archesgob* as 'high lord, chief lord', or else correct it to *archaddon* (cf. BBC p. 71, l. 5), and translate it as a complimentary epithet of a lord famed for generous gifts.[13] In any case, the epithet has survived in the name *Llyn Archaeddon*, or rather *Llyn Archaddon*, for a lake on Bodafon Mountain. See Lewis Morris's *Celtic Remains*,[14] and also Dafydd ab Edmwnd's poem in the fifteenth century[15] where *Bodafon*, *Clorach*, *Penrhos*, *Dulas*, *Botffordd*, are mentioned, as well as *Llyn Archaddon* (so spelt).

If *aeddon* is a common noun, then the Llywy of line 26 is not a proper name but the adjective *llywy*, often used of a fair lady: it describes the mistress who held sway in the chief's court, before those four maidens complicated matters.

The only clue to the chief's real name is to be seen in line 15, *Cynaethwy*.[16] There we have a genuine unmistakable personal name, fairly common in the pedigrees, and elsewhere, see G p. 243. Can anyone help with an Anglesey reference? A Llys Cynaethwy near Mynydd Bodafon would be most acceptable.

12 G p. 11 (*arglwydd*).

13 Compare the *hael archaedon* of line 17, with the *haeladon* of CA l. 554, where it is used of a generous chieftain; see n. p. 208.

14 Lewis Morris, *Celtic Remains*, ed. Silvan Evans (London, 1878) p. 18.

15 *Gwaith Dafydd ab Edmwnd* ed. Thomas Roberts (Bangor, 1914), poem XVIII, p. 33.

[16] In a postscript to this article in TAAS 1942, 19–24, IW rejected the interpretation of *kyn aethwy* as a personal name, and understood it to be a verbal form 3sg. perfect *kyn aethyw* 'before he went' (i.e. 'died')—an emendation which, as he showed, is corroborated by the rhyme between the fourth and eighth syllables in each line throughout the poem. He took *archaedon* in l. 5 of the poem to be a miscopying of *archad(d)on*, an epithet for the chieftain praised—Aed(d)on 'the noble' or 'the just'. He regarded the place-name *Bodafon* as a modified form of *Bod Aed(d)on* 'the dwelling of A.' and hoped that post-war excavation of the site would reveal evidence that it was the *llys* of Aed(d)on. Unfortunately when this hoped-for excavation took place in 1954 no traces were found of any human habitation which could be associated with the eleventh-century date assigned to the poem (see excavation report by W. E. Griffiths, TAAS 1955, 12–26).

IV The englyn on St. Padarn's Staff. By permission of the Master and Fellows of Corpus Christi College, Cambridge.

# *Chapter X*

# AN OLD WELSH VERSE

THE Editor has asked me for a note on a scrap of Old Welsh poetry written on the top margin of fol. 11*a* in Corpus Christi College Cambridge MS. 199, written by Ieuan ap Sulien. Perhaps it would be convenient to begin with Bradshaw's remarks[1] on this manuscript:

> At the beginning are some introductory verses, and all through the volume there are invocations at the top of the pages, mostly where a fresh book begins. Sometimes they are addressed to God, once to St David, and once to St Paternus, to aid and encourage the scribe in continuing his work. These mostly have JO. (the scribe's name) prefixed. But in one case is a Welsh quatrain (without the JO.) docked by the binder of part of its last line, but much resembling some lines in the Gododin (*sic*), though not identical. Except the two poems in the Juvencus MS., it is the only scrap of verse written down before the twelfth century, as yet discovered, and so is most precious; especially as we can date it almost to a certainty, seeing it must have been written some time between 1080 and 1090. It is in this scrap that the letter *y* first appears in Welsh, a letter which forms such a prominent feature in all later Welsh writing.

The verse referred to is written across the top margin in one long line; but the end of each line of the quatrain is marked by a point, and the beginning of each has a coloured initial. The letters are beautifully formed, and all the words can be read without difficulty, except the last three which have suffered severely at the hands of the binder. From a study of the manuscript itself, and a photograph provided for me by the courtesy of the Librarian of Corpus Christi, *per* the Editor, I have managed to restore the missing portions of the letters in the last line with tolerable certainty. Enough is left of most of them to make identification certain, once the scribe's characteristic strokes and curves have been carefully studied. But an exception must be made of the first 'restored' letter, the *d* in *daul*. What I see is the lower part of a straight *d* (not a round ꝺ as elsewhere in the verse), the fellow of the *d* in lines 4, 11, 12, 16, of Lindsay's *Early Welsh Script*, plate XVII, a facsimile of a page

1 *Collected Papers of Henry Bradshaw* (Cambridge, 1889), p. 465. See also A. W. Haddan and W. Stubbs, *Councils and Ecclesiastical Documents relating to Great Britain and Ireland* (Oxford, 1869–78), I, 667; *Arch. Cam.* (1874), p. 340 (where the quatrain is printed); also LL p. xxv, n.

from the psalter written by Ieuan ap Sulien's brother, Rhygyfarch. On the same page there are sixteen round ꝺ's; this proves the indiscriminate use of the two types at this period, though ꝺ was more favoured.

My reading of the four lines is as follows:

Amdinnit trynit trylenn.
Amtrybann teirbann treisguenn.
Amcen creiriou gurth cyrrguenn.
Amdifuys *daul bacl patern.*

There are seven syllables in each line, the rhyme being -*enn* in 1, 2, 3, and -*ern* in 4. That -*ern* is a possible rhyme with -*enn* at this period is proved by Irish rhymes of a similar type in the *Book of Taliesin*, in a poem (*Arymes Prydein*) dated *circa* A.D. 900,[2] where -*yrn* rhymes with -*ynn*, -*yng*; and in the *Black Book of Carmarthen*, in a poem dated 1096–1106,[3] where *teeirn* (= *teyrn*) rhymes with *unbin* (= *unbynn*). If -*yrn*, -*ynn* were accounted good rhymes in 900 and 1100 by our early bards, it seems safe to assume that they would pass -*ern*, -*enn* as up to standard in our text.

The *Patern* mentioned is our modern *Padarn*, founder of Llanbadarn Fawr, where this manuscript was probably written.[4] His name is a Welshified form of the Latin *Paternus*, and the change of -*ern* to -*arn* is according to the rule by which Latin *taberna* gave *tafarn* in Welsh (not *tafern*). In Old Welsh, however, this change had not taken place, e.g. Cunedda's ancestor, *Padarn* Peisrudd, is called *Patern* Pesrut in the Harley MS. 3859 pedigrees, copied about A.D. 1100 from a tenth-century original.[5] Curiously enough Llan*badarn* is frequently written Llan *Badern*, and the patron saint called *Padern* in the *Brut y Tywysogion* text lately published by Mr Thomas Jones from Peniarth MS. 20, e.g. dewi *aphadern*.[6] Perhaps ecclesiastics bred at Llanbadarn, whose patron's name in its Latin form, *Paternus*, was regularly on their lips in the services of the church, may have been loth to follow the fashion of Welshmen elsewhere in calling him *Padarn*. Ieuan ap Sulien, at the top of folio 10*b*, invokes his patron saint,[7] *Auxilium...tuum fer scē paterne*. He then on the

2 AP pp. 17–18, *hyn–mechteyrn*; 99–100–101, *glywyssing–mechteyrn–ebryn*; 137, *gwrtheyrn–genhyn* (= BT p. 13, ll. 15–16; p. 15, ll. 26–16, 2; p. 17, l. 3). [On 'Irish Rhyme' see chapter VIII above, p. 126 and n. 15.]

3 BBC p. 73, l. 12. [The poem is a eulogy of Hywel ap Goronwy, died 1106 (HW p. 406, n.). For an edition and discussion see J. Vendryes, EC IV, 275 ff.]

4 Haddan and Stubbs, *op. cit.* I, 667.

5 EWGT pp. 9–13. See above, p. 73, n. 9.

[6] Thomas Jones, *Brut y Tywysogyon* (*Peniarth MS. 20*) (Caerdydd, 1941), fol. 46*a*. For this spelling cf. also 45*b*, 53*b*, 69*a*, 88*b*, 91*b*, 154*a*, 216*b*.

7 Cf. J. E. Lloyd, 'Bishop Sulien and his family', *Journal of the National Library of Wales* II, 1–6; ibid. *The Story of Ceredigion* (Cardiff, 1937), pp. 29 ff. Ieuan ap Sulien also invoked Dewi Sant, as on fol. 5*b* of this manuscript (*Corpus Christi College* MS. 199), Antistes *dauid* operi succurre precantis. [On the activities of Bishop Sulien and his sons, see now further N. K. Chadwick, 'Intellectual Life in West Wales in the Last Days of the Celtic Church', *Studies in the Early British Church* (Cambridge, 1958), pp. 162 ff.]

next page, fol. 11 *a*, writes a Welsh verse in his honour. It may be his own composition; in this very manuscript there is a long Latin poem from his pen, which proves at any rate that he was very fond of alliteration as a poetic ornament. Or it may be an apt quotation from a long poem sung in honour of Padarn by an Old Welsh bard. I favour the second alternative.

Preceding *Patern* in l. 4, I read *daul bacl* which with *amdifuys* complete the line of seven syllables required by the metre.

**daul.** On *d-*, see above. *-a-*, cf. the *a* in *trybann teirbann*, l. 2. *-u-*, cf. *creiriou*, l. 3. *-l*; the angular curve remaining here is exactly like the lower portion of the *l* in *trylenn*, l. 1.

**bacl.** *b-*, cf. the *b* in line 2. *-a-*; what remains agrees with the *a* in *trybann teirbann*, l. 2. *-c-*; there is very little of it left, but cf. the *c* in *cyrrguenn*, l. 3. *-l*, cf. the *l* of *trylenn*, l. 2, and the remnant of an *l* in *daul*.

Old Welsh *bacl* is borrowed from the Latin *baculus* 'staff', and gave us the modern *bagl*. In Medieval Welsh an inorganic vowel, usually written *y*, appears in the orthography between a mute and a liquid, in such words; so we get *bagyl*, *dadyl*, *crwydyr*, etc. But in Old Welsh glosses of the ninth and tenth centuries, the inorganic vowel is not shown in *datl*, *dadl*, *cruitr*. Thus *bacl* is a possible orthography for 1080. And not only is it a possible form here, but its meaning links line 4 with line 3, which ends with *cyrrguenn*. In the *Life of St Padarn*[8] we are told that the three saints, David, Padarn, and Teilaw went to Jerusalem to be ordained by the chief archbishop. They were ordained by him, and received three gifts, Padarn being honoured with a double one, '*baculo* videlicet, et tunica ex toto contexta'. According to the Life of Teilaw in the *Book of Llan Dâv*[9] David received an altar, Teilaw a bell, and Padarn '*baculus* et choralis cappa pretiosissimo serico contexta, eoquod illum egregium cantorem uidebant'. In the *Life of St Padarn*, before the journey to Jerusalem is mentioned, there is an account of the saint's successful intervention in a destructive civil war in Ireland. Everyone praised the Lord in his servant, and blessed the saint, saying, 'Sit semper tibi signum pacis, per quod clarescat nomen tuum in terra dum vivas, et post mortem, quod impletur in munere *Cerirguen*'. This is translated by Rees, 'Mayest thou always have the sign of peace, whereby thy name may become famous upon earth whilst thou dost live, and after death mayest be filled with the reward of *Cerrigwen*'.[10] According to Kuno Meyer, however, the correct reading in the manuscript is not *Cerirguen* but *cirguen*, with *nomen baculi pacificantur* in the margin.[11] It is difficult to accept *pacificantur* as the correct reading here, though one is glad to be rid of *Cerirguen* (and *Cerrigwen*!) as the name of the 'pacifying' (if I may read *pacificantis*) *baculus* or staff.

8 W. J. Rees, *The Lives of the Cambro-British Saints* (Llandovery, 1853), p. 193; [A. W. Wade-Evans, *Vitae Sanctorum Britanniae et Genealogiae* (Cardiff, 1944), pp. 258–60].

9 LL p. 106.

10 Rees, *Cambro-British Saints*, pp. 190, 505–6.

11 *Cy.* XIII, 88. [Wade-Evans, *op. cit.* p. 256, adopts the reading *Cirguen*.]

And it seems more sensible to put the second quotation marks after *mortem*, and not *Cirguen*. With these emendations, the passage would run: '"Mayest thou always have a symbol of peace, by which thy name may be illustrious on earth while thou livest, and (also) after death!"—and this is fulfilled in the gift of *Cirguen*.' The marginal note emphasises that *Cirguen* is the *signum pacis* referred to; it is the name of the 'pacifying *baculus*'. The *Life* then runs on, 'Tanta namque utilitas *baculi* istius est, ut si qui duo discordantes sint, per eius conjurationem pacentur.' 'For such is the virtue of that *staff* that if two quarrel, by its means[12] they are reconciled.'

From this it appears that Padarn's episcopal staff was famed as a peacemaker, that it was called *Cirguen*, and that it was said to be the gift of the Archbishop of Jerusalem. In the Welsh verse, l. 3, the last word is *cyrrguenn*; in the last line we have *bacl Patern*, following a parenthesis, *amdifuys daul*. And *daul*, 'dawl', connects the verse very nicely with the *Life*, for it means 'share, part, gift', cf. the compound *gwa-ddawl*, 'gwaddol', used now for 'dowry, endowment'; and the Irish *dáil* 'share'; or the Old Welsh *di-daul* 'diddawl', a gloss on the Latin *expers*[13] 'having no share in'. *Cyrrguen* was an *amdifuys daul*: here *amddiffwys* must mean 'eminent, remarkable, wonderful'. As a noun *diffwys* meant 'height, precipice'; as an adjective 'mountainous, wild', with 'desolate, solitary' as a secondary meaning. Sometimes it was used like 'awful, dreadful', for anything 'extraordinary'. For the double meaning, cf. L. *eminens* 'standing out, projecting, high, lofty', and, figuratively, 'distinguished, eminent'. To describe Padarn's staff, his 'share' of the *tria munera* 'the three gifts' made to the three saints at Jerusalem,[14] I can think of nothing more apt than *amdifuys daul*, 'a wonderful gift', for it stresses the awe-inspiring qualities of the staff given to him and its 'uniqueness'. Nowadays it is difficult for us to realise the awe with which our forefathers looked upon this symbol of ecclesiastical authority. It was more than a symbol; it was the saint's weapon of offence and defence invested with miraculous powers. Two quotations may be given here. The first is from an ode by Gwynfardd Brycheiniog, a bard of the thirteenth century, to Dewi Sant. He is referring to the saint's staff or *bagl*:

> Ar *uagyl* eur y phenn ffowch recdi
> Val rac tan tost yd wan tyst duw idi.[15]

'And the golden-headed staff, flee from it as from fire : grievously does it smite. God testifies to it.'

The second is from Llywelyn Fardd's ode to St Cadfan of Tywyn:

> Ar *uagyl* uerth werthuawr wyrtheu newyt.
> a llut yr gelyn lat y gilyt.[16]

12 I take *conjuratio* here to be a translation of *tynghedu*.
13 VVB p. 100 (Ox. II).
14 LL p. 106, l. 16.
15 MA p. 195*b*, ll. 13–14 [= HGCr. XVIII, pp. 186–7].
16 H p. 43, ll. 27–8. Read *lut* (= 'ludd') in the second line.

'And the fine, precious staff, with new miracles, prevents a man from murdering his enemy.'

The name *Cyrrguenn* would be written *Cyrwen* in the modern orthography; it is a compound of *cwrr* and *gwenn* 'white, pure, holy, sacred', the feminine adjective being used, as *bagl* is a feminine noun. The first element, *cwrr*, is cognate with Irish *corr*, a word with various meanings. To quote a few:[17] *corr*, 'prow or stern of a ship' (cf. Welsh, *cwrr* ôl y llong); 'corner' (cf. *cyrrau'r ddaear*); 'snout' (cf. Llywarch Hen's reference to the *gylfin* 'beak' of his *baglan brenn* 'wooden crutch, or staff', CLlH II, 70): *corrán* 'a corner, angle'; also 'a hook, sickle': *corr-bacc* 'bent like a hook' (cf. our *cyrfach*): *corr-cháel* 'crooked and slender'; *corr-derg* 'red-snouted'. As *bagl* (dialectal, *bagal*) in Welsh is used to this day for 'the crook of a walking stick', and *baglan* for 'crutch', I think we can safely say that Padarn's Cyrwen was a 'holy staff with a crooked head', a real shepherd's crook.

The rest of the two last lines needs little comment or explanation.

**amcen,** 'amgen'. The old meaning was 'other, different',[18] not 'better' as in some of our modern phrases: *nid amgen* meant 'namely, no other, not different'. In the Mabinogi, Gwydion 'changed' his appearance, and that of Lleu: this is called '*amgenu* eu pryd'. In the text we can 'understand' *yw* after *amcen.*

**creiriou,** 'creiriau', not merely 'relics', but 'holy or sacred objects, treasures'. The bards even used the singular *crair* as a synonym for 'darling, lady-love': and Christ is called the *crair* of the believer. Church bells are called *creiriau.*[19]

**gurth,** the full form of the preposition 'wrth', used here with the meaning of 'in comparison with, compared with', cf. the ninth-century Juvencus englynion[20] or *Llawysgrif Hendregadredd*, p. 288, where a generous patron is said to be *wrth* Mordaf, Nudd and Rhydderch (the Three Generous Ones of the Isle of Britain)[21] as a giver of gold (*wrth* uordaf a nut pan roted ruteur / a rydderch afneued), i.e. he was 'comparable' to them.

So the two lines can be paraphrased as follows: 'Though sacred relics, holy treasures, abound, though Dewi had his altar, and Teilo his bell, etc. yet in comparison with Cyrwen they are all "different", they are not quite like Cyrwen, that pre-eminent *gift*, the staff (*bagl*) of Padarn.' The poet is careful not to disparage (too much) the relics of other saints—he may need their help—but yet, Cyrwen stands alone! Cyrwen is unique, without a peer.

I have dealt with the second half of the quatrain first, because every word in these two lines can be satisfactorily explained, and they prove that the subject of the stanza is St Padarn's Staff, a eulogy of Cyrwen. The first line, on the other hand, is exceedingly difficult; every word is ambiguous, and the interpretation amounts to a series of guesses. The second is not so bad, if we assume that *treisguenn* is an epithet

[17] See CIL pp. 491–3 for these examples.
18 H p. 47, l. 12; p. 85, l. 22.
19 H p. 44, l. 26, *y chreiryeu bangleu bann glyhwitor* [see GPC p. 579].
[20] See n. to line 7*c* of the Nine englynion, chapter VII, p. 115 above.
[21] TYP no. 2.

of *bacl Patern*, but even so *trybann* and *teirbann* are not free from ambiguity. I shall deal as briefly as I can with the difficulties of these two lines.

The first line seems to be an echo or imitation of the first line of two stanzas in the Gododdin poems. Of each of these there is a variant version in older ortho-graphy, but so much conflation and textual corruption has taken place that we seem to be reading four different stanzas jumbled together! Three of them, how-ever, agree in their first line:

Am drynni drylaw drylenn.[22]

though one has *drylav drylen*, a variation without significance. The second line (l. 460) in one reads:

Am lwys amdiffwys dywarchen.

So also in another (l. 471), but with *am diffwys* as two separate words. The resemblance is sufficient to make it likely that the author of our quatrain was familiar with the Gododdin, and used it as a model—this suggests that he was one of the professional bards, for the Gododdin was part of their stock-in-trade.[23] The stanzas in the Gododdin are *not* in honour of Padarn, or his Staff, but fragments of war poems; and so we cannot take them as stray pieces of the Ode to Padarn whence our quatrain probably derives.

To save space, I shall give only one or two guesses at the meanings of each word.

**Amdinnit.** May be a compound verb, with *am-* as prefix, rather than the preposition *am* followed by a noun. In Old Welsh verbs the termination *-it* is seen in the pres. indic., 3rd sing.; pres. subj. 3rd sing. (or imperative); and in the imperfect impersonal. The stem of the verb, *-dinn*, recalls Old Welsh *dinn*, modern, *dynn*, seen in ty-*ddyn*, etc.; cognate with Irish *dinn* 'a height, a fortified hill, fort'. Cf. *cae* 'hedge'; *cae-u* (now *cau*) 'to shut, to enclose'; gwar-*chae* 'besiege'; *ar-gae* 'dam'. Remembering the pacifying attributes of Cyrwen, I suggest that *am-dinn-it* means 'defends'. But there is also in Irish an adjective *dinn* meaning 'pleasant, delightful'.[24]

**trynit.** There are old compound nouns in which *try-* means 'three', or 'triple', e.g. *trywyr* 'three men', *trychant* '300', *trybedd* 'tripod', *tryfer* 'trident, fishing spear with three prongs'. In others *try-* means 'through, thorough', an intensive prefix; with a verb, cf. *try-wan-u* 'strike through, pierce'; with an adjective, *try-loyw*, 'pellucid'; *try-lew* 'very brave'; *try-frith* 'spotted all over'. As epithets of a shattered or pierced shield I have seen *try-wan*, *trydoll* (fem. of *trydwll*), *tryfriw*, *tryfrwyd*. When this *try-* is compounded with a noun, the meaning is usually adjectival; possible exceptions are *tryblith*, *trydar*. The chances are that *trynit* also is an adjective, with *try-* intensive preflxed to *gnit* (for the loss of *g-*, cf.

22 CA lines 459, 470, 478; cf. l. 486.

[23] See chapter v, p. 60 above, for the prose note in the *Book of Aneirin* which refers to the value of the poem in bardic contests.

[24] O'Davoren's Glossary, p. 735 (ACL II, 317). *dinn.i.aibhinn*. *Contribb. degra-dodelbtha* (1959), p. 124.

*try-lew* from *glew*), and this *gnit* may be from the same root as *gnif* 'work, toil', cf. Old Breton, *Uur-gnit.*[25] In Welsh, with the prefix *gwo-* it gave *gweinid*, as in *gweinid-*farch 'a working horse': *gweinid-awl*, *gweinid-awg*, 'servant', cf. *gwo-gnif*, 'gweini(f)'. The simple noun *gnid*, I think, is preserved in a poem by Prydydd y Moch,[26] where it is mutated after the pers. pron. *y* (*i*, our *ei*] cf. DGVB 177a. The poet addresses God:

Am parabyl oth dawn ym perid
parhawd o nebawd *y nid.*

His gift of words is from God: its *gnid* 'work' will continue *o nebawd*, i.e. to describe somebody or something. This cryptic saying is clarified by the following lines, 'so let the generous hero receive his praise, and the miser his satire'. He goes on to warn his lord, Gruffudd ap Cynan, not to be niggardly, or else he will bring the blush of shame to his face, etc.

But *nit*, (or *nid*) is possible from the same root as *nydd-u* 'to spin'; cf. *nidro* 'to twist round, to entangle'. Or from the same root as Irish *níth* 'conflict, mortal wounding of a man'. What is the origin of the name *Nidan*?

**trylenn.** The modern *trylen* 'well read, learned', is barred by the double *nn* in the text: it cannot be derived from *llên*. In Peniarth 51, a bard of the fifteenth century explains *trylenn* in the Gododdin poem quoted above, as *cad* 'battle, host'.[27] This may or may not preserve an old tradition, but the same bard is demonstrably wrong in so many of his 'shots' that I cannot feel any confidence in his correctness with regard to this particular word. The occurrence, however, of *trylenn* in the Gododdin makes it quite certain that in the verse we are now discussing it does *not* refer to the other Jerusalem gift to Padarn, viz. the *tunica* or *cappa*, mentioned in the *Life*. If *try-* is the intensive prefix, the second element is *glenn* or *lenn*. The first is unknown to me, but we have a Welsh *llenn* cognate with Irish *lenn*, both meaning 'mantle'. Sometimes, however, the poets used it for 'covering' (cf. *to* 'roof', *am-do* 'shroud'; Latin *toga*), cf. RBP col. 1430, ll. 30–1, *deyerin lenn* 'earthly covering', used of the grave: col. 1431, l. 8 *gwydlenn*, a *llen* of wood 'coffin'. So *trylenn* might be used for 'protection, refuge'. In the Gododdin it is associated with another rare word, *trylaw*,[28] which helps not at all. There is also another Irish word which may be useful, *lennán* 'love, sweetheart'. Can *trylenn* be explained as *tra chu*, 'much loved, very dear', or something of that sort? For the Welsh *dilenn* 'concealment' or 'disappearance', cf. G 353; *tryleu* 'heaps', given by Davies, Salesbury, T. Jones, does not appear too promising. T. Williams (on *acervatim*) evidently took it to be

25 *Chr. Br.* p. 133.

26 H p. 283, ll. 21–2. Cf. also p. 175, l. 10, llew toryf teryan eur *gynnid* (? *eurwaith*, i.e. decorated with gold).

[27] See B I, 218 (= IW's edition of Gwilym Tew's glossary) and cf. TYP p. XXXIV on the contents of Gwilym Tew's MS., Peniarth 51.

28 Cf. H p. 142, ll. 12–14, peir *pedrylaw* / *pedriliw* y lauyn... / *pedrylef* kwynuan; and p. 136, l. 18, y daryan *dryliw*. Such forms show how hard it is to separate *try-* 'very' from *try-* 'triple'.

for *tyrryleu*, from *twrr* 'heap', and formed like *mydyleu*. As for the construction, I take *trynit trylenn* to be the subject of *amdinnit*.

**am.** Here a preposition, 'about, all round'.

**trybann,** tryfan. On *try-*, see above. *bann* has a number of meanings, and several derivations. It occurs as a masculine noun, a feminine noun, and as an adjective. As a noun, one meaning is 'point, horn'; common in names of mountain peaks (*Y Fan*, *Bannau* Brycheiniog, etc.). The battlements of a castle or fort are called *bann*. From *bann* 'horn' is derived *bann* 'drinking horn', and the adj. *bannog* 'with long horns', e.g. Ychen *Bannog*; or 'with high peaks', e.g. y Mynydd *Bannog*. A derivative use is *bann* for the arm of a cross; a stave of a verse, line, syllable: also the *ban-* in *bangor*, the cross-bar in a wattle. As an adjective, *bann* means 'loud, clear', as in *banllef*; 'high', as in lloer *uann*, H p. 262, l. 8; probably 'melodious, tuneful', as in *Bangu*, St David's Bell (cf. Old Breton *bann*, glossing *canora*;[29] and Irish *bind* 'melodious'). See below on *teirbann*, and Meyer, CIL p. 198, on Irish *benn*; also, p. 175, *band* 'distance, extent'.

On *tryfan*, cf. Dr Davies, 'dail y *tryfan*, *v*. Alan Mawr: Petasites'. So H. Davies, *Welsh Botanology*,[30] 'Tussilago, Petasites, Butter-bur': T. Jones, 'Lug-wort, Butter-bur'. This *tryfan* seems to be the lance-like stalk, which thrusts itself out of the soil, and flowers before the leaves arrive, cf. the shape of the mountain called *Y Tryfan* in Nant Ffrancon, a fine peak. *Rhostryfan*, *Moeltryfan* (? Moel-y-Tryfan) near Caernarvon, I think, got their names from the house close by known as *Y Tryfan*; otherwise one would have expected *Foel-dryfan*, as the noun *Moel*, 'summit', is feminine, and causes soft mutation after it, e.g. *Moel Fenlli*, *Moel Wnion*. No instance of *tryfan* indicates sound of any sort, and so it seems safe to take it as 'a point'.

In the medieval poets I have noted some instances where *tryfan* seems to be an adjective, as in RBP col. 1234, ll. 23–4, Gwae dic...gwael drauael *dryuan*. Seven castles were captured in Powys by the men of Gwynedd, col. 1405, ll. 25 f., Kawssam ar bowys...gestyll

*tri tryua*n kyuan kyuoeth.
*pedwar* ennwawc peithyawc poeth.

'Three *tryfan*, with all their wealth, and four famous ones, ravaged, and burnt.' Were these three round towers with conical roofs? Cf. also col. 1420, ll. 14–15, uch deudraeth *dryuan*, probably Penrhyn*deudraeth*, with *tryfan* describing the long narrow *traeth* on each side.

**teirbann.** In modern Welsh *pedwar bann byd* is used for the four corners of the world; also *pedryfan*; cf. AL I, 346, gwialen ariant...a *thri bann* y erni a thri y deni 'a silver rod with three "points" (or "branches") above, and three below'; and the Glamorgan *triban* 'a three-line verse'. In these *bann* is masculine. But Lewys

[29] DGVB p. 78.
30 Hugh Davies, *Welsh Botanology* (London, 1813).

Glyn Cothi has *teirban y grog* 'the three arms of the Cross';[31] Peniarth 14, 168, rodi arnaw arwyd y *teir ban*, 'the sign of the Cross'; *Campeu Charlymaen*, 7, *pedeir bann* y gadair 'four corners of the chair'; Hafod 1, 80b, *pedeir bannoed y byt*, and *pedeir-uannoed*. In these *bann* is feminine. Both forms occur on the same page in *Llyfr yr Ancr*, 19, yr prynv *petwarbenn* (corrected to *-bann*) *y byt*, and lower down, *pedeir-bann y byt* (translating *quadrifidum* mundus, and *quatuor partes* mundi, p. 187). On p. 97, however, *teirbann y vedyssyawt* is explained as *nef a dayar ac uffernn* (the three parts of the universe, heaven, earth and hell).

What have we in our verse? The three arms of the Cross, or the three parts of the universe? Neither seems very appropriate, and so I favour the three parts of the world. Compare the *Book of Taliesin*, p. 80, where the world is said to be divided into three parts:

yn tri yt rannat.
yn amgen pwyllat.
vn yw yr asia.
deu yw yr affrica.
Tri yw europa.

'It is divided into three, variously named. One is Asia, Two is Africa, Three is Europa.' So also BT p. 5, l. 3. With this cf. the *Epitome Historiae Britanniae*.[32] Post mortem vero Noe, tres dicti filii diviserunt inter se universum orbem, videlicet Sem Asiam, Cam Affricam, Japhet Europam, 'After the death of Noah, the three abovementioned sons divided between them the whole world, Shem receiving Asia, Ham Africa, and Japheth Europe'. Only three continents were known in 1100!

**treisguenn.** This compound adjective describes Cyrwen, *treis*, because of the force, power, that was in it, and *guenn*, 'white, holy', because the power was used for holy purposes. *treis* 'trais' usually means 'force, violence' in a bad sense, but cf. H p. 182, l. 11, *treis duw* 'God's might'; and the compound adjective *treis-uawr* used to compliment Llywelyn (ibid. p. 308, l. 17): if the secular prince could be called *treisfawr* 'of great violence, might, force', so could St Padarn's Staff be called *treiswenn* 'of holy might'.

From this medley of possibles, one has to choose a probable. My choice (at the moment!) is something like this. The first two lines must be in praise of Cyrwen, and so I read the quatrain thus:

Much accomplishing, much loved, it gives protection,
Its holy power reaching the limits of three continents.
No other relic can be compared with Cyrwen—
A wonderful gift—Padarn's Staff.

31 *Gwaith Lewis Glyn Cothi* (ed. Hon. Soc. Cymmrodorion, Oxford, 1837), II, p. 364.
32 Rees, *Cambro-British Saints*, p. 286 (from Cotton MS. Titus D xxii).

# INDEX

# INDEX

# INDEX

# INDEX

INDEX